West Virginia's Criminal Justice System

Carolina Academic Press

State-Specific Criminal Justice Series

Criminal Justice Basics and Concerns
William G. Doerner, ed.

Alabama's Criminal Justice System
Vicki Lindsay and Jeffrey P. Rush, eds.

Arkansas's Criminal Justice System
Edward Powers and Janet K. Wilson

California's Criminal Justice System
Third Edition
Christine L. Gardiner and Georgia Spiropoulos, eds.

Florida's Criminal Justice System
Second Edition
William G. Doerner

Georgia's Criminal Justice System
Deborah Mitchell Robinson

Illinois's Criminal Justice System
Jill Joline Myers and Todd Lough, eds.

Maryland's Criminal Justice System
Debra L. Stanley, ed.

Massachusetts's Criminal Justice System
Lorenzo M. Boyd and Francesca Spina

Minnesota's Criminal Justice System
Jeff Bumgarner, Susan Hilal, and James Densley

Missouri's Criminal Justice System
Frances P. Reddington, ed.

New York's Criminal Justice System
Robert Costello

North Carolina's Criminal Justice System
Second Edition
Paul E. Knepper and Mark Jones

Ohio's Criminal Justice System
Joshua B. Hill, Nancy E. Marion, Kevin M. Cashen, R. James Orr, III, and Kendra J. Kec

Pennsylvania's Criminal Justice System
Mary P. Brewster and Harry R. Dammer, eds.

Texas's Criminal Justice System
Durant Frantzen and Marshall Lloyd

West Virginia's Criminal Justice System
Second Edition
Kimberly A. DeTardo-Bora, Dhruba J. Bora, and Wendy Perkins

West Virginia's Criminal Justice System

SECOND EDITION

Kimberly A. DeTardo-Bora
PROFESSOR OF CRIMINAL JUSTICE AND CRIMINOLOGY
MARSHALL UNIVERSITY

Dhruba J. Bora
PROFESSOR OF CRIMINAL JUSTICE AND CRIMINOLOGY AND
DIRECTOR OF THE SCHOOL OF FORENSIC AND CRIMINAL JUSTICE SCIENCES
MARSHALL UNIVERSITY

Wendy Perkins
ASSISTANT PROFESSOR OF CRIMINAL JUSTICE AND CRIMINOLOGY
MARSHALL UNIVERSITY

CAROLINA ACADEMIC PRESS
Durham, North Carolina

Library of Congress Cataloging-in-Publication Data

Names: DeTardo-Bora, Kimberly A., author. | Bora, Dhruba J., author.
Title: West Virginia's criminal justice system / Kimberly A. DeTardo-Bora, Dhruba J. Bora, and Wendy Perkins.
Description: Second Edition. | Durham, NC : Carolina Academic Press, [2019] |
Series: State-specific criminal justice series | Revised edition of West Virginia's criminal justice system, [2015] | Includes bibliographical references and index.
Identifiers: LCCN 2018047426 | ISBN 9781531002275 (alk. paper)
Subjects: LCSH: Criminal justice, Administration of--West Virginia. | Crime--West Virginia. | Criminology--West Virginia. | Law enforcement--West Virginia.
Classification: LCC HV9955.W42 D47 2019 | DDC 364.9754--dc23
LC record available at https://lccn.loc.gov/2018047426

eISBN 978-1-5310-1151-2

Carolina Academic Press, LLC
700 Kent Street
Durham, North Carolina 27701
Telephone (919) 489-7486
Fax (919) 493-5668
www.cap-press.com

Printed in the United States of America

To our daughter, Asha

—Kimberly A. DeTardo-Bora & Dhruba J. Bora

To my children and my students, who inspire me
to be a better version of myself.

—Wendy Perkins

Contents

Series Note

Carolina Academic Press's state-specific criminal justice series fills a gap in the field of criminal justice education. One drawback with many current introduction to criminal justice texts is that they pertain to the essentially non-existent "American" criminal justice system and ignore the local landscape. Each state has its unique legislature, executive branch, law enforcement system, court and appellate review system, state supreme court, correctional system, and juvenile justice apparatus. Since many criminal justice students embark upon careers in their home states, they are better served by being exposed to their own states' criminal justice systems. Texts in this series are designed to be used as primary texts or as supplements to more general introductory criminal justice texts.

Acknowledgments

A number of people have helped in the preparation of the second edition of this book. For their assistance, we would like to thank our graduate assistants: Erica Clark, Dylan Schaffer, and Matthew Vanden Bosch. We are also truly appreciative of the support from our dear colleague Dr. Sam Dameron and to those who helped us with obtaining pictures. Last, we would like to thank the following individuals and reviewers for their many helpful suggestions and constructive feedback:

Alex Facemyer, Probation Officer, West Virginia Supreme Court of Appeals
Jessica Napier-Eagle, Consumer Advocate and Compliance Specialist for the West Virginia Attorney General
Amy Sadler, Juvenile Probation Officer for the 29th Circuit of West Virginia
Steve Smith, Adult Probation Officer for the 13th Circuit of West Virginia
Erika Elswick, Juvenile Probation Officer for the 13th Circuit of West Virginia
Kaitlin Watson, Parole Region 1, Regional Director
Scott Lemley, Executive Director, Department of Development and Planning at City of Huntington
Jessica Underwood, Research Specialist II, West Virginia Department of Corrections
Chuck Sadler, Law Enforcement Professional Standards Coordinator, Division of Justice and Community services

West Virginia's Criminal Justice System

Chapter 1

History and Overview of the Criminal Justice System in West Virginia

West Virginia coal miner statue, Capitol Complex.
Courtesy of Sam Dameron.

During the formation of the United States, the founding fathers used their significant knowledge of British parliamentary democracy in the development of the American system of government. Moreover, they used the English system of law and order as the foundation for establishing a new criminal justice system in the former colonies. However, unlike England's unitary system, the United States was formed as a federated country. This meant we had a dual system of federal and state governments, compared to that of a singular English government. This posed unique challenges in regard to establishing each state's criminal justice process. While the fundamental concepts of a criminal justice system, by way of law enforcement, courts, and corrections, remained the same, each state's history and evolution had an independent impact on the development of their own systems of justice. However, the justice system as we know it today did not emerge in an orderly or predictable fashion. Instead, it developed haphazardly and, looking back, it was not much of a "system" at all. This chapter will provide a brief history and overview of the criminal justice system in West Virginia, as well as a current description of how the system is organized.

A Brief History of West Virginia's Criminal Justice System

The development of West Virginia's criminal justice system was largely an outgrowth of the Virginia system. A large number of the counties that we have in the state today were, in part, comprised of two earlier counties created in the State of Virginia, named Frederick and Augusta ("Counties," 2013). In the mid-to-late 1700s, some of the earliest counties were established, including Hampshire County in 1754, Berkeley County in 1772, and Ohio and Monongalia Counties in 1776.[1] At that time, some of these early Virginia colonies had their own county court, which performed a variety of executive, legislative, and judicial functions. Keep in mind that these court systems still favored the English model that was directly in line with and of service to the King of England (Oliver & Hilgenberg, 2010). This did not sit well for most colonists, and there was a growing mistrust of judges, who were lower-level justices of the peace, and for lawyers, many of whom were not legally trained. The court system was messy, misguided, and fraught with much injustice in comparison to the more refined system we know today.

With the secession of the state from Virginia, as well as the fundamental differences between the two states as a result of the American Civil War (1861–1865), a distinctive system emerged. After statehood was achieved on June 20, 1863, one of the earliest issues to be addressed was that of a state penitentiary. Small county jails simply would not suffice for the newly formed state, especially after the war.[2] After several years of construction, the Moundsville State Pen-

1. Today, West Virginia has 55 counties. The last five counties to be formed were Lincoln, Grant, Mineral, Logan, and Mingo.

2. At that time, Governor Boreman mandated that all state prisoners be held in Ohio County jails (Bumgardner, 2013). The only military prison in operation in the mid-1800s, named Atheneum, was located in Wheeling (Brennan, 2010).

itentiary, modeled after the Auburn system, was opened in 1876. Even though it served its purpose in warehousing dangerous criminals for more than 100 years, the prison had its share of problems. As the facility fell into a state of decay and disrepair, coupled with numerous lawsuits and habeas corpus petitions, the institution ceased operation in 1995.

In addition, two facilities were constructed for juveniles. In 1891, the West Virginia Reform School for boys was opened in Taylor County. Shortly thereafter, in 1913, it became known as the Industrial Home for Boys ("Pruntytown Correctional Center," 2013). The facility was designed for males under the age of 16. It was not to be a prison, per se, but a place for reformation and rigid discipline. Here they received at least a fourth grade education, training, and performed farm work. Boys as young as age six were sentenced to the reform school by court order, or by the parents, if they believed their son was unruly. The facility housed juvenile boys until 1983, when they were moved to the Industrial Home in Salem (formerly the Industrial Home for Girls), which became a co-ed facility.

In 1899, the Industrial Home for Girls (later known as the Salem Industrial Home for Youth) in Harrison County was opened. Not uncommon for this time, girls were sentenced for being incorrigible or for immoral acts, as well as crimes that were more serious. As the term "industrial" implies, the girls were taught a trade in order to become respectable citizens with honorable occupations. Harriet Jones, President of the Board of Directors, submitted the proposal for the facility and requested appropriations for the building. In her proposal, she wrote:

> We feel that we have been reasonable in our estimates, and are exceedingly anxious that this much needed institution be a success, and not handicapped for want of means to carry out the proposed plans, that our State may be able to rescue girls still innocent, but thoughtless and ignorant; to place them under good influences before they sink into lives of shame, while life with all its possibilities is open to them; to take them from the evil that surrounds them which must eventually bring them to jails, penitentiaries, and places of vice, then turned out to be a menace to society and bringing into the world men and women ten times worse than themselves, to continue to fill our public institutions in County and State (Jones, 1899, "Appropriations for the Fiscal Year," para. 10).

One of the most prominent agencies of law enforcement, the West Virginia State Police, was established in 1919 as a result of conflicts related to the coal industry (Cole, 2012). As a state deeply entrenched on its dependence for coal, unionized organizations quickly surfaced. It was not unusual for violent incidents to occur in the coalfields during these times, along with labor strikes. A few historic events serve as examples where police intervention was necessary: the Paint Creek-Cabin Creek mine war from 1912 to 1913, the Mingo mine wars from 1919 to 1921, the Battle of Blair Mountain, and the Matewan Massacre (Lewis, 2010). How the state police evolved from these conditions is explained in the passages below:

> Governor John Jacob Cornwell was the leading advocate of a state police force. He found sheriffs and constables ineffective, having to face periodic reelection and tending to take sides in labor struggles. Coal companies paid some deputy salaries in coalfield counties, and deputies moonlighted as private security guards. The private guard system angered workers and labor leaders, as did use of the National Guard during the bloody Paint Creek-Cabin Creek strike of 1912–13. Besides, the process of reestablishing the National Guard after World War I did not begin until April 1921.
>
> Labor leaders ardently opposed the police bill, but the legislature passed it anyway. Cornwell signed it into law on March 31, 1919, effective June 29. The agency was designated the Department of Public Safety. The governor appointed Jackson Arnold, grand-nephew of Gen. Thomas J. "Stonewall" Jackson and former executive officer of the 1st West Virginia Infantry, as first superintendent. Departmental headquarters was located in Charleston, and there were two field companies, with an authorized strength of 125 men. The first trooper, Sam Taylor, enlisted on July 24 (Cole, 2012, para. 2–3).

As mentioned, although local police agencies dealt with most of these incidents, the militia or National Guard was often called into areas to settle labor unrest. Formed in 1735, the primary purpose of the militia company was to protect colonists from Indian raids, and then later, during times of war (Bailey, 2015). In fact, federal troops and an air squadron were sent by President Harding during the Blair Mountain labor march (Corbin, 2016).

Throughout the years, the West Virginia criminal justice system continued to evolve amidst the backdrop of immigration, urbanization, and industrialization. This growth and change was not exclusive to the United States, but evident in industrializing countries in Europe and Asia (Walker, 1998). As the state progressed, changes were made to the system as a result of landmark events at the federal level. For example, the Civil Rights Movement, the women's movement, and the numerous reforms as a result of Supreme Court decisions involving juvenile rights (i.e., *In re Gault*, *Kent v. United States*, *Shall v. Martin*, etc.) clearly affected the state's justice system. In addition, legal

Police officer on horseback. Courtesy of the West Virginia Archives, Norma Shuck Levy Collection.

action within the state served as the impetus for change and even led to recent changes in both the adult and juvenile correctional systems. The state has had to take a deeper look into what the future holds—incarceration rates continue to climb, and drug crimes and drug dependency permeate numerous counties. These issues led the state to develop a justice reinvestment strategy in 2014, which resulted in adopting evidence-based practices, increasing access to substance abuse treatment programs, and mandating the supervision of violent offenders up to one year after incarceration. Finally, it can be said that the state's justice system continues to transform given the latest advancements with computers and technology.

The Department of Military Affairs and Public Safety

The West Virginia Department of Military Affairs and Public Safety (DMAPS) is spearheaded by a cabinet secretary, who is appointed by the governor, and a deputy secretary, who also serves as general legal counsel. The role of cabinet secretary was created by the legislature in 1989 and serves as one of the cabinet departments of the executive branch. The overarching mission of the DMAPS is "to provide a safe and secure state by ensuring the proper response to all levels, manners and phases of emergencies, disasters and crimes" (DMAPS, 2018, para. 1). Included in the Office of the Secretary are the Division of Homeland Security and Emergency Management and the West Virginia Intelligence Fusion Center. There are 10 other state agencies, and several of them make up the central agencies or public safety divisions that largely administer the justice system. They are the State Police, Division of Protective Services (which includes the Capitol Police), the Division of Corrections, the Parole Board, the Regional Jail and Correctional Facilities Authority, and the Division of Juvenile Services. The State Fire Marshal and the Adjutant General/National Guard are the other entities and, while important, are not included in this book. The remaining agency is the Division of Justice and Community Services. Brief descriptions of these agencies are presented below, with more detailed information provided in each respective chapter.

What resonates with all of these agencies is the emphasis on public safety and service; however, it is obvious that each organizational component operates independently and serves an important function in controlling, preventing, and reducing crime. For example, the West Virginia State Police, which has existed since the early 1900s, not only provides citizens with the necessary protections from criminals, but also ensures that safety is maintained on our state's streets, roads, and highways. The largest division within the state police is field services (WVSP, 2016). Within this division are seven field troops that are further divided into 20 districts, which are comprised of 59 detachments. Moreover, the field services division includes special operations, the training academy, public affairs, and the crimes against children unit. The West Virginia State Police are known to have one of the nation's most respected training academies, located in the city of Institute, which is near Charleston.

The Regional Jail and Correctional Facilities Authority Management, established in 1985, serves the public by detaining alleged and convicted offenders (WVRJA & CFA, 2016). At the same time, one of the important functions for the jails is to provide a safe, humane, and secure environment for inmates. Presently, there are 10 regional jails, serving multiple counties where pretrial detainees, misdemeanants, and inmates awaiting transfer to a state or federal institution are held.

The Division of Corrections (WVDOC) also contributes to crime control and risk containment, namely with respect to violent offenders, drug dealers, and career criminals. Equally, the role of corrections is one that is entrenched in treatment and rehabilitation, so that offenders will not return to the system once released. In addition to the Central Office, the WVDOC is comprised of

16 correctional institutions, four work release centers, two work camps, and 14 parole offices (WVDOC, 2017). Parole Services, which is instrumental in assisting inmates as they reenter society, consists of two parole districts—one in the north and one in the south, and eight parole regions (WVDOC, 2007–2017). Aside from these agencies, the WVDOC has a corrections academy and professional development center, which is currently located in Glenville in Gilmer County.

Distinct and separate from the adult system is the state's Division of Juvenile Services (DJS), which provides correctional services and treatment to the juvenile population. There are 10 juvenile detention centers (one of which is under private contract), and 13 youth day reporting centers (WVDJS, 2017). Since most youth commit minor offenses and are deemed nonviolent or status offenders, DJS often works jointly with the Department of Health and Human Resources (DHHR).

The Division of Homeland Security and Emergency Management (DHSEM) (2018) is comprised of several branches, but three primary units are relevant in this context: mitigation and recovery, preparedness and response, and technological hazards. The first two branches serve an important function in assisting with floodplain management, hazard mitigation, and emergency planning and reaction to natural as well as man-made disasters. The third branch, technological hazards, revolves more around coordination of activities in planning for and responding to radiological and hazardous materials. Also included here is the State Emergency Response Commission (SERC). The other relevant entity working closely with DHSEM is the West Virginia Intelligence Fusion Center. These entities, although separate, work to collect and filter information and intelligence to assist in identifying and preventing criminal activity and provide a comprehensive response plan for protecting citizens (West Virginia Intelligence Fusion Center, 2018).

Established in 1966, the Division of Justice and Community Services (DCJS) is an agency devoted to statewide planning and policy development to ensure that the justice system remains fair and efficient and to provide evidence-based practice and training to criminal justice professionals. The mission of DJCS is:

> to assist criminal and juvenile justice agencies and local government with research and performance data, planning, funding, and management of programs supported with granted funds, and to provide regulatory oversight of basic and annual in-service law enforcement training and certification; Community Corrections; Law Enforcement Response to Domestic Violence; and, juvenile detention facility standards compliance (DMAPS, DCJS, 2018, para. 1).

Some of the special projects and programs of the division have included the Justice Assistance Grant Program; the National Criminal History Improvement

Grant Program (NCHIP); the Child Advocacy Centers Grant Program; the Residential Substance Abuse Treatment for State Prisoners; and the Rural Domestic Violence, Dating Violence, Sexual Assault and Stalking Grant Program, just to name a few.

In addition, the division also houses the Criminal Justice Statistical Analysis Center (CJSAC), which is a member of the national Justice Research and Statistical Association (JRSA). The connection to the criminal justice system may not be as obvious, because the CJSAC is not directly a part of the "traditional" system described in this book. Yet, its importance and utility lies with the fact that the research produced from this office greatly influences practice and policy. In other words, before policies are adopted, before programs are implemented, or before training approaches are considered, analysts will conduct the necessary research to inform change. The research carried out by the research analysts is overseen by a director, and some of the research is funded by the Bureau of Justice Statistics as well as other federal agencies. In addition, residents in the state can access an interactive crime database. Some of the recent publications from this office are titled:

- "Recidivism by Direct Sentence Clients Released from Day Report Centers in 2011: Predictors and Patterns over Time" (2016, January)
- "Evidence-Based Offender Assessment: A Comparative Analysis of West Virginia and U.S. Risk Scores" (2015, October)
- "Predicting Recidivism of Offenders Released from the West Virginia Division of Corrections: Validation of the Level of Service/Case Management Inventory" (2015, September)
- "The Predictive Utility of Risk and Needs Assessment" (2015, June)

Although it is confusing, the state's criminal justice system is not neatly bundled into one single administrative unit or managed by one state-level office. In addition to the agencies just mentioned under the umbrella of DMAPS, magistrates, judges, prosecutors, defense counsel, and numerous officers of the court in all 55 counties also carry out justice. Furthermore, services are provided by the (DHHR) for juveniles who are neglected or abused as well as for status offenders. The West Virginia Supreme Court of Appeals administers another important aspect of the system, that is, adult and juvenile probation. The Division of Probation Services extends further into the management of both the adult and juvenile drug courts. Last, victims, who are often neglected in a discussion about the system, are served in part by the WVDOC in addition to several nonprofit advocacy centers.

Overview of *West Virginia's Criminal Justice System*

The purpose of this book is to provide a deeper look into the criminal justice system in the Mountain State, as most introductory textbooks about the system cover each area at a surface level with sweeping generalizations that do little to capture the nuances of each state's system. In addition, for students of criminal justice and criminology and members of the general public alike, it is important to learn about the state-specific system in an effort to dispel some of the myths often portrayed by prime-time crime dramas and local news stations. Thus, this text gives readers a realistic view of the justice system, specifically in the context of West Virginia. Some caution must be exercised before beginning, however. While the basis for the state's justice system is described and defined in much of the West Virginia legal code, how justice is carried out in practice may differ from county to county. In other words, there are distinct differences that are not addressed in this book, as it would not be feasible to describe how justice is administered in every single county. The common denominator is that each person who works in and for the system plays an important role and function within the purview of the law. The common goal or objective of each justice agency can be found in its mission statement, which is often centered on the administration of fair and humane practices while ensuring the safety and protection of the citizens.

Each chapter includes key terms and definitions, a set of review questions, and Internet resources. Where appropriate, information is provided in a "spotlight" section at the end of each chapter about a compelling or challenging issue that faces the West Virginia criminal justice system in the twenty-first century.

Aside from the organizational structure of the justice system and overview provided in this chapter, the second chapter provides a detailed description of West Virginia's crime rates in comparison to the rest of the United States. An examination of Part I index offenses is included, as well as an overview of the Uniform Crime Report (UCR) and the National Incident Based Reporting System (NIBRS). The chapter concludes with a discussion about the rise of Internet-related and computer crimes, and the ways in which data about these crimes are compiled.

In the third chapter, the state's legal authority is presented, with an overview of the formation and creation of the West Virginia constitution. A great deal of the discussion is placed in a historical framework, affording readers the opportunity to make comparisons between the United States Constitution and the West Virginia Constitution. Other important topics, such as the West

Virginia Bill of Rights and the separation of powers, are covered. In addition, an insightful special feature about the separation of the state from Virginia is provided at the end of the chapter.

Chapter 4 highlights the history of policing and the state's main policing agencies, that is, state, county, and municipal law enforcement. A great deal of coverage is given to one of the most notable and nationally reputable law enforcement programs—the West Virginia State Police. Essential to policing and prosecution, the forensic laboratory is also discussed. Professionally trained and armed officers who serve some of our numerous college campuses and federal law enforcement agencies also are covered. The chapter includes an overview of the process for becoming a police officer and the physical fitness requirements for entry into the police academy. The chapter ends with a spotlight discussion about police training.

Chapter 5, which delves into the state court structure, examines the courts from a historical perspective to its current status today. In addition, the key players in the courts process are introduced. Then, the structure of the current state system, which flows from the West Virginia Supreme Court of Appeals all the way down to the magistrate courts, is presented. The chapter concludes by highlighting some of the specialty courts and programs, such as drug courts. As a "spotlight," the chapter poses the question of whether an intermediate appellate court is necessary.

Topics related to adult corrections are discussed in Chapter 6. An organizational overview of the West Virginia Division of Corrections, the Regional Jail Authority, and Division of Probation Services is included. Then, details are presented about the different types of state prisons and jail facilities, including community corrections and prison industries. State prison data are provided where readers will gain a sense of the common types of offenses for which most people are incarcerated in the state. Despite the fact that the state has relatively low recidivism rates compared to others, reinvestment strategies undertaken by the state are discussed briefly. Also, descriptions of officer training, inmate programs, and the Federal Bureau of Prisons are included. While not all offenders are behind bars, special attention is given to the role of parole and probation officers. Given the impact of incarceration on children and the realization that some women enter prison while pregnant, the chapter ends with a description of the prison nursery program at Lakin Correctional Center for Women.

While much of the text is centered on adults, Chapter 7 addresses West Virginia's juvenile justice system. A portion of the chapter is devoted to key concepts such as "juvenile delinquent," "status offender," and "juvenile petition." It also provides the reader with a sense of the process, mainly involving the courts and hearings. Attention is given to adjudicated delinquents as well as detention and other dispositions. Furthermore, drug courts are described along with teen courts. To conclude, the chapter provides an insightful look into juvenile waiver to adult court.

Chapter 8 begins with a historical background on the victims' rights movement and the Victim Protection Act in West Virginia. Important legal definitions and penalties for domestic violence and sexual assault are presented. Moreover, the chapter includes a discussion about the prevalence of domestic violence and sexual assault in the state. State-driven services and programs are described, including the West Virginia Department of Corrections' Victims Services, the VINE system (Victim Information and Notification Everyday), the victim's compensation fund, and the assistance from victims' advocates who are housed in some of the counties' prosecuting attorney offices. In addition, the efforts and contributions of nonprofit agencies are recognized, including the West Virginia Coalition Against Domestic Violence, the West Virginia Foundation for Rape Information and Services, TEAM for West Virginia Children, and the West Virginia Child Advocacy Network. The last part of the chapter covers elder abuse and mistreatment.

The next chapter explains the multifaceted issues that coincide with drug and alcohol abuse. Incorporated is a brief discussion of the drug-crime connection. Moreover, drug addiction and drug abuse are defined and the West Virginia penalties for drug crimes are discussed. Furthermore, the chapter highlights several types of drugs and their damaging effects, such as marijuana, methamphetamine, heroin, cocaine, and crack cocaine, among others. Readers also learn about the federal Controlled Substances Act in addition to West Virginia's Uniform Controlled Substances Act. Information about drug arrests and seizures by the state police are also shared. Aside from the newly implemented West Virginia hotline to combat drug addiction, the chapter ends with a glimpse of the devastating effects of how drugs can impact a pregnancy and the ways in which neonatal abstinence syndrome are being addressed in our area hospitals and by our non-profit agencies.

To conclude, Chapter 10 takes a brief look at counterterrorism and homeland security. While the policy and mission of these areas is not that different from the federal mandate, there are unique situations in the state that exist in regard to homeland security that are identified. The chapter includes the evolution of counterterrorism strategy from a broader perspective of the United States and then more specifically, the role of the West Virginia Division of Homeland Security and Emergency Management, as well as the state Intelligence Fusion Center that exists to assist federal and local agencies in not only homeland security issues, but local criminal activity as well. Finally, the chapter concludes with an innovative program that has been developed among the United States Department of Homeland Security (DHS), the Fusion Center, and several state universities that operate Open Source Intelligence Exchange (OSIX) labs, which utilize college student analysts.

Select Internet Sources

West Virginia Division of Corrections (WVDOC): http://www.wvdoc.com/wvdoc/.
West Virginia Division of Juvenile Services: http://djs.wv.gov/Pages/default.aspx.
West Virginia Division of Probation Services: http://www.courtswv.gov/court-administration/probation/probation-services.html.
West Virginia Regional Jail & Correctional Facility Authority: http://www.rja.wv.gov/Pages/default.aspx.
West Virginia State Police: http://www.wvsp.gov/Pages/default.aspx.

References

Bailey, K. R. (2015, November). West Virginia National Guard. *e-WV: The West Virginia Encyclopedia.* Charleston, WV: West Virginia Humanities Council. Retrieved from http://www.wvencyclopedia.org/articles/1074.

Brennan, M. (2010, December). Atheneum prison. *e-WV: The West Virginia Encyclopedia.* Charleston, WV: West Virginia Humanities Council. Retrieved from http://www.wvencyclopedia.org/articles/305.

Bumgardner, S. (2013, May). Moundsville penitentiary. *e-WV: The West Virginia Encyclopedia.* Charleston, WV: West Virginia Humanities Council. Retrieved from http://www.wvencyclopedia.org/articles/1427.

Cole, M. T. (2012, September). State police. *e-WV: The West Virginia Encyclopedia.* Charleston, WV: West Virginia Humanities Council. Retrieved from http://www.wvencyclopedia.org/articles/573.

Corbin, D.A. (2016, December). The mine wars. *e-WV: The West Virginia Encyclopedia.* Charleston, WV: West Virginia Humanities Council. Retrieved from https://www.wvencyclopedia.org/articles/1799.

Counties. (2013, February). *e-WV: The West Virginia Encyclopedia.* Charleston, WV: West Virginia Humanities Council. Retrieved from http://www.wvencyclopedia.org/articles/1624.

Jones, H. B. (1899). *West Virginia Industrial Home for Girls: Biennial report, West Virginia Industrial Home for Girls Salem, West Virginia, 1899.* Charleston, WV: West Virginia Archives and History, West Virginia Division of Culture and History. Retrieved from http://www.wvculture.org/history/government/salem05.html.

Lewis, R. L. (2010). Labor history. *e-WV: The West Virginia Encyclopedia.* Charleston, WV: West Virginia Humanities Council. Retrieved from https://www.wvencyclopedia.org/articles/1271.

Oliver, W. M., & Hilgenberg, J. F., Jr. (2010). *A history of crime and criminal justice in America* (2nd ed.). Durham, NC: Carolina Academic Press.

Pruntytown Correctional Center. (2013, June). *e-WV: The West Virginia Encyclopedia.* Charleston, WV: West Virginia Humanities Council. Retrieved from http://www.wvencyclopedia.org/articles/1935.

Walker, S. (1998). *Popular justice: A history of American criminal justice.* NY: Oxford University Press.

West Virginia Department of Military Affairs and Public Safety (DMAPS). (2018). Retrieved from https://dmaps.wv.gov/Pages/default.aspx.

West Virginia Division of Corrections (WVDOC). (2007–2017). *Parole services overview.* Retrieved from http://www.wvdoc.com/wvdoc/ParoleServicesResources/ParoleServicesOverview/tabid/41/Default.aspx.

West Virginia Division of Corrections (WVDOC). (2017). *Annual report: 2017.* Charleston, WV: Office of Research and Planning. Retrieved from http://www.wvdoc.com/wvdoc/Portals/0/documents/2017-Annual-Report.pdf.

West Virginia Division of Homeland Security and Emergency Management (DHSEM). (2018). Retrieved from http://dhsem.wv.gov/About/Pages/default.aspx.

West Virginia Division of Juvenile Services (WVDJS). (2017, January). *West Virginia Division of Juvenile Services annual report for fiscal year 2016.* Retrieved from http://djs.wv.gov/annualreport/Documents/Annual%20Report%202016.pdf.

West Virginia Intelligence Fusion Center. (2018). Retrieved from http://www.wv.gov/fusioncenter/pages/default.aspx.

West Virginia Regional Jail and Correctional Facility Authority (WVRJA & CFA). (2016). *Annual report FY 2016.* Retrieved from http://rja.wv.gov/Documents/Annual%20Reports%20and%20Inmate%20Resources/The%20RJA%20Annual%20Report%20FY%202016%20revised.pdf.

West Virginia State Police (WVSP). (2016). *West Virginia State Police AY 2015–2016 annual report.* Retrieved from https://www.wvsp.gov/about/Documents/AnnualReports/2016annualReport.pdf.

Legal References

In re Gault, 387 U.S. 1 (1967).
Kent v. United States, 383 U.S. 541 (1966).
Schall v. Martin, 467 U.S. 253 (1984).

Chapter 2

Crime in West Virginia

Members of the Hatfield family. Courtesy of the West Virginia Archives.

Given the history of West Virginia, its secession from Virginia, and its position in the southeastern part of the United States, one would assume that it is plagued with high crime rates. In recent years, it can be said that this is partially true as certain types of crimes in West Virginia mirror in number, and in frequency, the rest of the country as a whole. It would be misleading, however, to assume that this is the case for all types of crimes. There are some remarkable differences signaling that West Virginia's crime rate for many types of offenses is much lower than the rest of the country. Specifically, West Virginia ranks 28th in violent crimes and 36th in property crimes in the United States, according to 2016 estimates (USDOJ/FBI, 2017).

Using crime data to examine rates and trends is of utmost importance to criminologists, legislators, and criminal justice professionals alike. Such an examination assists state and local law enforcement agencies in identifying "hot spots," or areas where crime is concentrated, in addition to analyzing whether increases or decreases among certain types of crimes (i.e., homicide, sexual assault, arson, drug crimes, property crimes, etc.) have occurred over a certain period. However, this type of analysis must be conducted with caution. Naturally, a notable increase or decrease in crime rates can be impacted by a number of factors, such as poverty, unemployment, population, availability of drugs, demographics, and police resources, among other causes (McDowall & Loftin, 2009). Another issue, discussed later in this chapter, is that the collection of official statistics is not without limitations. Thus, before examining violent and property crime rate trends, it is essential to put the state's social, racial, and economic factors into context.

In 2017, the population of West Virginia was estimated to be 1,815,857, according to the United States Census Bureau (2017). Similar to the rest of the United States, data from 2016 show that West Virginia is mostly comprised of whites (93.6% in West Virginia; 76.9% in the United States). The state is clearly one of the least diverse among the 50 states (Maine, Vermont, and New Hampshire have a white population that ranges from 93.8% to 94.8%). For example, the population of African Americans in West Virginia is 3.6% compared to the national percentage of 13.3%. In terms of age, there are slightly fewer younger people under the age of 18 (20.5%) compared to the rest of the country (22.8%). In turn, there is a larger percentage of people 65 and older (18.8% in West Virginia; 15.2% in the United States). One of the other major differences is that the median household income in West Virginia from 2012 to 2016 was far below the national average at $42,644 while the United States as a whole was $55,322. With such a low median income, it is not surprising that the number of people who live below the poverty level is higher in West Virginia (17.9% in West Virginia; 12.7% in the United States). In terms of education, West Virginia has a relatively similar number of high school graduates (85.3% in West Virginia; 87.0% in the United States); however, there are substantially fewer who have earned a bachelor's degree or higher (19.6% in West Virginia; 30.3% in the United States).

Measuring Crime

Official Crime Data: The Uniform Crime Report

Every year, the U.S. Justice Department's Federal Bureau of Investigation (FBI) compiles information from the nation's police departments on the number of criminal acts reported by citizens and number of persons arrested each year. These official statistics are called the **UCR**, or known formally as the Uniform Crime Report. The idea to compile crime statistics began in 1929 by the International Association of Chiefs of Police and, in 1930, the FBI was assigned to collect and archive the data. Annually, about 18,000 agencies report to the UCR Program. There are two parts of the UCR: Part I offenses and Part II offenses. ***Part I***, also known as index offenses, includes eight crime categories consisting of criminal homicide (murder and nonnegligent manslaughter), rape, robbery, aggravated assault, burglary, larceny-theft, arson, and motor vehicle theft. ***Part II***, or nonindex offenses, include crimes such as simple assault, forgery, fraud, gambling, embezzlement, vandalism, drug abuse violations, and drunkenness, among others. In regard to index offenses, participating law enforcement agencies are expected to report only the highest ranking offense of a crime event, even though multiple offenses may have been committed during the commission of a single crime event (called the Hierarchal Rule). However, there are three crimes in which there is an exception—arson, human trafficking involving commercial sex acts, and human trafficking involving involuntary servitude. Hence, these offenses are always counted even when multiple offenses may have occurred within one single incident.

The UCR is one of the few ways by which we can ascertain the amount of crime that occurs in our country; however, as stated earlier, the data generated by the UCR can be problematic. First, a number of crimes are not reported to the FBI. For example, a number of cybercrimes are presently unknown. Also, staff from local police departments may make data entry errors and it is possible that some police departments manipulate statistics in order to show a reduction or effort to fight crime. Moreover, records only show those who were "caught." Not all crimes are reported to the police, known as the ***dark figure of crime***, suggesting that the crime data provided from the UCR is in fact lower or not indicative of the true number of crimes that occur in the country. As mentioned above, using the hierarchal system, only the most serious offense during the commission of a single crime incident is reported, despite the fact that about 15% of crime incidents involve multiple offenses. Additionally, a great deal of classification error has been known to take place. This is particularly the case when a police officer records a crime in a certain category given local criminal statutes that may vary from the UCR's definition and categories (Nolan, Hass, & Napier, 2011). Last, not all police departments have the necessary resources for compiling data or data entry, which means that not all municipalities across the United States report crime. However, accuracy is improving, and the UCR Program continues to adjust the ways in which data are collected and how crimes are defined given the changing social climate.

One of the most important improvements and changes to the UCR is the definition of rape. The term originally used was "forcible rape," and it was defined in 1929 as "the carnal knowledge of a female forcibly and against her will" (LESS & CSMU, 2013, p. 34). For the 2013 reporting year, the definition was changed to "penetration, no matter how slight, of the vagina or anus with any body part or object, or oral penetration by a sex organ of another person, without the consent of the victim" (LESS & CSMU, 2013, p. 32). The modifications resulted in the omission of the term "forcible" and the phrase "against the person's will." In turn, the revised definition includes the phrase, "without the consent of the victim." This allows for instances where the victim may be mentally or physically incapacitated on a temporary or permanent basis (e.g., due to the influence of drugs or alcohol or because of age). Moreover, the definition is not gender exclusive as it was before; that is, both male and female victims and/or offenders are included.

Second, and also effective in 2013, the UCR Program changed the racial and ethnic categories. These changes are now more consistent with the definitions of race and ethnicity used by the United States Census Bureau. For instance, the four racial categories of White, Black, American Indian/Alaskan Native, Asian/Other Pacific Islander were altered by creating a separate category for Asian, thereby resulting in a fifth racial category, "Native Hawaiian/Other Pacific Islander." To more accurately report a person's ethnicity, the category "Hispanic" was expanded to "Hispanic/Latino Origin" or "Not of Hispanic/Latino Origin."

The last set of changes to the UCR is the way in which data are collected regarding human trafficking and hate crimes. As part of the William Wilberforce Trafficking Victims Protection Reauthorization Act of 2008 and the Matthew Shepard and James Byrd, Jr. Hate Crime Prevention Act of 2009, these data will be exclusively compiled by the FBI. Such data will allow law enforcement officials to gain more insight into crimes that involve the trafficking of humans in our country and across state and international lines, as well as the number of crimes motivated by gender and/or gender identity bias.

NIBRS Data

When examining crime trends, what typically comes to mind is the Uniform Crime Report. However, there are additional data sets that are equally as important when examining the crime phenomenon. One example is the ***National Incident-Based Reporting System (NIBRS)***, which was created in 1988 in an effort to provide more detailed crime data. Instead of Part I and Part II offenses, NIBRS has Group A and Group B offense categories. Group A is comprised of 52 different offenses in 24 different categories and Group B contains 10 offense categories (see Table 2.1) (LESS & CSMU, 2017). Every offense is counted, unlike the hierarchal system employed by the UCR. Group A offenses are further subdivided into three additional categories (not shown in Table 2.1). They are: "Crimes Against Persons," "Crimes Against Property," and "Crimes Against Society." Clearly, crimes such as murder, rape, and assault fall under the Crimes Against Persons category as the victims are always individuals. Robbery, bribery, and burglary are crimes committed for some purpose or benefit and are categorized as "Crimes Against Property." Last, the category, "Crimes Against Society" includes behaviors that are offensive to society in general, but are often victimless crimes and includes crimes like gambling, prostitution, and drug violations.

There are numerous advantages to using NIBRS. For example, more detailed information pertaining to specific crimes can be obtained, arrest information can be linked to a specific crime incident, plus a deeper analysis can be conducted as to the attempted and completed crimes not just within, but across law enforcement jurisdictions (James & Rishard, 2008). Given the detailed nature of NIBRS, additional analyses can be performed to examine the interrelationships among offenses, offenders, and victims. Contrary to the advantages listed here, there are also disadvantages to using NIBRS; many of these fall in line with the limitations of the UCR. Even with NIBRS data, there are crimes unreported to law enforcement, definitional variations across jurisdictions and at the state level, and data classification issues. Also, in order to be eligible to use NIBRS, states must be certified, mainly by demonstrating a very low error rate among incident reports. Last, 2016 NIBRS data showed that only 37.1% (6,849 law enforcement agencies) provided crime data. Because there are fewer agencies that report to NIBRS, ranking West Virginia among the other states in the country serves no real purpose, but the data are useful at the state level in some regards (see Chapter 4). Widespread adoption of NIBRS among all law enforcement agencies will certainly be fruitful; adoption of a NIBRS-only data collection system is scheduled for 2021. For this chapter, mostly UCR data are used to analyze crime trends.[1]

1. While NIBRS and the UCR provide us with certain trends and insights, the National Crime Victimization Survey is yet another, which is explained in more detail in Chapter 8.

Table 2.1. NIBRS Group A and Group B Offenses

Group A Offenses	Group B Offenses
Animal Cruelty	Bad Checks
Arson	Curfew/Loitering/Vagrancy Violations
Assault Offenses: Aggravated Assault, Simple Assault, Intimidation	Disorderly Conduct
Bribery	Driving Under the Influence
Burglary/Break and Entering	Drunkenness
Counterfeiting/Forgery	Family Offenses, Nonviolent
Destruction/Damage/ Vandalism of Property	Liquor Law Violations
Drug/Narcotic Offense: Drug/Narcotic Violations, Drug Equipment Violations	Peeping Tom
Embezzlement	Trespass of Real Property
Extortion/Blackmail	All Other Offenses
Fraud Offenses: False Pretenses/Swindle/ Confidence Game, Credit Card/Automatic Teller Machine Fraud, Impersonation, Welfare Fraud, Wire Fraud, Identity Theft, Hacking/Computer Invasion	
Gambling Offenses: Betting/Wagering, Operating/Promoting/Assisting Gambling, Gambling Equipment Violations, Sports Tampering	
Homicide Offenses: Murder and Non-Negligent Manslaughter, Negligent Manslaughter, Justifiable Homicide	
Human Trafficking: Human Trafficking, Commercial Sex Acts, Human Trafficking, Involuntary Servitude	
Kidnapping/Abduction	
Larceny/Theft Offenses: Pocket-picking, Purse-snatching, Shoplifting, Theft from Building, Theft from Coin-Operated Machine or Device, Theft from Motor Vehicle, Theft of Motor Vehicle Parts or Accessories, All Other Larceny	

Group A Offenses	Group B Offenses
Motor Vehicle Theft	
Pornography/Obscene Material	
Prostitution Offenses: Prostitution, Assisting or Promoting Prostitution, Purchasing Prostitution	
Robbery	
Sex Offenses, Rape, Sodomy, Sexual Assault With An Object, Fondling	
Sex Offenses, Consensual: Incest, Statutory Rape	
Stolen Property Offenses	
Weapon Law Violations	

Source: Law Enforcement Support Section (LESS), Crime Statistics Management Unit (CSMU). (2017). *Criminal Justice Information Services (CJIS) Division Uniform Crime Reporting (UCR) Program: National Incident-Based Reporting System (NIBRS) user manual.* Retrieved from http://www.fbi.gov/about-us/cjis/ucr/nibrs/nibrs-user-manual (pp.15–18).

Crime Trends in West Virginia

As shown in Table 2.2, in 2016 there were 6,557 violent crimes in West Virginia at a rate of 358.1. This means that for every 100,000 people in West Virginia, there were a little over 358 violent crimes. Here, ***crime rates*** are used because it helps practitioners, legislators, and researchers put the actual number of crimes into perspective with regard to the number of people in the population. This allows for more precise comparisons across states, municipalities, and counties. It can be argued that crime in West Virginia is relatively lower across most crime categories in comparison to the United States as a whole. Upon inspection, even though there were a reasonably lower number of actual offenses compared to the rest of the nation, a few of the rates are similar when adjusting for population size. For example, the 2016 murder rate in West Virginia is relatively close to the national rate (4.4 per 100,000 in the population in West Virginia versus 5.3 per 100,000 in the population in the United States) as well as the rape rate using the new definition (35.9 per 100,000 in the population in West Virginia versus 40.9 per 100,000 in the population in the United States). The two exceptions are the rates of aggravated assault and burglary, both of which were higher in 2016 in the state compared to the rest of the country. A

Table 2.2. Comparison of Violent and Property Crime Rates in the United States and West Virginia, 2016

Offenses	United States		West Virginia	
	Number of Offenses	Rate per 100,000	Number of Offenses	Rate per 100,000
Violent crime	1,248,185	386.3	6,557	358.1
Murder and nonnegligent manslaughter	17,250	5.3	81	4.4
Rape	130,603	40.9	657	35.9
Robbery	332,198	102.8	720	39.3
Aggravated assault	803,007	248.5	5,099	278.5
Property crime	7,919,035	2,450.7	37,487	2,047.20
Burglary	1,515,095	468.9	9,301	507.9
Larceny-theft	5,638,455	1,745.0	25,677	1,402.30
Motor vehicle theft	765,484	236.9	2,509	137

Source: United States Department of Justice, Federal Bureau of Investigation. (2017, September). *Crime in the United States, 2016 (by Region, Geographic Division, and State, 2015–2016; Table 1).* Retrieved from https://ucr.fbi.gov/crime-in-the-u.s/2016/crime-in-the-u.s.-2016/tables/table-2.

comparison of property crime rates reveals that West Virginia is substantially below the national level. The state rate of larceny-theft is significantly lower (1,402.3 per 100,000 in the population in West Virginia versus 1,745 per 100,000 in the population in the United States) than the rest of the United States, including motor vehicle theft (137 per 100,000 in the population in West Virginia versus 236.9 per 100,000 in the population in the United States).

On the other hand, while West Virginia's violent crime rate overall was lower than the national rate, data from the FBI's UCR shows that in 2016, 23 states had violent crime rates lower than West Virginia. In terms of states with a similar population, West Virginia had a considerably larger violent crime rate in comparison to states like Maine, Rhode Island, Idaho, Nebraska, and New Hampshire. Examining all of the states in the Southern Atlantic region as shown in Table 2.3, West Virginia's overall violent crime rate ranked among one of the lowest (358.1 per 100,000 in the population) in 2016. The state of Virginia had the lowest violent crime rate of 217.6 per 100,000 people in the

Table 2.3. Comparison of Violent and Property Crime Rates among South Atlantic States, 2016

	Population	Violent crime	Murder and non-negligent man-slaughter	Rape (revised definition)	Robbery	Aggravated assault	Property crime	Burglary	Larceny-theft	Motor vehicle theft
	Rate per 100,000	Rate per 100,000	Rate per 100,000	Rate per 100,000	Rate per 100,000	Rate per 100,000	Rate per 100,000	Rate per 100,000	Rate per 100,000	Rate per 100,000
South Atlantic	63,923,309	404.7	6.4	34.9	103.9	259.5	2,648.0	516.4	1,931.6	199.9
Delaware	952,065	508.8	5.9	32.4	142.7	327.8	2,766.0	527.6	2,078.7	159.7
Washington, DC	681,170	1,205.9	20.4	78.1	510.9	596.5	4,802.9	346.6	4,019.8	436.5
Florida	20,612,439	430.3	5.4	36.9	97.9	290.2	2,686.8	486.7	1,990.8	209.3
Georgia	10,310,371	397.6	6.6	34.0	118.4	238.5	3,004.5	614.4	2,130.1	259.9
Maryland	6,016,447	472.0	8.0	29.2	171.0	263.8	2,284.5	410.4	1,677.4	196.7
North Carolina	10,146,788	372.2	6.7	28.1	92.0	245.5	2,737.5	710.4	1,876.2	150.8
South Carolina	4,961,119	501.8	7.4	48.1	81.3	365.0	3,243.8	664.7	2,298.5	280.6
Virginia	8,411,808	217.6	5.8	32.5	57.1	122.2	1,859.4	238.0	1,505.1	116.4
West Virginia	1,831,102	358.1	4.4	35.9	39.3	278.5	2,047.2	507.9	1,402.3	137.0

Source: United States Department of Justice, Federal Bureau of Investigation. (2017, September). *Crime in the United States, 2016 (by region, geographic division, and state, 2015–2016; Table 2).* Retrieved from https://ucr.fbi.gov/crime-in-the-u.s/2016/crime-in-the-u.s.-2016/topic-pages/tables/table-2.

population. In this region alone, West Virginia also had the lowest rates of murder and nonnegligent manslaughter robbery, larceny-theft, and motor vehicle theft. Out of the eight states shown in the table, plus the District of Columbia, West Virginia had a higher rape rate (35.9 per 100,000 in the population) using the revised definition, and ranked fifth highest in aggravated assault (278.5 per 100,000 in the population) and burglary (507.9 per 100,000 in the population).

Detailed Examination of Crime Rates and Trends

A more detailed examination of crime rates and trends is warranted to capture a better understanding of how West Virginia compares to the rest of the country with regard to specific types of violent and property offenses. The next set of figures depicts crime trends from 1996 to 2016, using data obtained from the UCR.[2]

Violent Crimes

Murder

The homicide data in Figure 2.1 are defined by the FBI as "criminal homicide." There are two types of homicide included in this category. The first is ***murder and nonnegligent manslaughter***, which is "the willful (nonnegligent) killing of one human being by another" (LESS & CSMU, 2013, p. 28). It is important to note that there are several types of deaths that are excluded. These are deaths due to negligence, attempts to kill, assaults to kill, suicides, as well as accidental deaths. The second type is ***negligent manslaughter*** and it is defined as "the killing of another person through gross negligence" (LESS & CSMU, 2013, p. 31). Again, there are types of deaths that are excluded. These are deaths of persons caused by their own negligence, an accidental death that does not result from gross negligence, and traffic-related fatalities.

Figure 2.1 shows a declining trend in the murder rate in the United States over the past 20 years, with the exception of a slight increase starting in 2014. West Virginia has traditionally held a lower murder rate than the rate in the

---

2. In order to compare data and trends over the past 20 years, the FBI's Crime Data Explorer was used as a resource for developing the figures presented in this chapter (see https://crime-data-explorer.fr.cloud.gov/).

Figure 2.1. Estimated Murder Rate in West Virginia Compared to the United States, 1996–2016

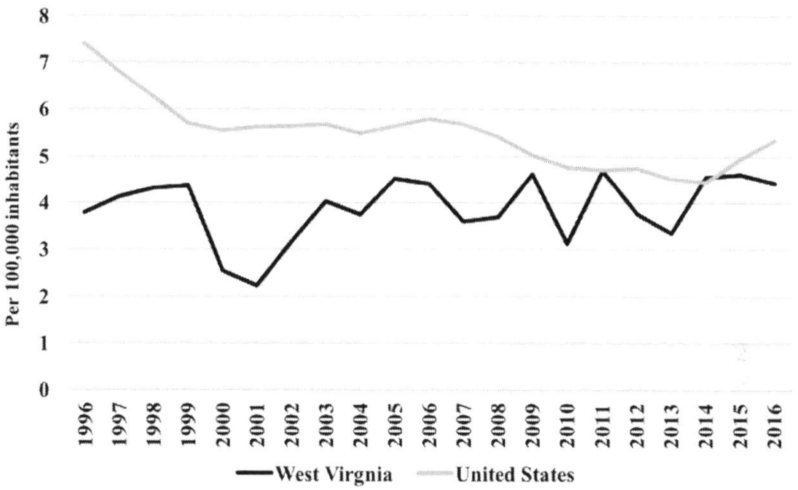

Source: Federal Bureau of Investigation (FBI), Crime Data Explorer. (2018). *Homicide rate in West Virginia, 1996–2016*. Retrieved from https://crime-data-explorer.fr.cloud.gov/explorer/state/west-virginia/homicide?placeId=WV&since=1996&until=2016.

entire United States. It can be seen that the murder rate appeared to steadily increase over the late 1990s and then took a sharp decline to the lowest rate of 2.2 in 2001. The rate remained lower than the United States until it converged with the rate of the nation in 2011 (4.6 per 100,000 in the population for West Virginia and 4.7 per 100,000 in the population for the United States) and then nudged past it in 2014 (4.5 per 100,000 in the population for West Virginia and 4.4 per 100,000 in the population for the United States). Recent data show that in 2016 the murder rate for the state was actually below the national average (4.4 per 100,000 in the population for West Virginia and 5.3 per 100,000 in the population for the United States). In terms of actual numbers and not rates, there were 81 reported homicides in West Virginia in 2016, compared to the 17,250 documented homicides that took place in the entire country. Despite these differences, the murder rate in West Virginia is still alarming.

Additional analyses about homicide can be drawn using NIBRS data, but caution is necessary as not all West Virginia police agencies report NIBRS data to the FBI. Nonetheless, the data show that since 1998, 79% of homicide offenders in West Virginia were male versus 82% of homicide offenders in the United States. Also, this means that in West Virginia, there has been a slightly

Table 2.4. Comparison of Types of Weapons Used in Murder Cases, United States and West Virginia, 2016

	West Virginia	United States
Total Murders[1]	76	15,028
Total firearms	47	10,970
Handguns	30	7,102
Rifles	2	374
Shotguns	0	262
Firearms (type unknown)	15	3,232
Knives or cutting instruments	4	1,604
Other weapons	21	1,798
Hands, fists, feet, etc.[2]	4	656

Source: United States Department of Justice, Federal Bureau of Investigation. (2017, September). *Crime in the United States, 2016* (*Murder, by State, Types of Weapons, 2016; Table 12* modified). Retrieved from https://ucr.fbi.gov/crime-in-the-u.s/2016/crime-in-the-u.s.-2016/tables/table-12.

Note: [1] Total number of murders for which supplemental homicide data were received. [2] Pushed is included in hands, fists, feet, etc.

larger percentage of females who commit homicide (17% of homicide offenders in West Virginia were female versus 11% of homicide offenders overall in the United States). Moreover, data show that 69% of homicide crime victims were male and 30% were female. Similar to the rest of the country, the most common age range of the offender was 20–29 and the most common age range of the victim was 20–29. Homicides were reported to most likely occur in a residence or home. This was true for both West Virginia and the rest of the country. Given the racial demographic of West Virginia being predominantly white, it makes sense that the homicide offender was typically white as opposed to African American (74% of homicide offenders were white in West Virginia versus 38% of homicide offenders in the United States).

From Figure 2.1 alone, criminal justice professionals and researchers are unable to tell how these murders were carried out. Additional data are presented in Table 2.4 regarding the types of murder weapons used. Instead of rates, raw numbers are presented. Unarguably, in both West Virginia and the United States, firearms, namely handguns, are the most common weapons used in the case of murder. The least common type of weapon used was a shotgun. In addition, what can be seen here is that West Virginia ranks far

Figure 2.2. Estimated Robbery Rate in West Virginia Compared to the United States, 1996–2016

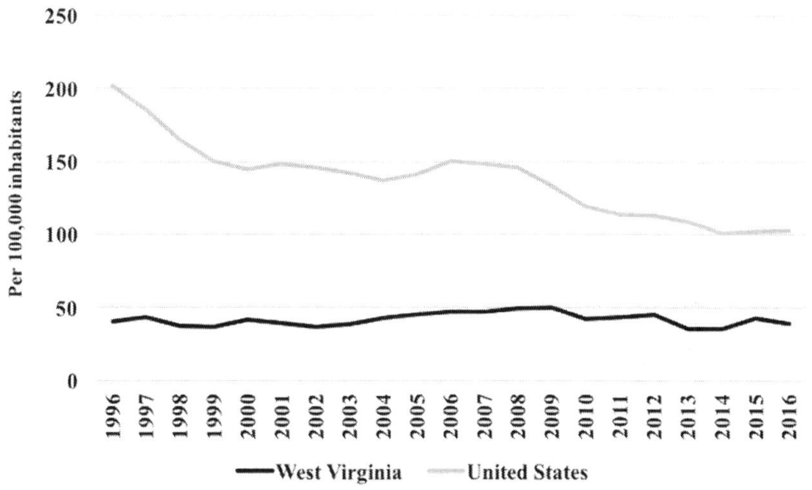

Source: Federal Bureau of Investigation (FBI), Crime Data Explorer. (2018*). Robbery rate in West Virginia, 1996–2016.* Retrieved from https://crime-data-explorer.fr.cloud.gov/explorer/state/west-virginia/robbery?placeId=WV&since=1996&until=2016.

below the average in the number of total firearms used for the commission of a murder. While 47 murders involved some type of firearm in 2016, the average number of firearms used to commit murder in the United States was 219 (FBI, 2017).

Robbery

According to the UCR, ***robbery*** refers to "the taking or attempting to take anything of value from the care, custody, or control of a person or persons by force or threat of force or violence and/or by putting the victim in fear" (LESS & CSMU, 2013, p. 35). As depicted in Figure 2.2, robbery in the United States has been decreasing since 1996 and in West Virginia the rate has been considerably and consistently lower when compared to the rest of the nation. The highest robbery rate occurred in West Virginia in 2009 at 50.2 per 100,000 in the population. More recently, in 2016 the rate was 39.3 in West Virginia compared to 102.8 in the United States.

Figure 2.3. Estimated Rape Rate in West Virginia Compared to the United States, 1996–2016

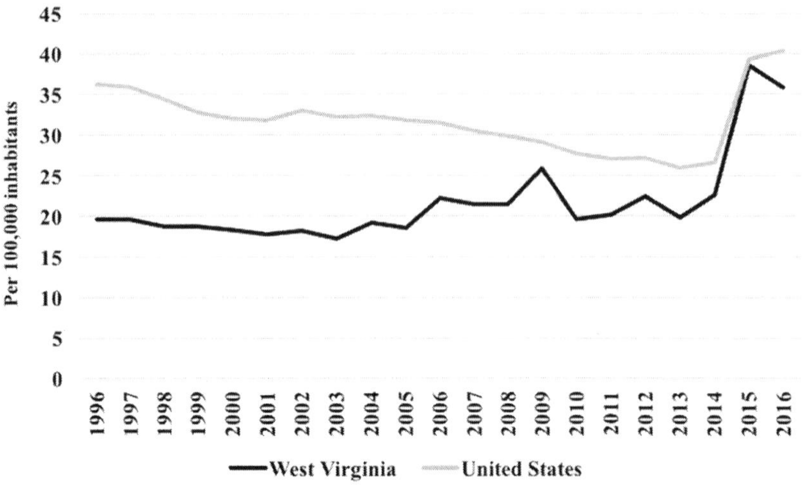

Source: Federal Bureau of Investigation (FBI), Crime Data Explorer. (2018). *Rape rate in West Virginia, 1996–2016.* Retrieved from https://crime-data-explorer.fr.cloud.gov/explorer/state/west-virginia/rape?placeId=WV&since=1996&until=2016.

Rape/Forcible Rape

As mentioned earlier, the term ***forcible rape*** was used prior to 2013. Thus, drawing conclusions about trends reflected in the Figure 2.3 data is complicated. From 1996–2012, the term forcible rape (also referenced as the legacy definition) was used and defined as "the carnal knowledge of a female forcibly and against her will" (LESS & CMSU, 2013, p. 34). This included a rape that took place by force and any attempt or assault to rape despite the age of the victim. Recent data reflect the term rape, which is defined as "penetration, no matter how slight, of the vagina or anus with any body part or object, or oral penetration by a sex organ of another person, without the consent of the victim" (LESS & CMSU, 2013, p. 32). The expanded definition allows departments to report attempted rape and assault but statutory rapes and incest are excluded. It is assumed that the sharp increase in 2014 is largely a reflection of the new definition and a more accurate depiction of the extent of this crime. In 2016, the rate for West Virginia was lower than the rest of the nation at a rate of 35.8 per 100,000 in the population (40.4 per 100,000 in the population in the United States).

Figure 2.4. Estimated Aggravated Assault Rate in West Virginia Compared to the United States, 1996–2016

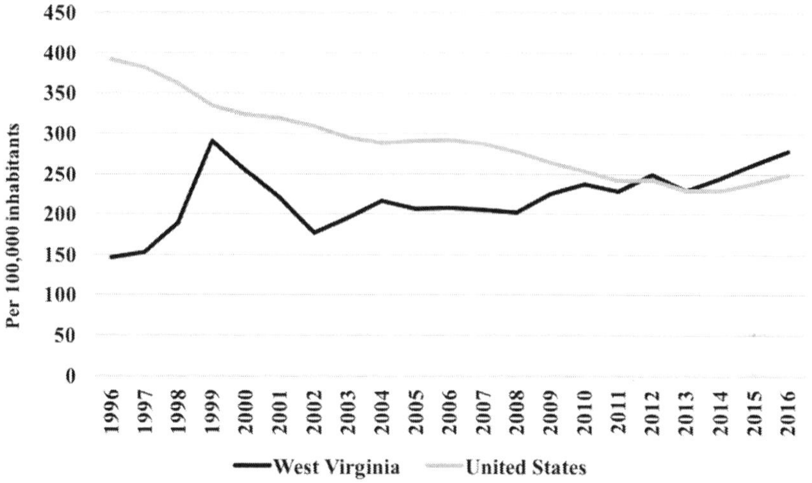

Source: Federal Bureau of Investigation (FBI), Crime Data Explorer. (2018). *Aggravated assault rate in West Virginia, 1996–2016*. Retrieved from https://crime-data-explorer.fr.cloud.gov/explorer/state/west-virginia/aggravated-assault?placeId=WV&since=1996&until=2016.

Aggravated Assault

As presented in Figure 2.4, one of the most interesting trends is how the national and state rates for aggravated assault converged in 2012 and 2013. ***Aggravated assault*** is known as "an unlawful attack by one person upon another for the purpose of inflicting severe or aggravated bodily injury. This type of assault usually is accompanied by the use of a weapon or by means likely to produce death or great bodily harm" (LESS & CSMU, 2013, p. 37). It is important to note that the act of simple assault does not involve an attempt to commit serious bodily harm or the commission of an act where a person is put in fear of being seriously harmed or injured; these acts are not included in this crime category. As displayed in Figure 2.4, the nation's rate of aggravated assaults has been steadily declining, despite a small upward trend in 2014. Also notable in this figure, aggravated assault in West Virginia reached a rate of 244.6 per 100,000 in the population in 2012, surpassing the national rate of 242.3 per 100,000 in the population. Similar rates existed at the state and national levels in 2013 (228.8 per 100,000 in the population in West Virginia

Figure 2.5. Estimated Property Crime Rate in West Virginia Compared to the United States, 1996–2016

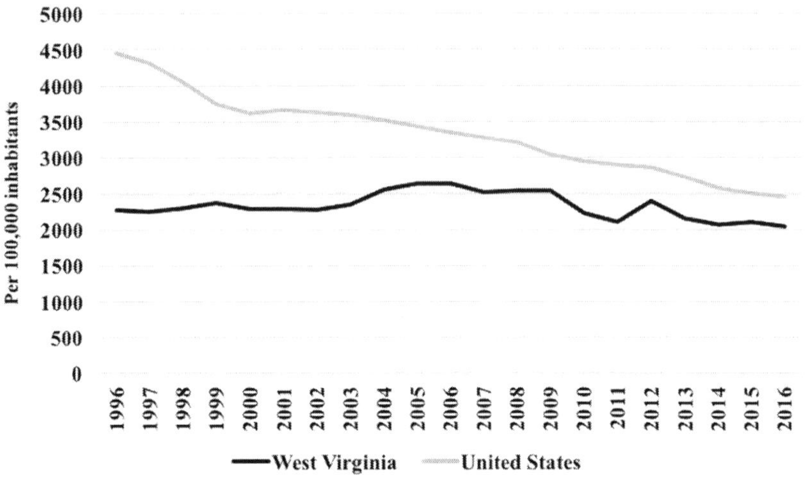

Source: Federal Bureau of Investigation (FBI), Crime Data Explorer. (2018). *Property crime rate in West Virginia, 1996–2016*. Retrieved from https://crime-data-explorer.fr.cloud.gov/explorer/state/west-virginia/property-crime?placeId=WV&since=1996&until=2016.

and 229.6 per 100,000 in the United States). However, the national rate climbed slightly, while the rate in West Virginia since 2014 has increased more substantially. In 2016, the aggravated assault rate climbed to 278.4 in West Virginia, compared to 248.5 for the United States.

Property Crimes

A summary of ***property crimes***, including burglary, larceny-theft, motor vehicle theft, and arson are included in Figure 2.5. These crimes are often combined as they involve property that is either taken or damaged, as is the case with arson. As can be seen from this figure, property crime rates in the United States have been steadily declining over the past two decades. Since 1996, the rates in the state have been lower in comparison to the rest of the nation and relatively stable. The state rate was at an all-time high in 2006 at 2,636.3 per 100,000 in the population, yet this was again below the nation's rate of 3,334.6 per 100,000 in the population. If the United States rate continues to decline, it is possible that West Virginia's property crime rate will converge with the

Figure 2.6. Estimated Burglary Rate in West Virginia Compared to the United States, 1996–2016

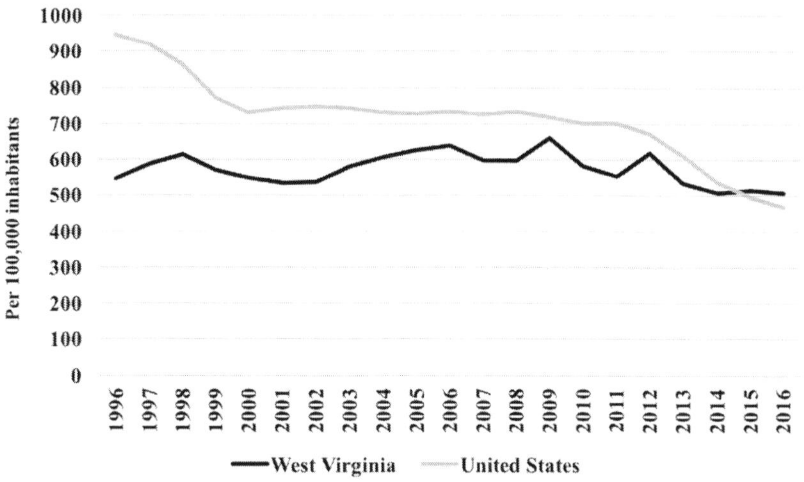

Source: Federal Bureau of Investigation (FBI), Crime Data Explorer. (2018). *Burglary rate in West Virginia, 1996–2016*. Retrieved from https://crime-data-explorer.fr.cloud.gov/explorer/state/west-virginia/burglary?placeId=WV&since=1996&until=2016.

nation's rate in the near future. In 2016, the rate in West Virginia was 2,154.1 per 100,000 in the population compared to the rate of the entire nation at 2,733.6 per 100,000 in the population.

Burglary

The FBI defines ***burglary*** (also known as breaking and entering) as "the unlawful entry of a structure to commit a felony or a theft" (LESS & CSMU, 2013, p. 42). A structure can range from an office, house, church, trailer, or apartment to a factory, garage, mill, or school. For the purposes of classifying burglary, this definition also includes forcible entry attempts where a tool of some sort is used to gain entrance to the structure. As shown in Figure 2.6, and similar to other crimes that have been declining in the United States as a whole, the burglary rate has been decreasing since the year 2000. For West Virginia, the burglary rate has been shaky at best, with periods of stability marked by increases and decreases. The highest rate in the state occurred in 2009 (659.7 per 100,000 in the population). In comparison to the rest of the country; however, it was still slightly lower (717.7 per 100,000 in the population

Figure 2.7. Estimated Larceny-Theft Rate in West Virginia Compared to the United States, 1996–2016

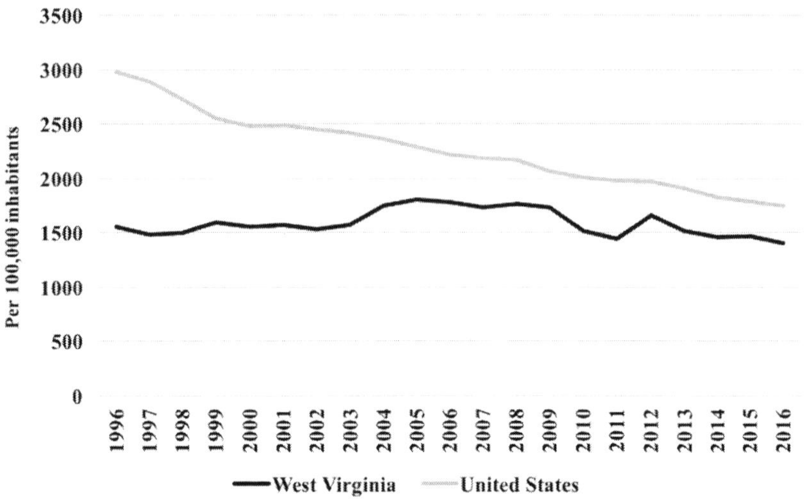

Source: Federal Bureau of Investigation (FBI), Crime Data Explorer. (2018). *Larceny theft rate in West Virginia, 1996–2016*. Retrieved from https://crime-data-explorer.fr.cloud.gov/explorer/state/west-virginia/larceny?page=crime&placeId=WV&placeid=usa&since=1996&until=2016.

in the United States). Since then, West Virginia's burglary rate has been dropping, but not enough to match the declining rate in the United Sates. The rate was 507.9 per 100,000 in the population for West Virginia and 468.8 per 100,000 in the population in the United States in 2016.

Larceny-Theft

As shown in Figure 2.7, rates of ***larceny-theft*** or "the unlawful taking, carrying, leading, or riding away of property from the possession or constructive possession of another" have been steadily rising over the past 50 years (LESS & CSMU, 2013, p. 46). Crimes represented here include those such as bicycle theft, theft of motor vehicle parts and accessories, shoplifting, pocket picking, or theft of property that is not taken by force, violence, or fraud. It is important to note that these figures include attempted larcenies. Similar to several crimes discussed previously, the trend for larceny-thefts in the United States has been declining while the rate in West Virginia has remained fairly steady, until a recent decline. In 2005, the rate reached an all-time high of 1,797 per 100,000 in the population in West Virginia. In addition, while the rate has continued to decline for the country as a whole,

Figure 2.8. Estimated Motor Vehicle Theft Rate in West Virginia Compared to the United States, 1996–2016

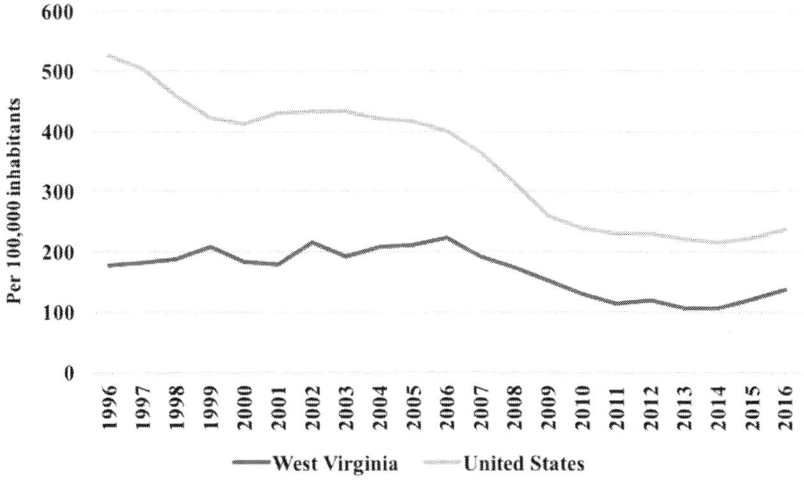

Source: Federal Bureau of Investigation (FBI), Crime Data Explorer. (2018). *Motor vehicle theft rate in West Virginia, 1996–2016*. Retrieved from https://crime-data-explorer.fr.cloud.gov/explorer/state/west-virginia/motor-vehicle-theft?placeId=WV&since=1996&until=2016.

in 2012, the rate in West Virginia increased slightly to 1,658.8 per 100,000 in the population whereas in the rest of the nation it fell. The lowest rate on record in the state was in 2016 with a rate of 1,402 per 100,000 in the population.

Motor Vehicle Theft

When examining trends of ***motor vehicle theft***, West Virginia has much smaller rates compared to the rest of the nation. As stated in the UCR handbook, motor vehicle theft is "the theft or attempted theft of a motor vehicle" (LESS & CSMU, 2013, p. 51). To be considered a motor vehicle, it is essential that it is self-propelled and operates on land and not on the rail system. Moreover, this category excludes motorboats, construction equipment, airplanes, and motorized equipment used in farming. Figure 2.8 shows that, in West Virginia, motor vehicle theft rates were the highest in 2006 (223.09 per 100,000 in the population) but have since declined. Yet again there is a notable downward trend for the United States, which has stabilized since 2010. The rate in West Virginia in 2016 was again considerably lower than the country as a whole at a rate of 137.02 per 100,000 in the population.

Arson

According to the FBI, ***arson*** is "any willful or malicious burning or attempt to burn, with or without intent to defraud, a dwelling house, public building, motor vehicle or aircraft, personal property of another, etc." (LESS & CSMU, 2013, p. 52). The crime of arson is further classified into the categories "structural" (i.e., residential dwelling, apartment, hotels, dormitories, storage facility, commercial building, restaurant, church, school, hospital, etc.), "mobile" (i.e., automobiles, trucks, buses, motorcycles, boats, etc.), or "other" (i.e., signs, fences, crops, merchandise, etc.). Despite this definition, the UCR does not take much stock in arson estimates due to the disparities in the definitions among law enforcement agencies. This makes compiling arson data not only difficult but highly unreliable. Nonetheless, arson is still a serious offense that warrants further attention. Nationally in 2016, there were a total of 43,119 arsons committed in the United States (a rate of 13.3 per 100,000 in the population), which is a significant decline as the rate in 1996 was 33.6. At the state level, data reveal mostly a decline as well. In 2016, West Virginia's arson rate was 2.9. The highest rate was noted in 2003 at 31.5.

Offenses Known to Law Enforcement in West Virginia

As shown in Table 2.5, the greatest number (not rates) of violent offenses known to law enforcement in 2016 took place in the state's capital, Charleston ($n = 767$), followed by Huntington ($n = 378$), and then by Wheeling ($n = 266$), which is located in the northern panhandle of the state. When inspecting each specific type of violent crime, aggravated assaults were the most numerous. Population density appears to be correlated with crime as Charleston had the largest number of aggravated assaults ($n = 566$), followed by Wheeling ($N = 223$), and Huntington ($n = 217$), respectively. Granted, the number of violent offenses for the state seems remarkably high, but still, property offenses outnumbered violent crimes by comparison. Among the property crimes listed, larceny-theft was the most common. The highest number of larceny-thefts reportedly took place in Charleston ($n = 2{,}694$), followed by Huntington ($n = 1{,}497$), and Beckley ($n = 984$).

Table 2.5. Offenses Known to Law Enforcement by Major Cities, 2016

City	Population	Violent crime	Murder and nonnegligent manslaughter	Rape (revised definition)	Robbery	Aggravated assault	Property crime	Burglary	Larceny-theft	Motor vehicle theft	Arson
Beckley	16,940	214	3	14	38	159	1,278	246	984	48	2
Bluefield	10,298	113	1	2	5	105	208	51	136	21	3
Charleston	49,429	767	13	36	152	566	3,939	947	2,694	298	28
Fairmont	18,733	79	0	13	17	49	329	77	224	28	6
Huntington	48,540	378	3	33	125	217			1,497	115	20
Martinsburg	17,789	81	0	13	25	43	882	117	740	25	3
Morgantown	31,109	89	2	12	19	56	674	129	517	28	3
Parkersburg	30,913	206	4	27	19	156	1,373	371	923	79	6
South Charleston	12,957	91	1	9	6	75	914	113	754	47	5
St. Albans	10,635	37	0	1	6	30	486	100	340	46	0
Vienna	10,537	20	0	4	1	15	447	29	415	3	0
Weirton	19,067	22	0	4	7	11	209	41	152	16	5
Wheeling	27,486	266	1	12	30	223	669	183	453	33	1

Source: United States Department of Justice, Federal Bureau of Investigation. (2017, September). *Crime in the United States, 2016.* Retrieved from https://ucr.fbi.gov/crime-in-the-u.s/2016/crime-in-the-u.s.-2016/tables/table-6/table-6-state-cuts/west-virginia.xls (table 6 modified).

Note: The FBI excluded statistics from Huntington, West Virginia, regarding property crimes and burglaries, as it was believed to be underreported.

Spotlight: Internet Crimes in West Virginia

While the FBI has been collecting violent and property crime data for nearly 85 years, little is known about crimes that are committed using a computer or crimes that are committed in cyberspace. As of 2015, estimates indicate that nearly 77% of American households had access to the Internet from home, compared to 18% of households in 1997 (Ryan & Lewis, 2017). Households in states such as West Virginia, Kentucky, and Tennessee are among those states that have lower percentages of Internet broadband subscriptions, ranging from 60–70.9%. As we continue to thrive in the digital age, the differences between age groups with access to a computer is also disappearing. Among those 15–34 years in age, 80.6% reside in a household with a desktop or laptop computer, while those ages 35–44 years in age reported a higher percentage of access (84.7%). Handheld devices were reported to be in 90.3% of households among 15- to 34-year-olds, followed by 89% of households among 35–44 year olds. Fewer individuals ages 45 to 64 or 65 and older reported having a handheld device in their house (78.5%, and 47.1%, respectively). Given the increased use of mobile devices and increased access to the Internet in the twenty-first century, there are additional avenues to commit crime. Because of this, some mechanisms are in place to collect information and to combat computer crimes. New legal codes and definitions and enhanced practices to combat cybercrimes are in place among law enforcement agencies, but these methods are still in their infancy as we navigate how we are to govern both the physical world and the virtual world.

An important data source for documenting and reporting Internet crimes is the Internet Crime Complaint Center (IC3), which originated in 2000 as the Internet Fraud Complaint Center. Within three years, the center changed its name to reflect the growing number of various cybercrimes. This entity operates in partnership with the FBI, the National White Collar Crime Center (NW3C), and with funding from the Bureau of Justice Assistance. The reporting system is largely dependent on victims to file a complaint on the IC3 website. From there, the victim is directed to enter more detailed information into the IC3 database. Then, IC3 analysts review the victim's complaint, and using an automated matching system, compare the individual's complaint to other reported Internet crimes that are similar in nature. This data can be accessed by law enforcement to provide more awareness of the computer crime activities within their state or jurisdiction.

For more than 18 years, IC3 has been gathering information about Internet crimes with most of the focus on fraudulent activities and scams. ***Internet crime*** is defined "as any illegal activity involving one or more components of the

Table 2.6. Reported Internet Crime Complaints Filed and Losses in West Virginia, 2016

	Victim Counts	Victim Loss
Non-payment/non-delivery	324	$511,952
Social Media	124	$107,180
419/Overpayment	115	$157,847
Personal Data Breach	109	$73,843
Auction	81	$82,641
Confidence Fraud/Romance	80	$343,130
Extortion	76	$15,598
Advanced Fee	71	$690,531
Employment	71	$157,961
Harassment/Threats of Violence	67	$41,880

Source: Internet Crime Complaint Center (IC3). (2016). *2016 State reports*. National White Collar Crime Center, Federal Bureau of Investigation, and Bureau of Justice Assistance. Retrieved from https://www.ic3.gov/media/annualreport/2016State/StateReport.aspx#?s=55.

Internet, such as websites, chat rooms, and/or email. Internet crime involves the use of the Internet to communicate false or fraudulent representations to consumers" (NW3C, 2013, para. 1). Included in the IC3 report are scams involving real estate, timeshares, email impersonation (e.g., FBI impersonators or impersonators of famous individuals), and romance or dating scams, just to name a few. While the IC3 report is very limited, and does not include computer crimes such as cyberbullying, cyberstalking, online child pornography and exploitation, and digital piracy, the NW3C has produced a series of prevention tips that are accessible to the general public, which provide more information about these computer crimes that have become a growing concern.

Data from the *Internet Crime Report* (IC3, 2016a) showed that nationally, California, Texas, Florida, and New York had the largest number of reported Internet crime complaints. Nationally, more than 298,000 complaints were filed, with a reported total of $1.33 billion in losses. Individuals over the age of 60 filed the majority of complaints and suffered the most in losses.

In West Virginia, as shown in Table 2.6, the most complaints were filed regarding non-payment/non-delivery (n = 324), which was defined as "goods and services are shipped, and payment is never rendered (non-payment).

Payment is sent, and goods and services are never received (non-delivery)" (IC3, 2016b, p. 27). However, the greatest amount in losses was reported for the category advanced fee, totaling $690,531. Advanced fee occurs when "an individual pays money to someone in anticipation of receiving something of greater in return, but instead, receives significantly less than expected or nothing" (IC3, 2016b, p. 23). Social media was the second most common category for complaints ($n = 124$), where victims reported fraudulent activity of a social networking site such as Facebook, Twitter, or Instagram. The third highest Internet crime category in terms of losses was confidence fraud/romance schemes, with a total reported loss among victims of $343,130. However, the third largest number of complaints came from 419/Overpayment ($n = 115$). These scams are also known as a 419 Nigerian scam, where the victim is asked to assist in the transfer of money in return for a future share in any profits. Overpayment occurs when "an individual is sent a payment and instructed to keep a portion of the payment, but send the rest on to another individual or business" (IC3, 2016b, p. 23).

Key Terms and Definitions

Aggravated assault: An unlawful attack by one person upon another for the purpose of inflicting severe or aggravated bodily injury.

Arson: Any willful or malicious burning or attempt to burn, with or without intent to defraud, a dwelling house, public building, motor vehicle or aircraft, personal property of another, etc.

Burglary: The unlawful entry of a structure to commit a felony or a theft.

Crime rate: The number of actual crimes that take place in a given period divided by the total number of people in the population.

Dark figure of crime: Unreported or unknown crimes to law enforcement.

Forcible rape (legacy definition): The carnal knowledge of a female forcibly and against her will.

Hate crime: Criminal offense committed against a person, property, or society that is motivated, in whole or in part, by the offender's bias against a race, religion, disability, sexual orientation, or ethnicity/national origin; also known as a bias crime.

Internet crime: Any illegal activity involving one or more components of the Internet, such as websites, chat rooms, and/or email. Internet crime involves the use of the Internet to communicate false or fraudulent representations to consumers.

Larceny-theft: The unlawful taking, carrying, leading, or riding away of property from the possession or constructive possession of another.

Motor vehicle theft: The theft or attempted theft of a motor vehicle.

Murder (nonnegligent manslaughter): The willful (nonnegligent) killing of one human being by another.

National Incident-Based Reporting System (NIBRS): An automated mechanism for local, state, and federal law enforcement agencies to compile information about a single crime incident and arrest within the specified 22 offense categories.

Negligent manslaughter: The killing of another person through gross negligence.

Part I offenses (index offenses): The first of two main groupings of UCR crime classifications consisting of eight offenses (criminal homicide, forcible rape, aggravated assault, robbery, burglary, larceny-theft, motor vehicle theft, and arson).

Part II offenses (nonindex offenses): The second of two main UCR groupings of crime classifications not already designated in Part I. Agencies are limited to reporting arrest information only for Part I offenses with the exception of simple assault.

Property crimes: Crimes that include burglary, larceny-theft, motor vehicle theft, and arson.

Rape (revised definition): Penetration, no matter how slight, of the vagina or anus with any body part or object, or oral penetration by a sexual organ of another person, without the consent of the victim.

Robbery: The taking or attempted taking of anything of value from the care, custody, or control of a person or persons by force or threat of force or violence and/or by putting the victim in fear.

Uniform Crime Report (UCR): Crime statistics from local, state, and federal law enforcement agencies that are submitted annually by way of an automated system to the Federal Bureau of Investigation.

Select Internet Sources

Crime in the United States, FBI (UCR): https://ucr.fbi.gov/ucr-publications.

National Incident-Based Reporting System (NIBRS) (2016): https://ucr.fbi.gov/nibrs/2016.

National White Collar Crime Center: http://www.nw3c.org/.

West Virginia Division of Justice and Community Services, Statistical Analysis Center: https://djcs.wv.gov/ORSP/SAC/Pages/default.aspx.

West Virginia State Police: http://www.wvsp.gov/.

Review and Critical Thinking Questions

1. What methods are used to compile crime data? What are the strengths and limitations of these data sets?
2. What is a crime rate? How is it calculated?
3. Why does the FBI update and make definitional changes for some types of crimes, such as forcible rape? Are there other definitions of crime that should be modified? Why or why not?
4. Considering the rate of aggravated assault has continued to increase substantially in the state, what prevention efforts can be put into place to reduce this crime?
5. How does West Virginia compare to the rest of the nation in terms of violent crime rates and property crime rates? What crimes are the highest? Which ones are the lowest?

References

Federal Bureau of Investigation (FBI). (2018). *Crime data explorer.* Retrieved from https://crime-data-explorer.fr.cloud.gov/.

Internet Crime Complaint Center (IC3). (2016a). *2016 Internet crime report.* National White Collar Crime Center, Federal Bureau of Investigation, and Bureau of Justice Assistance. Retrieved from https://pdf.ic3.gov/2016_IC3Report.pdf.

Internet Crime Complaint Center (IC3). (2016b). *2016 State reports.* National White Collar Crime Center, Federal Bureau of Investigation, and Bureau of Justice Assistance. Retrieved from https://www.ic3.gov/media/annualreport/2016State/StateReport.aspx#?s=55.

James, N., & Rishard, L. (2008, January). *CRS report for Congress: How crime in the United States is measured.* Prepared for members and committees of Congress. Retrieved from: http://www.fas.org/sgp/crs/misc/RL34309.pdf.

Law Enforcement Support Section (LESS) and the Crime Statistics Management Unit (CSMU) (2013). *Criminal Justice Information Services (CJIS) Division Uniform Crime Reporting (UCR) Program: Summary Reporting System (SRS) user manual.* Retrieved from http://www.fbi.gov/about-us/cjis/ucr/nibrs/summary-reporting-system-srs-user-manual.

Law Enforcement Support Section (LESS) and the Crime Statistics Management Unit (CSMU). (2017). *Criminal Justice Information Services (CJIS) Division*

Uniform Crime Reporting (UCR) Program: National Incident-Based Reporting System (NIBRS) user manual. Retrieved from http://www.fbi.gov/about-us/cjis/ucr/nibrs/nibrs-user-manual.

McDowall, D., & Loftin, C. (2009). Do US city crime rates follow a national trend? The influence of nationwide conditions on local crime patterns. *Journal of Quantitative Criminology, 25*, 307–324. doi: 10.1007/s10940-009-9071-0.

National White Collar Crime Center (NWC3). (2013). *Internet fraud 2013.* Retrieved from http://www.nw3c.org/docs/whitepapers/internet_fraud.pdf?sfvrsn=8.

Nolan, J.J., Haas, S.M., & Napier, J.S. (2011). Estimating the impact of classification error on the "statistical accuracy" of Uniform Crime Reports. *Journal of Quantitative Criminology, 24*, 497–519. doi: 10.1007/s10940-011-9135-9.

Ryan, C., & Lewis, J.M. (2017, September). *Computer and internet use in the United States: 2015.* Washington, DC: U.S. Census Bureau. Retrieved from https://www.census.gov/content/dam/Census/library/publications/2017/acs/acs-37.pdf.

United States Census Bureau. (2017). *State and county quickfacts.* Retrieved from https://www.census.gov/quickfacts/fact/table/WV,US/PST045217.

United States Department of Justice, Federal Bureau of Investigation (USDOJ/FBI). (2017, September). *Crime in the United States, 2016.* Retrieved from https://ucr.fbi.gov/crime-in-the-u.s/2016/crime-in-the-u.s.-2016/cius-2016.

Chapter 3

State Legal Authority

Delegates meeting at the Custom House in Wheeling from Harper's Weekly, July 6, 1861. Courtesy of the West Virginia Archives.

The supreme law of West Virginia is found in the Constitution of West Virginia, which was ratified in 1872, and since amended. The West Virginia Constitution divides the government into three divisions—legislative, executive, and judicial. It specifies the powers and limitations of each of these three divisions of government. For criminal justice in the state of West Virginia, the legislature determines what behavior is criminal, the executive division enforces these laws and sometimes refines their definitions through administrative laws, and the judiciary determines guilt or innocence of those accused and whether the laws were written and applied fairly. The West Virginia Constitution, Article 3, is the most important to the criminal justice system because it includes the

Bill of Rights for West Virginia citizens. All laws and their enforcement must adhere to the constitution, especially Article 3.

What makes the West Virginia Constitution unique is the fact that it is a constitution written by representatives of another state. West Virginia removed itself from Virginia while Virginia was seceded from the United States during the Civil War. Citizens of Virginia, mostly from the western counties, formed the Restored Government of Virginia, made up of representatives and a governor loyal to the Union. Once this government was recognized as the legitimate government of Virginia by Congress, 44 of the western counties of Virginia[1] wrote a new constitution and petitioned Congress for recognition as the 35th state of the Union. Congress voted to accept the state if it agreed to "gradual emancipation" of slaves (Stealey, 2011, p. 44), which it did (Ambler & Summers, 1958; Bailey, 2015; Bastress, 2010; Rice & Brown, 2014; Stealey, 2011).

The U.S. Constitution, Article IV, Section 3 required new states that were made up of part of another state(s) to have the approval of each state's legislature and Congress. Approval by Virginia's Legislature was unlikely. Therefore, the western counties sought approval from the recognized legislature of the Restored Government of Virginia, which they granted. Thus, the new state arguably met the requirements of the U.S. Constitution. The vote of the Reorganized Government of Virginia cleared the way for a petition to Congress that West Virginia be recognized as a new state. In response, Congress and President Lincoln recognized the State of West Virginia (Bailey, 2015; Rice & Brown, 2014; Stealey, 2011) on June 20, 1863. The new state was born.

West Virginia law was developed from a long line of legal codes. However, the primary derivation for the code is from English Common Law, which was in effect when the colonies separated from England. The ***Common Law*** was an unwritten set of laws that judges and the English people were expected to know and follow. In the colonies, the Common Law was modified and supplemented by the colonists. New laws were based upon the unique challenges of the new world by each colony and their respective ideological, religious, and philosophical beliefs (Friedman, 2005).

English Common Law evolved from the influence of earlier and ancient laws (i.e., Code of Hammurabi, Mosaic Code, etc.). However, it differed from

1. These counties included: Barbour, Boone, Braxton, Brooke, Cabell, Calhoun, Clay, Doddridge, Fayette, Gilmer, Greenbrier, Hancock, Harrison, Jackson, Kanawha, Lewis, Logan, Marion, Marshall, Mason, McDowell, Mercer, Monongalia, Monroe, Nicholas, Ohio, Pleasants, Pocahontas, Preston, Putnam, Raleigh, Randolph, Ritchie, Roane, Taylor, Tucker, Tyler, Upshur, Wayne, Webster, Wetzel, Wirt, Wood and Wyoming (West Virginia Legislature, 2017–2018).

other European legal codes in that law enforcement and courts were localized by the king. The country was divided into ***tithings***, made up of 10 households. Tithings were combined into hundreds or parishes, and the hundreds were combined into shires, later called counties (Oliver & Hilgenberg, 2010). Since the Common Law was not a written code, the law enforcers and court justices in the hundreds and shires interpreted the law by local standards and traditions (Calvi & Coleman, 2016). Law enforcement groups within hundreds and shires were assisted by magistrates and justices of the peace for court proceedings. This made the English tradition different from other European countries where the courts and law were more closely controlled by the king.

A foundation of English law and legal authority came from the ***Magna Carta***, also called the Great Charter, of 1215, wrested from King John. The Magna Carta granted English noblemen certain rights and protections. These rights for the nobles, church, and foreign merchants later evolved to rights for all Englishmen. These rights eventually included the right to a trial by jury of one's peers, indictment by a grand jury based upon probable cause, and a fair and speedy trial (Johnson & Wolfe, 2003).

The English citizens by the sixteenth century were subjected to prosecution and punishment according to commonly accepted procedures under English law, known as the Common Law (Johnson & Wolfe, 2003). When English colonists came to the new world, they brought with them this sense of rights that should be afforded them by the government under the Common Law, the Magna Carta, and rights that had been granted them under the colonial charters by the King.

The ***Royal Charters of Virginia*** influenced the charters of other later colonies. This, in turn, influenced the constitutions of the colonies. There were three royal charters in Virginia, enacted in 1606, 1609, and 1611. The first charter kept the king as the landowner, the London Company as tenants, and the settlers as subtenants. At that time, the colony was governed by a council in London. The second charter gave rights of land ownership to the London Company and local government was transferred to the Governor and his council at Jamestowne [Jamestown]. The third charter went even farther in colonial rule. This charter recognized a representative assembly and put the authority of government in Virginia (Jamestowne Society, 2014). This third charter allowed the plantation/colony officers to make laws (as long as they were not contrary to English law), hold courts, and punish offenders (The Avalon Project, 2008).

After the settlement of the Virginia Colony, a debate began about the power of the government in Europe and the Americas. The ***Classical School of Philosophy*** was a school of thought that proposed limiting the power of government, the monarchy, and increasing the power of the people. It was very popular during the 1700s, and led to the American and French Revolutions because its concept favored the ***social contract***, an agreement between the citizens and the government of the country that specified the powers, rights, privileges, and obligations of citizens and the government, keeping the power of the government in the hands of the people.

The philosophers of the school originally argued from two opposite perspectives on what the nature of man would be if left alone without government. One perspective was based upon the idea that man's nature is one of peace and cooperation. The other was that the natural state of man was a state of war. The result was an argument over whether the monarch or the people should have the ultimate power in government. If the nature was one of peace, the people should have the power of government and the monarch's power should be limited. On the other hand, if man's nature was one of a state of war, the monarch should have absolute power to quell this nature.

The conflict nature of man was espoused in England by Thomas Hobbes. He believed that the natural state of man was a state of war and that life without government would be "solitary, poor, nasty, brutish, and short" (Hobbes, 1651 as cited in Owen, Fradella, Burke, & Joplin, 2015, p. 44). This view of the nature of man, therefore, would require the surrender of power to the monarch to ensure order in society. On the other hand, according to John Locke and other social philosophers of the Classical School of Philosophy, the state of nature was not a state of war. People in the state of nature were very social and got along well with one another. They only entered into government because of their desire to have their property protected. Therefore, government should only have enough power granted by the people to protect them and their property. The power of the government should lie in the people and not the monarch (Johnson & Wolfe, 2003). This concept of limiting governmental power and the power of government remaining with the citizens of the state was adopted by the American colonists and helped fuel the Declaration of Independence, the separation from England, and the Constitution. The social contract between the people and the government was believed to be the ultimate expression of societal beliefs. It represented the supreme law of the land to which all laws should adhere.

In the United States, the U.S. Constitution is the written expression of this social contract and is the supreme law of the United States, to which all federal laws must adhere. In West Virginia, the Constitution of West Virginia is the supreme law of the state to which all West Virginia laws must conform. However, the Constitution of West Virginia and its implementation also must ultimately adhere to the Constitution of the United States in matters specified as reserved for the federal government.

Laws are interpreted and employed both substantively and procedurally. In criminal laws, substantive ***due process*** generally requires that laws defining crimes must set forth the elements of the crime, including ***mens rea***, or evil intent; ***actus reus***, consisting of actions committed or omissions that constitute the crime itself; and ***concurrence***, meaning that both the act/omission and the evil intent take place at the same time (Gaines & Miller, 2015). In order for a crime to occur, a physical ***act*** prohibited by law must take place or an act required by law is not carried out (an ***omission***). Thinking about committing a crime is not a crime. In addition, the crime must have a prescribed penalty, and the punishment for the crime must be included in its definition. The definition of a crime must conform to constitutional requirements (Holten & Lamar, 1991).

The original constitution for what is now West Virginia was the Constitution of Virginia. However, after the secession of many of the southern states, including Virginia, from the Union, the northwestern counties of Virginia voted on dismemberment from the rest of Virginia and developed their own constitution beginning with the First Constitutional Convention. Delegates were elected on October 24, 1861, and met on November 26th to draft a constitution. The West Virginia Constitution was based heavily on the Virginia Constitution of 1851; however, it was changed to remove some of the aspects that the northwestern counties felt were egregious, specifically voting and representation requirements (Bastress, 2010). The petition to be acknowledged as a new state was adopted by both houses of Congress and approved by President Lincoln. As stated earlier, West Virginia became a state on June 20, 1863 (Ambler & Summers, 1958).

Constitutional Comparison

In order to see the similarities and differences in the United States and West Virginia constitutions, constitutional rights and limitations will be compared between the two, using tables to make the comparisons of constitutional authority easier to examine. Remember that the United States Constitution had been in place for about 80 years at the time of the adoption of the West Virginia Constitution and had influenced the state's constitutions and laws over that time.

The West Virginia Constitution covers many of the same areas as the U.S. Constitution; however, in some instances the West Virginia Constitution states things differently or in more detail. For instance, the West Virginia Constitution divides liberty into civil, political, and religious freedom and uses the term "security" instead of "common defense." Plus, it uses the term "common welfare" instead of "general welfare" and seeks to "promote, preserve and perpetuate

Table 3.1. Constitutional Comparison: Preamble

West Virginia Constitution	U.S. Constitution
"Since through Divine Providence we enjoy the blessings of civil, political and religious liberty, we, the people of West Virginia, in and through the provisions of this Constitution, reaffirm our faith in and constant reliance upon God and seek diligently to promote, preserve and perpetuate good government in the state of West Virginia for the common welfare, freedom and security of ourselves and our posterity" (Not originally a part of the original constitution, Added 1960).	"We the People of the United States, in Order to form a more perfect Union, establish Justice, insure domestic Tranquility, provide for the common defense, promote the general Welfare, and secure the Blessings of Liberty to ourselves and our Posterity, do ordain and establish this Constitution for the United States of America."

Sources: West Virginia Constitution, pmbl. and U.S. Constitution, pmbl.

good government" (see Table 3.1). Most important, the authors specifically mention Divine Providence and God in the preamble while the writers of the U.S. Constitution do not.[2]

Another aspect of the West Virginia Constitution is based upon its Civil War beginnings. In Article 1, Section 1, "Relations to the government of the United States," is a statement of allegiance to the United States of America.

> The state of West Virginia is, and shall remain, one of the United States of America. The constitution of the United States of America, and the laws and treaties made in pursuance thereof, shall be the supreme law of the land (West Virginia Legislature, 2018).

While the colonists were breaking away from England to form a new government, the citizens of West Virginia were dismembering themselves from Virginia, returning to the Union from which their previous state government had removed itself. Thus, the new state constitution was acknowledging its place in the Union and demonstrating a commitment to the U.S. Constitution. This commitment, however, was not absolute, as it was somewhat modified in Article

2. To help add some clarity, the U.S. Constitution articles and amendments will be listed in Roman Numerals (I, II, III, etc.) and the articles and amendments of the W. Va. Constitution will be listed in Arabic Numerals (1, 2, 3, etc.) in the text.

1, Sections 2 and 3, to ensure state's rights in peacetime and time of war. Article 1, Section 2, "Internal government and police," states:

> The government of the United States is a government of enumerated powers, and all powers not delegated to it, nor inhibited to the states, are reserved to the states or to the people thereof. Among the powers so reserved to the states is the exclusive regulation of their own internal government and police; and it is the high and solemn duty of the several departments of government, created by this constitution, to guard and protect the people of this state from all encroachments upon the rights so reserved (West Virginia Legislature, 2018).

Article 1, Section 3, continues with "Continuity of constitutional operation":

> The provisions of the constitution of the United States, and of this state, are operative alike in a period of war as in time of peace, and any departure therefrom, or violation thereof, under the plea of necessity, or any other plea, is subversive of good government, and tends to anarchy and despotism (West Virginia Legislature, 2018).

The State and National Bill of Rights

Of particular significance to criminal justice is the Bill of Rights of the U.S. Constitution and the Bill of Rights of the West Virginia Constitution. The Bill of Rights is found in the first 10 amendments to the U.S. Constitution and in Article 3 of the West Virginia Constitution. They are compared in Table 3.2. Originally, West Virginia also listed 10 rights in its Constitution (Article 2), but those rights were subsequently expanded ("*Constitution of West Virginia*"). The rights originally included the definition of treason and the penalties; however, this part was subsequently left in Article 2 and the rest of the Bill of Rights moved to Article 3. Most of the rights contained in the Bill of Rights were added and approved for the 1872 West Virginia Constitution, unless otherwise noted (West Virginia Legislature, 2017–2018; West Virginia Legislature, 2018).

Article 3, Section 1, which introduces the Bill of Rights for the West Virginia Constitution, is more in line with the beginning of the Declaration of Independence (see Table 3.2). It guarantees that all men are free, equal, independent, and have certain rights, such as the "enjoyment of life and liberty, with the means of acquiring and possessing property, and of pursuing and obtaining happiness and safety." These words not only mirror the Declaration of Independence, but also the precepts of the Classical School of Criminology espoused by Locke and other philosophers concerning the social contract.

Table 3.2. Bill of Rights Comparison between the Current West Virginia Constitution and the U.S. Constitution

West Virginia Constitution (Article-Section)	U.S. Constitution
3, §1. Bill of rights. "All men are, by nature, equally free and independent, and have certain inherent rights, of which, when they enter into a state of society, they cannot, by any compact, deprive or divest their posterity, namely: The enjoyment of life and liberty, with the means of acquiring and possessing property, and of pursuing and obtaining happiness and safety."	"We hold these truths to be self-evident, that all men are created equal, that they are endowed by their Creator with certain unalienable Rights, that among these are Life, Liberty and the pursuit of Happiness.—That to secure these rights, Governments are instituted among Men, deriving their just powers from the consent of the governed, ..." (*Declaration of Independence*, 1776).
3, §2. Magistrates servants of people. "All power is vested in, and consequently derived from, the people. Magistrates are their trustees and servants, and at all times amenable to them."	Article VI "This Constitution, and the Laws of the United States which shall be made in Pursuance thereof; and all Treaties made, or which shall be made, under the Authority of the United States, shall be the supreme Law of the Land; and the Judges in every State shall be bound thereby, any Thing in the Constitution or Laws of any state to the Contrary notwithstanding."
3, §3. Rights reserved to people. "Government is instituted for the common benefit, protection and security of the people, nation or community. Of all its various forms that is the best, which is capable of producing the greatest degree of happiness and safety, and is most effectually secured against the danger of maladministration; and when any government shall be found inadequate or contrary to these purposes, a majority of the community has an indubitable, inalienable, and indefeasible right to reform, alter or abolish it in such manner as shall be judged most conducive to the public weal."	"That whenever any Form of Government becomes destructive of these ends, it is the Right of the People to alter or to abolish it, and to institute new Government, laying its foundation on such principles and organizing its powers in such form, as to them shall seem most likely to effect their Safety and Happiness. Prudence, indeed, will dictate that Governments long established should not be changed for light and transient causes; and accordingly all experience hath shewn, that mankind are more disposed to suffer, while evils are sufferable, than to right themselves by abolishing the forms to which they are accustomed. But when a long train of abuses and usurpations, pursuing invariably the same Object evinces a design to reduce them under absolute Despotism, it is their right, it is their duty, to throw off such Government, and to provide new Guards for their future security" (*Declaration of Independence*, 1776).

Table 3.2. *Continued*

West Virginia Constitution (Article-Section)	U.S. Constitution
3, §4. *Writ of habeas corpus.* "The privilege of the writ of *habeas corpus* shall not be suspended. No person shall be held to answer for treason, felony or other crime, not cognizable by a justice, unless on presentment or indictment of a grand jury. No *bill of attainder, ex post facto law,* or law impairing the obligation of a contract, shall be passed" (Original 2-1).	Article I, §9 "The Privilege of the Writ of Habeas Corpus shall not be suspended, unless when in Cases of Rebellion or Invasion the public Safety may require it." "No Bill of Attainder or ex post facto Law shall be passed." Amendment V "No person shall be held to answer for a capital, or otherwise infamous crime, unless on a presentment or indictment of a Grand Jury, except in cases arising in the land or naval forces, or in the Militia, when in actual service in time of War or public danger; ..."
3, §5 Excessive bail not required "Excessive bail shall not be required, nor excessive fines imposed, nor cruel and unusual punishment inflicted. Penalties shall be proportioned to the character and degree of the offence. No person shall be transported out of, or forced to leave the state for any offence committed within the same; nor shall any person, in any criminal case, be compelled to be a witness against himself, or be twice put in jeopardy of life or liberty for the same offence" (Original 2-2, Amended).	Amendment VIII "Excessive bail shall not be required, nor excessive fines imposed, nor cruel and unusual punishments inflicted." Amendment V "... nor shall any person be subject for the same offence to be twice put in jeopardy of life or limb; nor shall be compelled in any criminal case to be a witness against himself ..."
3, §6. Unreasonable searches and seizures prohibited. "The rights of the citizens to be secure in their houses, persons, papers and effects, against unreasonable searches and seizures, shall not be violated. No warrant shall issue except upon probable cause, supported by oath or affirmation, particularly describing the place to be searched, or the person or thing to be seized" (Original 2-3).	Amendment IV (1791) "The right of the people to be secure in their persons, houses, papers, and effects, against unreasonable searches and seizures, shall not be violated, and no Warrants shall issue, but upon probable cause, supported by Oath or affirmation, and particularly describing the place to be searched, and the persons or things to be seized."

Table 3.2. *Continued*

West Virginia Constitution (Article-Section)	U.S. Constitution
3, §7. Freedom of speech and press guaranteed. "No law abridging the freedom of speech, or of the press, shall be passed; but the Legislature may, by suitable penalties, restrain the publication or sale of obscene books, papers, or pictures, and provide for the punishment of libel, and defamation of character, and for the recovery, in civil actions, by the aggrieved party, of suitable damages for such libel, or defamation" (Original 2-4, Amended).	Amendment I "Congress shall make no law respecting an establishment of religion, or prohibiting the free exercise thereof; or abridging the freedom of speech, or of the press; ..."
3, §8. Relating to civil suits for libel. "In prosecutions and civil suits for libel, the truth may be given in evidence; and if it shall appear to the jury, that the matter charged as libelous is true, and was published with good motives, and for justifiable ends, the verdict shall be for the defendant" (Original 2-5).	Not in the U.S. Constitution
3, §9. Private property, how taken. "Private property shall not be taken or damaged for public use, without just compensation; nor shall the same be taken by any company, incorporated for the purposes of internal improvement, until just compensation shall have been paid, or secured to be paid, to the owner; and when private property shall be taken, or damaged for public use, or for the use of such corporation, the compensation to the owner shall be ascertained in such manner as may be prescribed by general law: *Provided*, That when required by either of the parties, such compensation shall be ascertained by an impartial jury of twelve freeholders" (Original 2-6, Amended).	Amendment V "... nor be deprived of life, liberty, or property, without due process of law; nor shall private property be taken for public use, without just compensation ..."
3, §10. Safeguards for life, liberty and property. "No person shall be deprived of life, liberty, or property, without due process of law, and the judgment of his peers" (Original 2.6, Amended).	Amendment V "... nor be deprived of life, liberty, or property, without due process of law; ..."

Table 3.2. *Continued*

West Virginia Constitution (Article-Section)	U.S. Constitution
3, § 11. Political tests condemned. "Political tests, requiring persons, as a prerequisite to the enjoyment of their civil and political rights, to purge themselves by their own oaths, of past alleged offences, are repugnant to the principles of free government, and are cruel and oppressive. No religious or political test oath shall be required as a prerequisite or qualification to vote, serve as a juror, sue, plead, appeal, or pursue any profession or employment. Nor shall any person be deprived by law, of any right, or privilege, because of any act done prior to the passage of such law."	Not in the U.S. Constitution
3, § 12. Military subordinate to civil power. "Standing armies, in time of peace, should be avoided as dangerous to liberty. The military shall be subordinate to the civil power; and no citizen, unless engaged in the military service of the state, shall be tried or punished by any military court, for any offence that is cognizable by the civil courts of the state. No soldier shall, in time of peace, be quartered in any house, without consent of the owner; nor in time of war, except in the manner to be prescribed by law."	Amendment III "No Soldier shall, in time of peace be quartered in any house, without the consent of the Owner, nor in time of war, but in a manner to be prescribed by law." Amendment II "A well regulated Militia, being necessary to the security of a free State, the right of the people to keep and bear Arms, shall not be infringed."
3, § 13. Right of jury trial. "In suits at common law, where the value in controversy exceeds twenty dollars exclusive of interest and costs, the right of trial by jury, if required by either party, shall be preserved; and in such suit in a court of limited jurisdiction a jury shall consist of six persons. No fact tried by a jury shall be otherwise reexamined in any case than according to the rule of court or law" (Original 2-7, Amended 1880, 1974).	Amendment VII "In Suits at common law, where the value in controversy shall exceed twenty dollars, the right of trial by jury shall be preserved, and no fact tried by a jury, shall be otherwise re-examined in any Court of the United States, than according to the rules of the common law."

Table 3.2. *Continued*

West Virginia Constitution (Article-Section)	U.S. Constitution
3, § 14. Trials of crimes—Provisions in interest of accused. "Trials of crimes, and of misdemeanors, unless herein otherwise provided, shall be by a jury of twelve men, public, without unreasonable delay, and in the county where the alleged offence was committed, unless upon petition of the accused, and for good cause shown, it is removed to some other county. In all such trials, the accused shall be fully and plainly informed of the character and cause of the accusation, and be confronted with the witnesses against him, and shall have the assistance of counsel, and a reasonable time to prepare for his defence; and there shall be awarded to him compulsory process for obtaining witnesses in his favor" (Original 2-8, Amended).	Amendment VI "In all criminal prosecutions, the accused shall enjoy the right to a speedy and public trial, by an impartial jury of the State and district wherein the crime shall have been committed, which district shall have been previously ascertained by law, and to be informed of the nature and cause of the accusation; to be confronted with the witnesses against him; to have compulsory process for obtaining witnesses in his favor, and to have the Assistance of Counsel for his defence."
3, § 15. Religious freedom guaranteed. "No man shall be compelled to frequent or support any religious worship, place or ministry whatsoever; nor shall any man be enforced, restrained, molested or burthened, in his body or goods, or otherwise suffer, on account of his religious opinions or belief, but all men shall be free to profess and by argument, to maintain their opinions in matters of religion; and the same shall, in nowise, affect, diminish or enlarge their civil capacities; and the Legislature shall not prescribe any religious test whatever, or confer any peculiar privileges or advantages on any sect or denomination, or pass any law requiring or authorizing any religious society, or the people of any district within this state, to levy on themselves, or others, any tax for the erection or repair of any house for public worship, or for the support of any church or ministry, but it shall be left free for every person to select his religious instructor, and to make for his support, such private contracts as he shall please" (Original 2-9).	Amendment I "Congress shall make no law respecting an establishment of religion, or prohibiting the free exercise thereof; ..."

Table 3.2. *Continued*

West Virginia Constitution (Article-Section)	U.S. Constitution
3, § 15a. Voluntary contemplation, meditation or prayer in schools. "Public schools shall provide a designated brief time at the beginning of each school day for any student desiring to exercise their right to personal and private contemplation, meditation or prayer. No student of a public school may be denied the right to personal and private contemplation, meditation or prayer nor shall any student be required or encouraged to engage in any given contemplation, meditation or prayer as a part of the school curriculum" (1984).	Not in U.S. Constitution
3, § 16. Right of public assembly held inviolate. "The right of the people to assemble in a peaceable manner, to consult for the common good, to instruct their representatives, or to apply for redress of grievances, shall be held inviolate."	Amendment I "Congress shall make no law ... abridging ... the right of the people peaceably to assemble, and to petition the Government for a redress of grievances."
3, § 17. Courts open to all—Justice administered speedily. "The courts of this state shall be open, and every person, for an injury done to him, in his person, property or reputation, shall have remedy by due course of law; and justice shall be administered without sale, denial or delay."	Amendment VI "... public trial, by an impartial jury ..."
3, § 18. Conviction not to work corruption of blood or forfeiture. "No conviction shall work corruption of blood or forfeiture of estate."	Article III, Section 3 "The Congress shall have Power to declare the Punishment of Treason, but no Attainder of Treason shall work Corruption of Blood, or Forfeiture except during the Life of the Person attainted."
3, § 19. Hereditary emoluments, etc., provided against. "No hereditary emoluments, honors or privileges shall ever be granted or conferred in this state."	Article I, Section 9 "No Title of Nobility shall be granted by the United States: And no Person holding any Office of Profit or Trust under them, shall, without the Consent of the Congress, accept of any present, Emolument, Office, or Title, of any kind whatever, from any King, Prince, or foreign State."

Table 3.2. *Continued*

West Virginia Constitution (Article-Section)	U.S. Constitution
3, §20. Preservation of free government. "Free government and the blessings of liberty can be preserved to any people only by a firm adherence to justice, moderation, temperance, frugality and virtue, and by a frequent recurrence to fundamental principles."	Not in U.S. Constitution
3, §21. Jury service for women. "Regardless of sex all persons, who are otherwise qualified, shall be eligible to serve as petit jurors, in both civil and criminal cases, as grand jurors and as coroner's jurors" (1955).	Not in U.S. Constitution
3, §22. Right to keep and bear arms. "A person has the right to keep and bear arms for the defense of self, family, home and state, and for lawful hunting and recreational use" (1985).	Amendment II "A well regulated Militia, being necessary to the security of a free State, the right of the people to keep and bear Arms, shall not be infringed."

Sources: *Declaration of Independence*. (1776). Retrieved from http://www.archives.gov/exhibits/charters/declaration_transcript.html; United States Senate. (n.d.). *Constitution of the United States*. Retrieved from http://www.senate.gov/civics/constitution_item/constitution.htm; West Virginia Legislature. (2017–2018). *Manual of the house of delegates and senate, eighty-third legislature* Retrieved from http://www.wvlegislature.gov/Educational/publications/Manual_2017-2018.pdf; *Constitution of West Virginia*. Retrieved from http://www.legis.state.wv.us/WVCODE/WV_CON.cfm.

Note: * Amended means amended later to its present working.

The first of 22 rights enumerated for the citizens of West Virginia is Article 3, Section 2 of the West Virginia Constitution (see Table 3.2). It specifies that magistrates are subject to the will of the people, while Article VI of the U.S. Constitution holds that judges, at the federal and state levels, are subject to the U.S. Constitution. Again, the West Virginia Constitution has tied the limitation of government to the governed; however, as stated before, in Article 1, Section 1, the West Virginia Constitution acknowledges the U.S. Constitution as the supreme law of the land.

The second right specified in Article 2, Section 3 is the right to "abolish" a government that is "inadequate" or contrary to the purposes of producing the greatest "happiness and safety" (see Table 3.2). Again, this section is more in line with the Declaration of Independence than the Constitution.

The third set of rights in the West Virginia Constitution states the right of *habeas corpus* shall not be suspended, even in time of war, whereas the U.S. Constitution allows its suspension during time of war (Article I, §9) and that no "bill of attainder, ex post facto law, or law impairing the obligation of a contract, shall be passed" (see Table 3.2). The section mirrors the U.S. Constitution, but adds the provision prohibiting laws that would impair an obligation under contract. In addition, the West Virginia Constitution does not allow the suspension of indictment by grand jury even under time of war, while the U.S. Constitution allows the suspension of this right during time of war or rebellion. This grants protection to citizens beyond those afforded by the U.S. Constitution, which is permissible under the states' rights. It is only when the rights of citizens are curtailed by the state constitution, not expanded, that the U.S. Constitution would hold sway (Peltason, 1979). The states' rights are found in the Tenth Amendment of the U.S. Constitution. "The powers not delegated to the United States by the Constitution, nor prohibited by it to the States, are reserved to the States respectively, or to the people" (U.S. Senate, n.d.).

Article 3, Section 5 prohibits excessive bail and fines and cruel and unusual punishment. These prohibitions are also found in the Eighth Amendment of the U.S. Constitution. Article 3, Section 5, also contains protection against being compelled to be a witness against oneself and a prohibition of double jeopardy. Those rights are present in the Fifth Amendment to the U.S. Constitution (see Table 3.2). Finally, the section also requires that penalties must fit the crime and that persons cannot be "transported out of, or forced to leave the state for any offence [sic] committed within the same."

Article 3, Section 6 gives people in West Virginia the right to be free from unreasonable searches and seizures, as does the Fourth Amendment to the U.S. Constitution (see Table 3.2). Both the state and federal provisions protect citizens' houses, persons, and papers from unreasonable searches or seizures, and requires a warrant that specifies the particular place to be searched and the person or thing to be seized. Both provisions require a warrant to be supported by oath or affirmation as well.

The next set of rights in Article 3, Section 7 provides for punishment of libel and defamation of character and the recovery of damages in civil action (see Table 3.2). It also allows the restraint of obscene books, papers, or pictures. In Article 3, Section 8, there is a restriction for libel convictions. For example, the verdict shall be in favor of the defendant in civil suits for libel if the publication was for "good motives and justifiable ends."

Next, Article 3, Section 9 contains rights concerning the protection of private property and the manner in which it can be taken for the state (see Table 3.2). It spells out in more detail the protection found in the Fifth Amendment of the U.S. Constitution and adds protection against private corporations and damage to the property as well. The value of property subject to eminent domain would be determined by law or a jury of 12 freeholders. Article 3, Section 10 also mirrors the Fifth Amendment's protection from deprivation of a citizen's life, liberty, or property without due process of law, but adds that the deprivation also must be made with the "judgment of his peers." This provides an additional protection to citizens of the State of West Virginia.

Article 3, Section 11, forbids the use of political or religious tests to allow citizens to vote, "serve as a juror, sue, plead, appeal, or pursue any profession or employment," and the section also prohibits *ex post facto* laws. ***Ex post facto* laws** are laws that criminalize, increase punishment, or lower the burden of proof on acts after those acts were already committed (see Table 3.2). It precludes civil disabilities based upon political or religious tests. The civil disabilities permitted are those generally found in laws concerning convicted felons and their subsequent loss of civil rights based upon their convictions.

Article 3, Section 12 makes the military subordinate to civil power and states that standing armies should be avoided, and citizens should not be tried or punished by any military, except when in military service, for any crime that is clearly in the civil law (see Table 3.2). Like Amendment III of the U.S. Constitution, it also precludes housing of soldiers in homes during times of peace or in war except in the manner prescribed in the law.

Article 3, Section 13, mirrors the Seventh Amendment in the Bill of Rights of the U.S. Constitution. It requires a six-person jury trial for any civil case involving $20 or more, "if required by either party" (see Table 3.2). The section also requires that cases be reexamined by other courts only according to the rule of "court of law," similar to the requirement in Amendment VII that requires re-examination according to the "rules of the common law."

Article 3, Section 14 is basically a restatement of Amendment VI to the U.S. Constitution (see Table 3.2). Article 3, Section 14 entitles defendants accused of felonies and misdemeanors to a trial before a 12-man jury (later amended to allow women on petit, grand, and coroner's juries, in Article 3, Section 21, 1955). It requires that a trial be public and without "unreasonable delay" (what is referred to as a speedy trial). It requires that the trial take place in the county where the crime is committed, unless the accused requests a change of venue with "good cause." It also requires that the accused be informed of the "character and cause of the accusation," be allowed to confront the witnesses against him or her, have the assistance of counsel, and time to prepare a "defence [sic]."

Finally, it mandates that the accused have a compulsory process to assure the presence of defense witnesses. This differs from Amendment VI, which does not designate the number of jurors in a jury trial. Amendment VI also does not specify that a defendant has time to prepare a defense or for a change of venue.

Article 3, Sections 15 and 15a guarantee religious freedom, as does the First Amendment to the U.S. Constitution (see Table 3.2). It specifies that no man can be compelled to "frequent" or support any religious worship, or be punished for not doing so. It also does not allow punishment for religious opinions or their expression. Furthermore, it does not allow any religious tests or taxes to support religions or their houses of worship. Section 3-15a requires a brief time at the beginning of each school day for students who wish to have "personal and private contemplation, meditation or prayer," but does not allow the requirement or encouragement of students to do so.

Article 3, Section 16 contains the right to public assembly, which is found in Amendment I to the U.S. Constitution (see Table 3.2). It gives the people the right to assemble in "a peaceable manner" so that they may "consult for the common good, to instruct their representatives, or to apply for redress of grievances." It is a broader statement of the rights for assembly and redress found in Amendment I.

Article 3, Section 17 provides the right to a public trial by an impartial jury, consistent with the same provision in Amendment VI (see Table 3.2). It expands this right to include the admonition that the courts should be open to every person who has been injured in his person, property, or reputation. The remedy should be done by "due course of law" and without "sale, denial, or delay."

Article 3, Section 18 precludes conviction from working corruption of blood or forfeiture of estate (see Table 3.2). This is similar to the U.S. Constitution's Article III, Section 3, which does not allow Congress to punish treason or ***corruption of blood*** or forfeiture except during the life of the person attained. These sections precluded a practice of English law in which not only the traitor, but the traitor's family was held responsible for treason. This allowed the king to take lands and titles without the eldest son demanding inheritance by right (Peltason, 1979). The U.S. Constitution, Article III, Section 3 also provides that convictions for treason were to be made by the courts and Congress was not to punish, which is a further separation of the legislative and judicial functions.

Article 3, Section 19 precludes any hereditary "emoluments, honors or privileges" from being bestowed by the state, similar to Article I, Section 9 of the U.S. Constitution. This precludes Congress from giving a title of nobility and any person who holds office from accepting ***emoluments*** (e.g., compensation, benefits, fees, rewards), office, or title of any kind from a foreign state or monarch (see Table 3.2). In the West Virginia Constitution, emoluments, honors, or privileges can be given, but only to the office holder and not that person's heirs as generational entitlements that would continue indefinitely from generation to generation. Emoluments have been given, for example, in various amendments for veterans.

Article 3, Section 20 admonishes the state to adhere to "moderation, temperance, frugality and virtue" and to use those qualities frequently (see Table 3.2). This is not mirrored in the U.S. Constitution and is more in line with Benjamin Franklin's admonitions in *Poor Richard's Almanac* (Morgan, 2008).

Finally, Article 3, Section 22, bestows the right to keep and bear arms, which is in line with Amendment II to the U.S. Constitution (see Table 3.2). However, instead of a "well regulated militia," it gives this right to "a person for the defense of self, family, home and state, and for lawful hunting and recreational use." This section of the West Virginia Constitution's Bill of Rights was added in 1985. It has been interpreted to generally allow ***open carry***; the carrying of a firearm in plain sight so that it is readily seen by those approached except for a few legal restrictions. By statute, West Virginia allows any legal citizen 21 years of age or older, who has no legal restrictions from doing so, to carry a concealed handgun without a license[3] (Office of the Attorney General, 2017).

> This authorization applies to all such persons regardless of his or her state of residence. This is commonly known as "constitutional carry" which indicates a form of permitless or unrestricted concealed carry of a deadly weapon. See W.Va. Code §61-7-7(c) (Office of the Attorney General, 2017, p. 3).

Before moving to the division of powers that exist within the West Virginia Government, there is one amendment to the U.S. Constitution that has great impact on the laws of West Virginia: The ***Fourteenth Amendment*** (Amendment XIV, §1).

> All persons born or naturalized in the United States and subject to the jurisdiction thereof, are citizens of the United States and of the State wherein they reside. No State shall make or enforce any law which shall abridge the privileges or immunities of citizens of the United States; nor shall any State deprive any person of life, liberty, or property,

3. For additional information about West Virginia's concealed handgun policy and opportunities for licensing, as well as laws and restrictions against carry and areas where it is unlawful to carry firearms, see the Office of the Attorney General's *Handbook on laws relating to firearms, July 2017.*

> without due process of law; nor deny to any person within its jurisdiction the equal protection of the laws (Amendment XIV, § 1).

This amendment, ratified in 1868, four years before the revised West Virginia Constitution, has resulted in the majority of the federal rights found in the Bill of Rights being selectively incorporated through the due process clause to the states through U.S. Supreme Court decisions (Congressional Research Service, Library of Congress, 2013).

Separation of Powers

Another aspect of the U.S. and West Virginia Constitutions is the separation of powers, which provides checks and balances. The ***separation of powers*** is the concept that the power of the government should be separated into three branches of government, the executive, legislative, and judicial (Congressional Research Service, Library of Congress, 2013; West Virginia Legislature, 2017–2018). This separation of powers gives each of the three branches the power to make law. The executive branch has the authority to issue executive orders, administrative laws, and directives. ***Administrative laws*** are regulations and requirements written by agencies or officials to carry out the agency's function—a good example of this would be the tax code. The legislative branch enacts ***statutory laws***, or statutes, which are the legal code of the state, and what most people think of when they think of laws. This includes both civil and criminal laws. The judicial branch creates ***case law***, which is law that is based upon a case finding. Although not technically a law, the courts follow precedents, or the decisions of other courts, and thus, the holding of cases from courts within the same jurisdiction has the same effect as law. An example of this type of case law is *Miranda* rights, which must be read to suspects during custodial interrogation. The original requirement was through a U.S. Supreme Court decision (*Miranda v. Arizona,* 384 U.S. 436, 1966). Once decided and applied in the federal and state courts, it had the effect of law. Each type of law affects the rights of individuals and must conform to the substantive and procedural due process of law requirements in their content and application. The law must be written fairly.

The West Virginia Constitution provides for the separation of powers in Article 5, Section 1, "Division of Powers," stating:

> The legislative, executive and judicial departments shall be separate and distinct, so that neither shall exercise the powers properly belonging to either of the others; nor shall any person exercise the powers of

> more than one of them at the same time, except that justices of the peace shall be eligible to the Legislature.

Since justices of the peace have been replaced with magistrates, this sole exception no longer applies. In the following pages, the powers and limitations of the Governor and Legislature are discussed from the West Virginia Constitution, whereas the judicial powers are discussed in Chapter 5.

The Constitution of West Virginia also shows this separation of power in Article 6, Section 13, which states that:

> No person holding any other lucrative office or employment under this state, the United States, or any foreign government; no member of Congress; and no person who is sheriff, constable, or clerk of any court of record, shall be eligible to a seat in the Legislature.

This mandates that the branches should be independent, not only from one another but from national or foreign influence.

As the chief executive of the state, the governor is given domain over the executive branch of government by the West Virginia Constitution. According to the constitution, "The chief executive power shall be vested in the governor, who shall take care that the laws be faithfully executed" (Article 7, §5). Additionally,

> The governor shall be commander-in-chief of the military forces of the state, (except when they shall be called into the service of the United States) and may call out the same to execute the laws, suppress insurrection and repel invasion (Article 7, §12).

The governor also predicts the state's revenue and puts forth a budget to be approved by the legislature (Article 6, §18), and approves contracts for printing (Article 6, §34). He or she also may nominate and

> … by and with the advice and consent of the Senate, (a majority of all the senators elected concurring by yeas and nays) appoint all officers whose offices are established by this constitution, or shall be created by law, and whose appointment or election is not otherwise provided for (Article 7, §8) and may … remove any officer whom he may appoint in case of incompetency, neglect of duty, gross immorality, or malfeasance in office; … (Article 7, §10).

Further, the governor can appoint the other executive officers mentioned in the constitution, including the secretary of state, auditor, treasurer, commissioner of agriculture, or attorney general (Article 7, §1), in situations when their position becomes vacant (Article 7, §17).

The governor does have some authority over the legislature. He or she has the power to call the legislature into session for a specific reason that needs to be addressed immediately, extend a legislative session to address the budget, and move the location of the legislature in times of danger (Article 6, §21; Article 6, §51, D, (8); Article 7, §7). The governor also can sign or veto the budget (Article 6, §51, D, (11)) or bills (Article 7, §14), and appoints the members of Citizens Legislative Compensation Commission, which suggests the levels of compensation for the legislature (Article 6, §33). The governor also has some authority over the judiciary in that he can remit fines and forfeitures, commute capital punishment, and grant reprieves and pardons after convictions (Article 7, §11), except for reprieves and pardons for prosecutions carried out by the House of Delegates (Article 7, §11). In addition, he proposes the budget for the judiciary and the legislature.

The governor's powers over the executive branch include a cabinet of the secretaries of each of the executive branch's main components. These secretaries aid the governor in overseeing the executive branch. The governor's cabinet includes the secretaries from the Department of Administration, Department of Commerce, Department of Education and the Arts, Department of Environmental Protection, Department of Health and Human Resources, Department of Military Affairs and Public Safety, Department of Revenue, Department of Transportation, and the Department of Veterans Assistance. While all of these departments have functions that are involved in the criminal justice area, the Department of Military Affairs and Public Safety has the most agencies directly providing criminal justice functions, especially in policing and corrections.

The West Virginia Department of Military Affairs and Public Safety (DMAPS) houses the Homeland Security State Administrative Agency, Intelligence Fusion Center, Adjutant General/National Guard, Division of Justice and Community Services, Division of Corrections, Division of Homeland Security and Emergency Management, Division of Juvenile Services, Parole Board, West Virginia Division of Protective Services, Regional Jail and Correctional Facilities Authority, State Fire Marshal, and the State Police. Created in 1989 by the Legislature (Barnes, 2015–2016), the Department's mission is:

> ... to provide a safe and secure state by ensuring the proper response to all levels, manners and phases of emergencies, disasters and crimes. The role of the Office of the Secretary is to provide support, oversight and guidance to agencies involved in all facets of public safety. This includes law enforcement and other first response agencies, as well as

the state's criminal justice, correctional and homeland security systems (DMAPS, 2018, para. 1).

As stated above, the emphasis of the Department is to support and oversee the criminal justice system. Therefore, each of the agencies listed under the department are discussed in the chapters that follow as they pertain to the criminal justice system.

In looking at the powers designated by the Constitution, the Legislature is given domain over writing the criminal code because the legislature passes, amends, or rejects bills and resolutions (Article 6, §28). The legislature also prescribes the "terms of office, powers, duties and compensation of all public officers and agents, and the manner in which they shall be elected, appointed and removed" (Article 4, §8). With the local law exceptions noted in Article 6, §39 and 39a,[4] the legislature also is supposed to write, when possible, general laws and not special laws for individual cases/circumstances. It also passes the budget (Article 6, §51), and determines voting laws, requirements for elections, and decides how to handle contested elections (Article 4, §1-11). In addition, it writes laws to protect the private property of married women from the debts of their husbands (Article 6, §49), and laws that govern the manufacture and sale of intoxicating liquor (Article 6, §46). Finally, it enacts laws for fish and wildlife conservation and nongame wildlife resources (Article 6, §56).

The Legislature also has some constitutional powers that limit the powers of the other two branches of government. These include passing or not passing the budget recommended by the governor, which involves the budgets for the

4. "Local laws not to be passed in enumerated cases. The Legislature shall not pass local or special laws in any of the following enumerated cases; that is to say, for granting divorces; laying out, opening, altering and working roads or highways; vacating roads, town plats, streets, alleys and public grounds; locating, or changing county seats; regulating or changing county or district affairs; providing for the sale of church property, or property held for charitable uses; regulating the practice in courts of justice; incorporating cities, towns or villages, or amending the charter of any city, town or village, containing a population of less than two thousand; summoning or impaneling grand or petit juries; the opening or conducting of any election, or designating the place of voting; the sale and mortgage of real estate belonging to minors, or others under disability; chartering, licensing, or establishing ferries or toll bridges; remitting fines, penalties or forfeitures; changing the law of descent; regulating the rate of interest; authorizing deeds to be made for land sold for taxes; releasing taxes; or releasing title to forfeited lands" (Article 6, §39). Also, "No local or special law shall hereafter be passed incorporating cities, towns or villages, or amending their charters. The Legislature shall provide by general laws for the incorporation and government of cities, towns and villages, and shall classify such municipal corporations, upon the basis of population, into not less than two nor more than five classes ..." (Article 6, §39a).

executive, judicial, and legislative branches; overseeing the governor's appointments; making temporary appointments of public offices when disasters are caused by enemy attack and "adopt[ing] such other measures as may be necessary and proper for insuring the continuity of governmental operations" (Article 6, §54), which would normally be an executive function; and the power of impeachment, trial being generally a judicial function. According to the Constitution, the Legislature has the power to impeach any officer of the state, including the governor. The charge is to be levied by the House, while the Senate has the power to try the case. The president of the Supreme Court of Appeals presides over the case or any other Supreme Court of Appeals justice official, in the event that the president of the Supreme Court is unable to do so. In brief, the Senators decide guilt or innocence. A two-thirds vote of the membership is required for impeachment (Article 4, §9).

Balancing the Powers of the Three Branches

As mentioned in the preceding paragraphs, the West Virginia Constitution's ***balancing of powers*** is in line with those of the U.S. Constitution's protection of the citizens from one branch's overreach of power. This is the concept that the powers of the three branches of government (legislative, executive, and judicial) should be balanced so that one part cannot gain excessive power over the other two or the people. This applies to criminal justice in that the constitutional requirements of each branch determines how laws are enacted by the legislative branch, enforced by the executive branch, and interpreted by the judicial branch. The functioning of each branch limits the functioning of the others, so that the criminal justice system operates in a constitutional manner. The constitutional requirements governing arrest, search and seizure, punishment, bail, fines, trials, and laws are subject to the control of the constitutions of the state and federal government through their bill of rights and powers bestowed on the branches of government. It is the balancing of these powers and their limitation that ensures that the rights of citizens are protected and that citizens receive equal protection under the law.

Spotlight: Dismemberment, the Establishment of the State of Kanawha

The final section of the chapter is about ***dismemberment***. It makes a very appropriate spotlight, because West Virginia, originally proposed as the ***State*** *of Kanawha*, is the only state to ever "dismember" itself from another. Its legality as a state is still debated even today, more than 150 years after its founding.

Article IV, Section 3 of the U.S. Constitution states that:

> New States may be admitted by the Congress into this Union; but no new State shall be formed or erected within the Jurisdiction of any other State; nor any State be formed by the Junction of two or more States, or Parts of States, without the Consent of the Legislatures of the States concerned as well as of the Congress.

This seems like a clear statement of how states will be admitted into the Union. Nonetheless, it becomes difficult to interpret when the state involved has removed itself from the Union through secession and when part of that state wishes to reform into a new state and be admitted into the Union while the rest of the state remains outside of that union. It seems confusing and indeed it was in 1861.

In 1861, several southern states seceded from the United States, and one of those was Virginia. In the vote to secede, the majority of representatives to the legislature voted in favor of it; however, the representatives from the western counties were generally against secession. Once the Civil War began, many of the mostly western counties who were opposed to seceding formed the Restored Government of Virginia and replaced the representatives who favored secession with members loyal to the Union. Thus, Virginia had two governments: the rebel government in Richmond and the Restored Government of Virginia.

In 1861, the Virginia Governor, John Letcher, summoned the General Assembly to an extra session to consider what to do in the crisis between the northern and southern states. At first, the delegates to the convention seemed to support a moderate stance; however, with the firing on Fort Sumter and President Lincoln calling for troops to put down the insurrection, the convention passed the ordinance of succession, which was to be voted on later by the citizens of Virginia (West Virginia Division of Culture and History, 2018). The long-standing disagreements between the western counties and the eastern counties over taxation, representation, and other issues were exacerbated by the passing of the ordinance (Stealey, 2011). As a result, the western delegates withdrew from the convention and would sow the seeds that led to the eventual formation of the State of West Virginia (West Virginia Division of Culture and History, 2018).

The western counties first met, filled all of the seats vacated by the rebel delegates, then formed the Restored Government of Virginia in Wheeling, July 1–26, 1861, and received recognition from Congress and President Lincoln.

This then evolved to the consideration of removing the western counties from Virginia and creating a new state, proposed to be the state of Kanawha, but discussions led to the proposal and adoption of West Virginia as the state name (Stealey, 2011; West Virginia Division of Culture and History, 2018). Since Article IV, Section III of the U.S. Constitution did not allow the creation or admission of a new state made from another state, or parts of states, without the approval of the state's legislature and Congress, the Restored Government of Virginia voted to allow West Virginia to dismember from Virginia and Congress agreed to accept the new state. The acceptance was then approved by President Lincoln. Thus, West Virginia became a new state on June 20, 1863 (Stealey, 2011; West Virginia Division of Culture and History, 2018).

Key Terms and Definitions

Act: A physical action that must be present for a crime to occur.

***Actus Reus*:** The act or omission that constitutes the crime itself.

Administrative laws: Laws written and enforced by government agencies.

Balancing of powers: The concept that the powers of the three branches of government (legislative, executive, and judiciary) should be balanced so that one part cannot gain excessive power over the other two or the people.

Case law: Case rulings by judges, especially those of an appeals court or Supreme Court, that have the same effect as a statutory or administrative law because they govern what behaviors are allowed or prohibited from government agents.

Classical School of Philosophy: The school of thought that proposed limiting the power of government, the monarchy, and increasing the power of the people.

Common law: The unwritten code of law enforced in England.

Concurrence: Requirement in law that the *mens rea* and *actus reus* take place at the same time for the act to be a crime.

Corruption of blood: The system of punishment in which not only were the traitor's lands and titles taken, but the heirs' rights to them were also forfeited. Thus, the heirs' blood was also corrupt.

Dismemberment: The splitting of one state into two or more states.

Due process: Required guidelines and procedures that must be followed in the implementation of a law.

Emolument: Wages or perks from an office or title.

***Ex post facto* laws:** Laws that criminalize, increase punishment, or lower the burden of proof on acts after those acts were committed.

Fourteenth Amendment: The constitutional amendment that was used to apply the majority of federal rights from the Bill of Rights to the states under the "due process" and "equal protection" clauses.

Magna Carta: The Great Charter, of 1215, wrested from King John, which granted English noblemen and then Englishmen certain rights and protections. These rights for the nobles, church, and foreign merchants later evolved to rights for all Englishmen. These rights eventually included the right to trial by a jury of one's peers, indictment by grand jury based upon probable cause, and a fair and speedy trial.

***Mens Rea*:** The state of mind of the actor in legal definitions. Generally held to be the evil intent of the actor.

Omission: A failure on the part of an actor to act when required by law to do so.

Open carry: The carrying of a firearm in plain sight so that it is readily seen by those approached.

Royal Charter(s) of Virginia: The three Charter(s) given to the London Company/Colony of Virginia by the King of England. They specified land ownership and tenant and subtenants' rights, law enforcement, and how courts would be established.

Separation of powers: The concept that the powers of government should be separated into three branches: legislative, executive, and judicial.

Social contract: An agreement between the citizens of a country and the government of the country that specified the powers, rights, privileges, and obligations of citizens and their government.

State of Kanawha: The original proposed name for the State of West Virginia.

Statutory laws: Laws enacted by elected officials, generally Congress and the state legislatures. However, they also can include laws written by county commissions, city councils, or other governing bodies with the power to enact legislation.

Tithings: Ten families pledged to support one another in crime prevention and enforcement.

Select Internet Sources

The Creation of the State of West Virginia: http://www.wvculture.org/history/statehood/statehoodtoc.html.

U.S. Constitution and Constitutional Analysis: https://www.congress.gov/constitution-annotated/.

The West Virginia Constitution: http://www.legis.state.wv.us/wvcode/wv_con.cfm#articleV.

Review and Critical Thinking Questions

1. What is the importance of the social contract? Why is it necessary?

2. How do the Bill of Rights of West Virginia and the Bill of Rights of the United States differ?

3. The rights specified in the West Virginia Bill of Rights tend to be more detailed than those from the U.S. Constitution. Do you think that this helps or hurts interpreting these rights?

4. What are the three branches of government? Should the balances be specified in the Constitution or should they develop over time? Why?

5. What are the three types of laws that each branch writes? Can you give an example of each? How do you think each influences criminal justice?

References

Ambler, C. H., & Summers, F. P. (1958). *West Virginia, the mountain state* (2nd ed.). Englewood Cliffs, NJ: Prentice Hall.

Bailey, K. R. (2015, August). Reorganized government of Virginia. *e-WV: The West Virginia Encyclopedia.* Charleston, WV: West Virginia Humanities Council. Retrieved from http://www.wvencyclopedia.org/articles/62.

Barnes, C. S. (2015–2016). *West Virginia blue book 2015–2016.* Retrieved from http://www.wvlegislature.gov/Educational/publications/pub.cfm.

Bastress, R. M. (2010, October). The Constitution of West Virginia. *e-WV: The West Virginia Encyclopedia.* Charleston, WV: West Virginia Humanities Council. Retrieved from http://www.wvencyclopedia.org/articles/1558.

Calvi, J. V., & Coleman, S. (2016). *American law and legal systems* (7th ed.). New York: Routledge.

Congressional Research Service, Library of Congress. (2013, June). *The Constitution of the United States: Analysis and interpretation, Centennial edition.* K. R. Thomas and L. M. Eig (Eds.). Washington, DC: U.S. Government Printing Office. Retrieved from https://www.gpo.gov/fdsys/pkg/GPO-CONAN-2013/pdf/GPO-CONAN-2013.pdf.

Constitution of West Virginia. Charleston, WV: West Virginia Division of Culture and History. Retrieved from http://www.wvculture.org/history/statehood/constitution.html.

Declaration of Independence. (1776). Washington, DC: The U.S. National Archives and Records Administration. Retrieved from http://www.archives.gov/exhibits/charters/declaration_transcript.html.

Friedman, L. M. (2005). *A history of American law* (3rd ed.). New York: Simon & Schuster.

Gaines, L. K., & Miller, R. L. (2015). *CJ 3*. Stamford, CT: Cengage Learning.

Holten, N. G., & Lamar, L. L. (1991). *The criminal courts: Structures, personnel, and procedures*. New York: McGraw-Hill.

Jamestowne Society. (2014). *Royal charters and ordinance for Virginia*. Retrieved from http://www.jamestowne.org/royal-charters.html.

Johnson, H. A., & Wolfe, N. T. (2003). *History of criminal justice* (3rd ed.). New York: Routledge/Taylor and Francis Group.

Morgan, L. (2008, Summer). *The prominent and prodigiously popular Poor Richard*. University Park, PA: Pennsylvania Center for the Book, The Pennsylvania State University. Retrieved from http://pabook.libraries.psu.edu/palitmap/PoorRichardsAlmanack.html.

Office of the Attorney General. (2017). *Handbook on laws relating to firearms, July 2017*. Charleston, WV: Author. Retrieved from http://ago.wv.gov/gunreciprocity/Documents/2016%20Firearms%20Handbook.pdf.

Oliver, W. M., & Hilgenberg, J. F., Jr. (2010). *A history of crime and criminal justice in America* (2nd ed.). Durham, NC: Carolina Academic Press.

Owen, S. S., Fradella, H. F., Burke, T. W., & Joplin, J. W. (2015). *Foundations of criminal justice*. New York: Oxford University Press.

Peltason, J. W. (1979). *Corwin & Peltason's understanding the Constitution* (8th ed.). New York: Holt, Rinehart & Wilson.

Rice, O. K., & Brown, S. W. (2014, October). History of West Virginia. *e-WV: The West Virginia Encyclopedia*. Charleston, WV: West Virginia Humanities Council. Retrieved from https://www.wvencyclopedia.org/articles/414.

Stealey, J. E. III. (2011). West Virginia's constitutional critique of Virginia: The revolution of 1861–1863. *Civil War History, 56*(1), 9–47.

The Avalon Project, Yale Law School, Lillian Goldman Law Library. (2008). *The third charter of Virginia; March 12, 1611*. Retrieved from http://avalon.law.yale.edu/17th_century/va03.asp.

United States Senate. (n.d.). *Constitution of the United States*. Retrieved from http://www.senate.gov/civics/constitution_item/constitution.htm.

West Virginia Department of Military Affairs and Public Safety (DMAPS). (2018). Retrieved from https://dmaps.wv.gov/Pages/default.aspx.

West Virginia Division of Culture and History. (2018). *A state of convenience: The creation of* West Virginia. Retrieved from http://www.wvculture.org/history/statehood/statehood.html.

West Virginia Legislature. (2017–2018). *Manual of the house of delegates and senate, eighty-third legislature.* Retrieved from http://www.wvlegislature.gov/Educational/publications/Manual_2017-2018.pdf.

West Virginia Legislature. (2018). *Constitution of West Virginia.* Retrieved from http://www.legis.state.wv.us/WVCODE/WV_CON.cfm.

Legal References

Miranda v. Arizona, 384 U.S. 436 (1966).
U.S. Const. amend. I
U.S. Const. amend. II
U.S. Const. amend. III
U.S. Const. amend. IV
U.S. Const. amend. V
U.S. Const. amend. VI
U.S. Const. amend. VII
U.S. Const. amend. VIII
U.S. Const. amend. XIV §1
U.S. Const. art. I §9
U.S. Const. art. II
U.S. Const. art. IV
U.S. Const. art. I1, §3
U.S. Const. pmbl.
West Virginia Const. art. I, §1
West Virginia Const. art. I, §2
West Virginia Const. art. I, §3
West Virginia Const. art. III, §1
West Virginia Const. art. III, §2
West Virginia Const. art. III, §3
West Virginia Const. art. III, §4
West Virginia Const. art. III, §5
West Virginia Const. art. III, §6
West Virginia Const. art. III, §7
West Virginia Const. art. III, §8
West Virginia Const. art. III, §9
West Virginia Const. art. III, §10
West Virginia Const. art. III, §11
West Virginia Const. art. III, §12
West Virginia Const. art. III, §13

West Virginia Const. art. III, § 14
West Virginia Const. art. III, § 15
West Virginia Const. art. III, § 15a
West Virginia Const. art. III, § 16
West Virginia Const. art. III, § 17
West Virginia Const. art. III, § 18
West Virginia Const. art. III, § 19
West Virginia Const. art. III, § 20
West Virginia Const. art. III, § 21
West Virginia Const. art. III, § 22
West Virginia Const. art. IV, § 8
West Virginia Const. art. IV, § 9
West Virginia Const. art. IV, § 11
West Virginia Const. art. VI, § 5
West Virginia Const. art. VI, § 13
West Virginia Const. art. VI, § 18
West Virginia Const. art. VI, § 21
West Virginia Const. art. VI, § 28
West Virginia Const. art. VI, § 31
West Virginia Const. art. VI, § 33
West Virginia Const. art. VI, § 39
West Virginia Const. art. VI, § 39a
West Virginia Const. art. VI, § 49
West Virginia Const. art. VI, § 51(D)(8)
West Virginia Const. art. VI, § 51(D)(11)
West Virginia Const. art. VI, § 54
West Virginia Const. art. VI, § 56
West Virginia Const. art. VII, § 1
West Virginia Const. art. VII, § 5
West Virginia Const. art. VII, § 7
West Virginia Const. art. VII, § 8
West Virginia Const. art. VII, § 10
West Virginia Const. art. VII, § 11
West Virginia Const. art. VII, § 12
West Virginia Const. art. VII, § 14
West Virginia Const. art. VII, § 17
West Virginia Constitution, Preamble

Chapter 4

Policing in West Virginia

Believed to be the Huntington Police Department, ca. early 1900s. Courtesy of the Marshall University Special Collections.

Policing in West Virginia developed much as it did in the rest of the country. Prior to industrialization and urbanization, communities were responsible for policing themselves. Reporting criminal activity, apprehending criminals, and maintaining order were community responsibilities. As the population of West Virginia grew, so did the need for a more organized form of social control. Huntington and Charleston hired police officers in the mid-1800s. Increased crime, disorder, and labor disputes predicated the organization of the West Virginia State Police in 1919. Currently, police in West Virginia face unique challenges that stem in part from the high rate of opioid usage in the state.

This chapter focuses on policing in West Virginia, beginning with an overview of the general development of policing in England and America. The chapter explores the eras of policing and the major developments during these periods. Next, the chapter focuses on policing in West Virginia, including police training and the hiring process. The chapter concludes with a discussion about police training in West Virginia.

Origins of Policing

Early Social Control

Social control is one way a society encourages its citizens to conform to norms, rules, and laws; and discourages behavior that deviates from said norms, rules, and laws. ***Informal social control*** is primarily exercised through socialization. Socialization is the process of teaching people about their culture and the accepted behaviors of their culture. When informal social control fails, ***formal social control*** may be used in an effort to force people to conform to social norms or to punish people for failing to conform to social norms. One form of social control is the criminal justice system (Chriss, 2010).

In ancient times, social control was largely maintained by individuals and retribution was frequently the penalty for wrongdoing. ***Lex talionis***, an eye for an eye, was one means of obtaining justice. As societies evolved and populations grew, codified laws were developed. One of the first known set of codified laws was ***Hammurabi's Code***. The Code of Hammurabi identified prohibited behavior and prescribed punishments for rule breakers. Punishments varied based upon the type of rule infraction, and included fines, the death penalty, and continued application of *lex talionis* (Oliver & Hilgenberg, 2010; Shelden, 2001). In Rome, the vigiles were akin to a city police force and were responsible for policing and firefighting (Shelden, 2001).

History of Policing in England

Policing in England developed over several centuries. Under the ***frankpledge system***, citizens were responsible for reporting local crime and apprehending lawbreakers within their own small communities, and failure to do so was considered a criminal act. These smaller communities were combined into larger communities called shires. Shires were overseen by the ***shire reeves*** (sheriffs) who were responsible for tax collection and maintaining order (Grant & Terry, 2017). Around 1285, the frankpledge system gave way to a more formalized manner of ensuring lawbreakers were brought to justice. One element of the new system was ***hue and cry***, which required men between the ages of 15 and 60 to respond to requests for assistance from the ***constables*** who were responsible for enforcing the law and organizing community night watches. ***Justices of the peace*** acted as judges, presiding over criminal trials (Grant & Terry, 2017; Uchida, 2015).

Several factors contributed to restructuring the policing system in England. First, constables and justices of the peace engaged in misconduct and corrupt activities. Second, industrialization resulted in more citizens moving from the countryside to larger cities for employment. Third, the aforementioned population growth contributed to an increase in crime and disorder. These developments led to the 1740s creation of the ***Bow Street Runners***. The Bow Street Runners were formed by Henry Fielding with permission from the London government. Members of the Bow Street Runners located stolen property, apprehended wanted persons, and engaged in patrol. The Bow Street Runners are considered to be England's first formal police force (Cox, 2008).

The Bow Street Runners were disbanded with the creation of the London Metropolitan Police (Cox, 2008). The ***London Metropolitan Police (LMP)*** were established by the London Metropolitan Police Act in 1829. The LMP was organized and led by Sir Robert Peel. Peel implemented a paramilitary structure that emphasized a chain of command and professionalism. Officers wore uniforms distinguishing them from the British military. Peel believed the police should act as a preventive agent, stopping criminal activity before it was started or completed. Thereby, Peel asserted the absence of crime is the most effective way to measure police efficiency. Peel also advocated for police hiring and training standards. Peel's guiding principles have a continued influence on policing in the United States of America (Grant & Terry, 2017; Uchida, 2015).

The Development of Policing in the United States of America

Policing in the United States is based upon practices and concepts originating in England. In less populated areas, sheriffs appointed by the governor enforced tax laws, apprehended persons wanted for crimes, and conducted court duties, such as serving subpoenas (Uchida, 2015). In larger cities, the focus of constables and the citizen night watch was to ensure fire alarms were sounded, suspicious persons were investigated, and that court duties were performed as needed. Eventually the ***night watch system*** became more organized and required citizens to patrol city streets and respond to criminal activity (Uchida, 2015). The night watch system and the paid daytime constables were the immediate precursors to the organization of the first policing agencies in the northern United States (Grant & Terry, 2017; Uchida, 2015).

Slave patrols were formed in the 1740s and were unique to the southern part of the United States. As the name implies, slave patrols were responsible for apprehending escaped slaves and returning them to their owners. As the slave patrols grew into a more organized entity, they were also responsible for enforcing slave codes and other laws. After the Civil War ended, slave patrols became responsible for enforcing Jim Crow Laws, thus setting the stage for the poor relationship between African Americans and the police.

Some scholars contend that slave patrols were the basis upon which all modern policing was formed (Williams & Murphy, 1990). Other scholars assert that the first organized police departments in the United States were formed in larger northeast cities in response to population growth and increases in crime and disorder stemming from the Industrial Revolution and urbanization. The first American police departments were loosely modeled after the London Metropolitan Police. New York City, Boston, Philadelphia, and Cincinnati were early adopters of the LMP model (Grant & Terry, 2017; Uchida, 2015). The development of American policing can be loosely divided into three periods.

Eras of Policing

The development of American policing has occurred over roughly three periods. The eras of policing do not have cut-and-dried starting and stopping points. Rather, these eras serve as general guidelines about the key developments in policing practice and function.

The ***political era of policing*** roughly extends from the 1840s to the early 1900s. This era of policing is largely known for the negative influence of politics on policing practice, in addition to the rampant corruption and misconduct engaged in by police officers. People often were awarded jobs as police officers based upon political affiliations and promotions to higher ranks were bought instead of earned, cementing political influence in policing (Perkins Gilbert, 2012). Police officers frequently overlooked vice crimes in exchange for personal gain, and sometimes charged business owners for protection (Uchida, 2015). Prohibition offered additional opportunities for corrupt police officers and politicians to engage in illegal activities (Perkins Gilbert, 2012). The extensive nature of misconduct and other behaviors prompted some police leaders to advocate for reforming existing police practices.

The ***reform/professionalization era of policing*** began in the early 1900s at the urging of citizen progressives who wanted to lessen the influence of politics and reduce corruption and misconduct in policing (Kelling & Moore, 1988). The public-initiated police reform effort gained little traction and policing reform remained stagnant until police leaders became involved in the movement. The reform/professionalization era is characterized by improvement in hiring processes and training. For example, Chief August Vollmer formalized the hiring process for police officers at the UC Berkeley Police Department and required prospective officers to have psychiatric screenings and take intelligence tests (Carte, Carte, & Robinson, 1983; Uchida, 2015). Vollmer was a proponent of technology, and the Berkeley Police Department was the first to develop a forensic laboratory and lie detector machine (Carte et al., 1983). Vollmer supported educating police officers and implemented the country's first training academy (Carte et al., 1983; Grant & Terry, 2017). Similar to Sir Robert Peel, Vollmer believed that the primary job of the police was crime control and prevention, beginning with juvenile interventions. He was also actively involved in academics and saw value in using empirical research to inform policing practices (Carte et al., 1983). Vollmer's protégé, O.W. Wilson, served as a police officer while attending Berkeley as a student. During his career, Wilson made numerous advances toward Vollmer's goal of professionalizing the police. Wilson served as chief of police in Fullerton, California; Wichita, Kansas; and Chicago, Illinois. Wilson also served as Dean of the School of Criminology at the University of California (Bopp, 1975). Wilson engaged in research activities to assess police practices and implemented new technology to improve police effectiveness (Sealock, 2012).

Several technological advances were made during the reform/professionalization era of policing that changed the way the police did business. The automobile became a police tool that was used to facilitate quick response to calls and conduct preventive police work. The invention of the telephone allowed citizens to immediately request assistance from the police. The telephone also provided a means of communication between police officers on the street and their headquarters. The handheld radio allowed police supervisors to have more oversight over patrol officers and served as a key safety tool for officers (Uchida, 2015).

Despite the positive changes in policing, the police found themselves at odds with the public during the 1960s and 1970s. Citizens protested the treatment of black Americans and the Vietnam War; some of these demonstrations resulted in direct confrontations with the police. At this point it became necessary for the police to assess and evaluate their response to the communities they served. This is generally accepted as the starting point of the ***community policing era.***

While the idea of community policing originated in the 1970s, it was not until the 1980s that the philosophy was promoted by the federal government as a way for the police to mend fences with the public. One guiding tenet of this era is that the police need to communicate and partner with the public to combat crime and disorder (Uchida, 2015). To further improve police-community relations, the ***Community Oriented Policing Office (COPS)*** was formed in 1994. As of 2018 the office still exists, and provides funding opportunities, training, program ideas, and technical assistance to police departments wishing to engage in COP activities.

Policing in West Virginia

The state of West Virginia was formally established in 1863 (Bastress, 2011) and the creation of municipal police and county sheriff's departments soon followed. Shepherdstown is the oldest city in West Virginia, founded in 1762. The Shepherdstown Police Department also is one of the oldest mentioned in the state, if one counts their original *constables* as the beginning of the police department. On June 15, 1801, the City Court of Shepherdstown appointed two Constables, James Nixon and Jacob Long. They were appointed by the court because of growing incidents of "Breach of the Sabbath" so that they could patrol the streets and alleyways to stop such misbehavior (Musser, 1931).

If one does not count the constables as a police department, then the oldest official department is probably the Wheeling Police Department, which was founded on January 16, 1806. It was headed by a sergeant, who was then the equivalent of a chief of police. The Huntington Police Department was formed in 1872 with the appointment of a town marshal, Isaac H. Mitchell (Huntington Police Department, 2016). The Charleston Police Department was officially established around 1873, although men served in the capacity of police officers prior to this date. The original charter called for a police force of at least six men, exclusive of the chief of police (Westfall, 2014). As of early 2018, West Virginia has approximately 3,700 police officers serving state, county, and municipal departments (Chuck Sadler, personal communication, March 17, 2018).

Policing in West Virginia—especially the West Virginia State Police, the county sheriffs, and city police departments in the Southern West Virginia coal fields—was greatly influenced by the labor strife at the turn of the twentieth century known as the Mine Wars (Corbin, 2016). One of the most famous clashes between labor workers and police was the Battle of Blair Mountain (Bailey, 2013). At Blair Mountain, in 1921 an original force of 5,000 miners wearing red bandanas around their necks (where the term "rednecks" may have been coined), converged on Logan County. Many of the miners did not march to Blair Mountain, but those who did were met by a large army of sheriff's deputies, mine guards, store clerks, and West Virginia State Police Officers led by Logan County Sheriff Don Chafin. Leadership of the miners' opposition was taken over by Colonel William Eubank of the National Guard and the two sides met at Blair Mountain. Over several days, there was intense fighting and Col. Eubank brought in airplanes to drop bombs on the miners to aid his troops. The battle ended at Blair Mountain when President Harding sent in federal troops from Fort Thomas, Kentucky and an air squadron from Langley Field in Virginia. When the federal troops arrived in Logan County, most of the miners surrendered and were returned home by train. There were at least

12 miners and four of Chafin's army killed in the fighting. The labor strife would continue throughout the modern history of West Virginia, calling on agencies such as the West Virginia State Police and the Department of Natural Resources, to try to keep order along with local police and sheriff's agencies during times of labor unrest.

Today, West Virginia Code §8-14-3 lists the powers, authority and duties of law-enforcement officials and policemen as follows.

> The chief and any member of the police force or department of a municipality and any municipal sergeant shall have all of the powers, authority, rights and privileges within the corporate limits of the municipality with regard to the arrest of persons, the collection of claims, and the execution and return of any search warrant, warrant of arrest or other process, which can legally be exercised or discharged by a deputy sheriff of a county. In order to arrest for the violation of municipal ordinances and as to all matters arising within the corporate limits and coming within the scope of his official duties, the powers of any chief, policeman or sergeant shall extend anywhere within the county or counties in which the municipality is located, and any such chief, policeman or sergeant shall have the same authority of pursuit and arrest beyond his normal jurisdiction as has a sheriff (W. Va. Code §8-14-3).

Currently there are several types of police agencies in West Virginia employing officers charged with the duties and responsibilities described in the West Virginia Code. While all these agencies share the goals of promoting public safety, maintaining order, and enforcing law, the agencies differ in several ways. Some agencies are under the purview of the state, while others are governed by counties and municipalities. These agencies often work together to achieve their goals, supporting each other with resources and expertise. A description of these agencies is discussed next.

West Virginia State Police

The ***West Virginia State Police (WVSP)*** was established in 1919 by Governor John. J. Cornwell and is the fourth oldest state police agency in the country (WVSP, 2018). The mission of the state police is stated in West Virginia Code §15-2-12(a):

> The West Virginia State Police shall have the mission of statewide enforcement of criminal and traffic laws with emphasis on providing basic enforcement and citizen protection from criminal depredation

throughout the state and maintaining the safety of the state's public streets, roads and highways.

Originally designated the West Virginia Department of Public Safety, the agency was formed in response to widespread labor disputes and political misconduct. Ten years after their formation, the WVSP became responsible for traffic enforcement and in 1934 began organized road patrols that also assisted in the enforcement of criminal laws (Cole, 1998). Currently the WVSP is an all-purpose agency that employs approximately 630 officers (referred to as troopers) who perform a variety of duties. State troopers engage in law and traffic enforcement, service calls, investigations, and provide support to local police agencies. WVSP troopers provide policing services in rural areas of the state that are unincorporated or have small numbers of local officers available to the public. The South Charleston field office serves the largest population of people at approximately 447,628. The Elkins field office serves the smallest population of people at approximately 142,470.

There are several divisions of the state police that provide specialized services. The investigative services field division focuses on investigating felony-level narcotics interdiction and investigation, often working in concert with local authorities and task forces. During the 2016 fiscal year, Bureau of Criminal Investigations activities resulted in 778 felony federal charges, 1,537 state felony charges, and nearly $2.3 million in property seizures (WVSP, 2016). The 15 teams that comprise the K-9 unit engage in searches for narcotics, explosives, and provide protection for officers in dangerous situations. During the 2016 fiscal year, the K-9 units contributed 7,574 service hours to missing persons searches, explosives searches, and narcotics searches. This activity resulted in more than $1.5 million of seized cash and contraband. The aviation unit completed 71 missions, including searching for missing persons, searching for fleeing fugitives, and marijuana eradication. The aviation unit, special response team, and explosives and dive team provide additional services, which include searching for missing persons, serving high-risk warrants, and searching for evidence in waterways (WVSP, 2016).

The WVSP are responsible for maintaining the state ***crime lab***, which provides free evidence processing services to all police agencies in West Virginia. The crime lab is accredited by the American Society of Crime Laboratory Directors Laboratory Accreditation Board (ASCLD/LAB). There are several sections in the crime lab. The central evidence receiving section stores all the evidence submitted to the lab in a central location and determines if evidence should be forwarded to the biochemistry lab for analysis. The biochemistry section is responsible for analysis of crime scene evidence that may contain DNA or other biological specimens. The latent prints section analyzes evidence that may be left by a person's bare fingers, hands, feet, and toes. The drug identification section identifies possible controlled substances submitted to the lab. The firearms and tool marks section analyzes evidence to identify what type of firearms or tools might have been used during the commission of a crime. The questioned document section is responsible for examining paper evidence such as receipts, checks, and prescriptions. Toxicology analyzes blood and urine for the presence of drugs and alcohol. Last, the trace evidence section examines pieces of evidence that are small, such as gun powder residue (West Virginia State Police, Crime Lab, 2018).

Sheriff's Departments

There are 55 counties in West Virginia, each served by a sheriff's department. There are approximately 1,100 deputies and 273 civilian personnel serving at these departments. The largest sheriff's department in West Virginia is Kanawha County, which employs 100 sheriff's deputies and 35 civilian employees. There are 19 sheriff's departments in West Virginia employing 10 or fewer deputies; Calhoun County has only two deputies (USDOJ/FBI, 2017). Some sheriff duties are different from those of state and municipal police officers. For example, the sheriff's department is responsible for enforcing tax laws, maintaining tax records, estate and trust management, serving court notices, and providing court bailiffs. Sheriff's departments sometimes work with municipal, state, and federal agencies to conduct investigations.

Municipal Departments

There are an estimated 204 municipal police agencies in West Virginia (Chuck Sadler, personal communication, March 19, 2018). One hundred forty-nine West Virginia municipal police agencies reported employee data to the Federal Bureau of Investigation Uniform Crime Report. These agencies employ an estimated 1,500 police officers and 204 civilian personnel. The largest of these departments is Charleston, which has 163 officers and 24 civilian personnel. The Huntington Police Department is the second largest city department in the state, with 105 officers and 11 civilian personnel. Most West Virginia municipal police departments have 10 or fewer sworn officers, and many operate without civilian support positions (USDOF/FBI, 2017). Municipal police officers perform a variety of peacekeeping/order maintenance, service, and law enforcement duties. They may also enforce local ordinances and building codes.

"Fallen Partner" Law Enforcement Officer Memorial, Capitol Complex. Courtesy of Sam Dameron.

Campus Police Agencies

According to the Uniform Crime Report (FBI, 2016), 11 colleges and universities in West Virginia employ their own police officers. The largest campus agency in the state is West Virginia University (WVU), which employs 56 officers and 23 civilians. The smallest campus agency in the state is Bluefield College, which employs two officers and has no civilian personnel. Some campus police departments serve as all-purpose police and are responsible for investigating criminal activity occurring on or near their campus. Other campus agencies, such as West Virginia State University (WVSU) and Glenville State College (GSC), employ full-service law enforcement officers and security staff to provide services to students (GSC, 2015–2016; WVSU, 2018). Campus departments may also provide security during campus events and offer safety education to the student population. For example, Marshall University's Office of Public Safety offers Rape Aggression Defense (RAD) classes, which students can take for credit. The WVU Police Department offers Flash Point training, which is designed to help students, faculty, and staff deescalate potentially

Figure 4.1. Higher Education, the Clery Act, and Title IX

During the 2015–2016 academic year, West Virginia institutions of higher learning were responsible for the safety and well-being of approximately 65,000 students (WVHEPC, 2017). Campus safety standards in West Virginia, and in the rest of the county, are guided by the Clery Act. The Clery Act is named after college student Jeanne Clery, who was raped and murdered in her LeHigh University dormitory room by another student in 1986 (Clery Center, 2018c). The ***Clery Act*** requires institutions of higher learning to take several steps to maintain a safe learning environment for students. Campuses are required to maintain publicly available information about campus crime; to issue yearly crime and safety reports; and to document policies and procedures for reporting criminal activity to proper authorities. The Clery Act also addresses rights and services for crime victims and mandates that institutions document programming designed to prevent dating violence and sexual assault. Campuses also are required to report arrests and disciplinary referrals for substance use. To further support student safety, institutions of higher education must notify students of any ongoing threats to safety on or near campus, such as immediate criminal activity or severe weather (Clery Center, 2018a).

Related to the Clery Act is a federal civil rights act known as Title IX. Title IX provides students with protection against sex and gender discrimination at educational institutions receiving federal funding (USDOJ, 2012). Title IX requires institutions of higher learning to provide fair treatment for alleged victims and alleged suspects of sexual assault, sexual harassment, and discrimination (USDOJ, 2012). Each university is required to have a Title IX officer and/or investigator who is responsible for conducting inquiries into any allegations. Title IX applies to events and activities that occur on campus and off campus.

Together the Clery Act and Title IX create a framework for institutions of higher learning regarding student safety and equal treatment. These regulations assist campuses with providing a positive and safe educational experience for the nearly 65,000 West Virginia college students. Further information about West Virginia campus crime statistics, policies, and procedures can be found on individual institution websites.

violent situations and identify people who might be at risk for committing violent acts (WVU, 2017). Campus police departments are responsible for notifying students of criminal activity occurring on or near campus and for maintaining annual crime statistics. All institutions of higher learning are required to publicly report criminal activity per the Clery Act (Clery Center, 2018b).

Division of Natural Resources

The West Virginia Division of Natural Resources Law Enforcement Section (DNR) was organized in 1897. The law enforcement section has the primary responsibility for the enforcement of game and fish laws and rules. DNR officers investigate hunting and boating accidents, forest fires, and assist the state police when needed (WVDNR, 2003). The section has the highest entrance requirements for any law enforcement officers in the state. Candidates must have graduated from an accredited four-year college or university and a degree in law enforcement, criminology, criminal justice, or natural sciences is preferred. There are some permitted exceptions to the four-year degree requirement (WVDNR, 2010).

Hatfield-McCoy Trail Rangers

The Hatfield-McCoy Trail Rangers is a small state-level agency, consisting of West Virginia Natural Resource Police Officers. The rangers patrol each of the trails in the Hatfield-McCoy off-highway managed vehicle trail system. Rangers also enforce all safety laws and policies on those trails (Hatfield-McCoy Trails, 2016). The trail system is named after the families and the feud between them, the Hatfields and McCoys, which occurred in southwestern West Virginia and southeastern Kentucky.

Federal Law Enforcement

Federal law enforcement agencies maintain a presence in West Virginia, sometimes working with local and state agencies to conduct investigations. The FBI's ***Criminal Justice Information Services Division (CJIS)*** is located in Clarksburg, West Virginia. CJIS is the hub for the ***Uniform Crime Report***, the ***National Instant Criminal Background Check System (NICS)***, ***National Crime Information Center (NCIC)***, ***National Data Exchange (N-Dex)***, and other programs designed to make policing and investigations more effective. The FBI also has several offices in West Virginia cities that participate in investigations activities. The ***Drug Enforcement Administration (DEA)***, the ***Alcohol Firearms Tobacco and Explosives Agency (ATF)***, ***Central Intelligence Agency (CIA)***, ***United States Marshals Service***, and the ***United States Customs and Border Protection (CBP)*** are some of the other federal agencies with a presence in West Virginia.

Police Activities in West Virginia

Police officers perform several duties, many of which do not involve enforcing the law. Police officers generally engage in two types of activities—proactive and reactive. ***Proactive policing*** involves officer-initiated activities, while ***reactive policing*** occurs at the request of someone else. Proactive and reactive activities can be generalized into three categories of police duties: order maintenance/peacekeeping, service, and law enforcement.

General Forms of Policing

Order maintenance and peacekeeping duties vary in scope but can generally be defined as police actions that ensure the interest of the general public is not disturbed by people or by events. Examples of order maintenance and peacekeeping duties include crowd dispersion, responding to loud noise complaints, mediating non-criminal disputes, and directing traffic. It is important to note that these activities do not necessarily involve enforcing the law (Brandl, 2018). However, some order maintenance and peacekeeping activities might result in a citizen being given a citation or being arrested. For example, if a police officer is requested by a business owner to disperse a crowd of people impeding entry to the business and the officer finds that the subjects have been engaging in illegal drug use, the officer may decide to make an arrest or issue a ticket.

Service duties include sponsoring community events, escorting funeral processions, assisting stranded motorists, and providing education at schools (Brandl, 2018). These duties rarely involve enforcement of the law but may also be categorized as order maintenance activities if the result of the service is the reduction of the likelihood of a disorderly event. For example, directing traffic at the scene of a traffic crash is a service that maintains order by ensuring the flow of traffic does not result in further accidents.

Law enforcement duties include a variety of activities that may result in the arrest of citizens for law-breaking activities (Grant & Terry, 2017). The law enforcement activity with which general citizens are most aware is traffic patrol. Some departments have dedicated traffic units, while other departments allow officers to engage in traffic work at their own discretion. While most citizens who are stopped by police are not engaging in criminal behavior, they may be issued a traffic citation. There are occasions when citizens are stopped by the police and are discovered to be transporting narcotics, driving under the influence, or engaged in some other form of criminal activity.

Another law enforcement activity is criminal investigation. Most investigations are short-term and involve misdemeanor crimes. Intimate partner violence, operating while intoxicated, and drug possession cases are examples of misdemeanor crimes that may be investigated and resolved during an officer's shift. Felony crimes and crimes committed by strangers may take longer to investigate. It is important to note that not all criminal investigations result in an arrest, and therefore may be classified as peacekeeping or order maintenance activities.

Police Tactics

The police use many tactics to accomplish their goals and fulfill their duties. The most obvious tactic used by the police is patrol. Police officers spend many hours patrolling their communities using several methods. The patrol method with which most people are familiar is ***vehicle patrol***, which involves police officers driving around their assigned areas to deter and detect instances of crime and disorder. Officers engaging in ***foot patrol*** may do so as part of their regular job duties or as part of a special assignment. Many large cities have regular foot patrols in downtown areas. Sometimes foot patrol is used during festivals, concerts, or other community events. One benefit of foot patrol is being able to interact with the public more frequently. ***Bicycle patrol*** is used in many jurisdictions and requires specialized training. Bicycle officers may ride during their regular shifts and may also engage in patrol during special events. One advantage of bicycle patrol is being able to travel to places vehicles cannot access, such as narrow alleyways. Other methods of patrol include waterway patrols and equine patrols.

Police patrol serves multiple purposes. First, police patrol deters some criminal and disorderly activities. Second, the public has come to associate police work with general patrol. Therefore, the public sees the police as "doing their job" when there is a visible police presence in a community. Police patrol also makes the public feel safer. Third, patrol is one way for the police to detect criminal activity. In particular, patrol is useful for apprehending citizens who are committing traffic violations or operating a vehicle while intoxicated or under the influence of narcotics.

Community Oriented Policing (COP)

Community Oriented Policing (COP) is a police strategy that began in earnest in the 1980s. The core component of COP strategy is engaging the public in a partnership to combat crime and disorder. Examples of COP programs include implementing a neighborhood watch program, hosting citizen police academies, hosting Police Explorer troops, school presentations, school resource officers, and partnering to provide after-school programs. To facilitate success of COP initiatives, it is important for officers to understand community needs. One strategy to accomplish this goal is to permanently assign officers to specific neighborhoods so that those officers can become well acquainted with more localized concerns (Brandl, 2018).

Problem Oriented Policing (POP)

Problem Oriented Policing (POP) is a policing strategy that hinges on police identifying problems in the community and addressing these problems at their sources. POP applies a form of the scientific method to accomplish its goal. POP encourages police agencies to "think outside of the box" and to work with non-criminal justice agencies to solve community problems. Examples of problems that may be addressed using the POP method include copper theft, sex offenses, and residential burglary (Center for Problem Oriented Policing, 2018).

Figure 4.2. Occupational Stress among Rural and Urban Officers in West Virginia

As in any job that involves emergency response calls, unpredictable situations, and potential danger, it is important to examine occupational stress experienced by men and women who serve in law enforcement. There are several factors compounding occupational stress resulting from police work. Research has shown that the size of a department and its organizational structure can negatively affect police officers in urban departments (Brooks & Piquero, 1998). On the other hand, environmental challenges and remoteness can affect officers stress levels in rural departments (Sandy & Devine, 1978). In addition, rural police officers are more prone to experiencing four additional factors related to stress than their urban counterparts. These factors are security (i.e., isolation as a result of the rural geographical area that the officer serves), social factors (i.e., the "fish bowl" environment), working conditions (i.e., limited resources), and inactivity (i.e., boredom) (Oliver & Meier, 2004; Sandy & Devine, 1978).

While West Virginia's unique landscape includes metropolitan areas (e.g., Charleston, Huntington, Morgantown, Wheeling, etc.), the majority of West Virginia citizens live in rural areas served by small police agencies. Because of this, the unique stress experienced by officers in a rural setting is important to study. As part of a graduate capstone project at Marshall University, West Virginia sheriff deputies employed in both rural and urban settings were surveyed about their stress levels. For the purpose of this study, rural areas in West Virginia were defined as those counties with a population of less than 50,000 people (Twardy, personal communication, December 14, 2017). Urban areas were defined as counties with more than 50,000 people. Twelve sheriff's departments from six urban areas and six rural areas were surveyed. The six urban departments were Kanawha County, Cabell County, Monongalia County, Wood County, Raleigh County, and Putnam County. The rural departments were Logan County, Mingo County, Boone County, Wyoming County, Lincoln County, and Braxton County.

Overall, a total of 63 deputies from five departments provided responses (Twardy, personal communication, December 14, 2017). Almost 90% of the respondents were male, and all of the deputies were white. The majority of deputies were married (70.5%) and their average age was 40 years. The officers reported about 15 years of service on average as an officer in some capacity. Most of the officers were deputies (32.8%) or sergeants (20.6%). Despite attempts to garner surveys equally from both urban and rural departments, the final sample was comprised of mostly urban officers (81%) versus rural officers (19%).

Despite the low response rate, some important findings about officer stress emerged. Officers in rural settings reported more stress than their urban counterparts (Twardy, personal communication, December 14, 2017). For example, rural deputies reported viewing their occupations as being more dangerous than urban deputies. This could be the result of rural deputies working in more isolated and remote areas where backup is not readily available. Rural officers were more likely to report that they were more often aggravated on the job, but urban officers reported higher percentages of feeling angry while they were working. Moreover, rural officers expressed that they had difficulty sleeping after witnessing a traumatic event. It is assumed that resources for coping after such tragedies and the companionship that is afforded in a larger urban department are lacking in rural departments. Last, rural officers responded that they had family members they could talk to about their problems, while urban officers were able to confide with a larger base of companions.

As West Virginia police officers continue to address crime and disorder in its communities, it is essential to provide these professionals the proper stress reduction resources. In the current study, exercise was shown to be a valuable method of reducing stress (Twardy, personal communication, December 14, 2017). Providing officers with a gym membership or access to a physical fitness facility could provide benefits such as stress reduction and fewer physical ailments. Also, opportunities to talk to spouses, co-workers, or licensed professionals are encouraged to relieve stress. One deputy suggested that some stress stems from police-community relations and suggested, "sporting events that allow departments to play against the community will allow officers to form a bond inside the community, thus relieving the tension between the community and the officers" (Twardy, personal communication, December 14, 2017).

Law Enforcement Activities in West Virginia

West Virginia police officers engage in a wide variety of law enforcement activities. As described in Chapter 2, the information in this section is largely derived from the Uniform Crime Report. The ***Uniform Crime Report*** includes information about serious personal and property crime offenses known to the police (USDOJ/FBI, 2017). Reporting data to the UCR is optional, and not all police agencies in West Virginia submitted their crime statistics. Based upon the number of agencies that did submit their crime data, several observations can be made.

In 2016, West Virginia police departments reported that their officers investigated 37,487 property crimes and 6,557 violent crimes. Property crimes include burglary, larceny-theft, and motor vehicle theft. Violent crimes include murder/negligent homicide, rape, aggravated assault, and robbery. These numbers underestimate the amount of criminal activity that police are responsible for investigating. The UCR only includes specific offenses considered to be the most serious and omits offenses that are likely to be misdemeanors. For example, the UCR does not include drug-related offenses or operating a vehicle while intoxicated (OWI). In 2015, the Huntington Police Department made 530 arrests for OWI, which was the highest in the state (Hessler & Nash, 2016). As explained in Chapter 2, another reason the UCR underestimates crime rates is the use of the hierarchy rule. The hierarchy rule states that only the most serious crime in any single incident will be recorded in the UCR database (USDOJ/FBI, 2017). Table 4.1 summarizes violent crime and property crime offenses known to law enforcement during 2016. It is important to remember that these estimates depend upon the voluntary submission of crime data from police agencies.

The drug problem poses unique challenges for West Virginia police officers. Officers address possible medical issues in addition to the potential for criminal activity when responding to overdose calls. West Virginia led the nation for drug overdoses in 2016 with 884 deaths (CDC, 2017). There are safety issues when officers respond to opioid cases. West Virginia police officers have been exposed to substances that have required them to be administered with Narcan (Nash, 2017). Drug use and abuse also contributes to the violent and property crime rates in the state. Drug users will often steal to supply their drug habit, and sometimes trade sex for a drug supply. Drug dealers may engage in violent crimes during the commission of drug deals. A deeper discussion about the drug problem is provided later in Chapter 9.

Becoming a Police Officer

Now that there is an understanding of police agencies and duties in West Virginia, it is time to consider the process for becoming a police officer. There are several steps to complete when applying for a job as a police officer. While each agency has specific requirements, there are some general steps that are part of the application process for most departments. The time required to participate in the hiring process varies. Some departments move very quickly

Table 4.1. Comparison of Violent and Property Crime Rates in the United States and West Virginia (2016) Using UCR Data, Offenses Known to Law Enforcement

	United States		West Virginia	
Offenses	Number of Offenses	Rate per 100,000	Number of Offenses	Rate per 100,000
Total Violent Crimes	1,248,185	386.3	6,557	358.1
Murder and Nonnegligent Manslaughter	17,250	5.3	81	4.4
Rape (revised definition)	130,603	40.4	657	35.9
Rape (legacy definition)	95,730	29.6	468	25.6
Robbery	332,198	102.8	720	39.3
Aggravated Assault	803,007	248.5	5,099	278.5
Total Crimes against Property	7,919,035	2450.7	37,487	2,047.2
Burglary	1,515,096	468.9	9,301	507.9
Larceny/Theft	5,638.455	1745.0	25,677	1,402.3
Motor Vehicle Theft	765,484	236.9	2,509	137

Source: United States Department of Justice, Federal Bureau of Investigation (USDOJ/FBI). (2017, September). *Crime in the United States, 2016*. Retrieved from https://ucr.fbi.gov/crime-in-the-u.s/2016/crime-in-the-u.s.-2016/cius-2016.

Note: The federal figures cover 323,127,518 people, while the state figures cover approximately 1.8 million people.

through the process, while the process might take months at larger departments. Please remember that the hiring activities discussed below may occur in a different order than presented.

a) *Application*. Completing an application is usually the first step in the police hiring process. Information required as part of the application will vary, but generally includes your personal information, level of education, references, and special skills. You may be required to include a resume and cover letter, or provide a personal statement about why you want to serve as a police officer. Many departments now have online applications, but be aware that some departments will require you to complete a paper application. Remember to submit your application before the deadline or you may be excluded from the current and future hiring processes.

Division of Protective Services, Capitol Complex.
Courtesy of Sam Dameron.

b) *Physical agility.* All recruits attending the basic police academy must meet the minimum physical fitness requirements as outlined in the police training section. The fitness standards are designed to assess your overall physical fitness, which is an indicator of success in the training academy and on the job. Some departments have more extensive physical fitness requirements that applicants are required to achieve during the hiring process.

c) *Civil service or police knowledge tests.* Some agencies are required to use a civil service test that is given to all public employees. Other agencies rely on specialized tests that are specific to the job of police officer or deputy. These tests are generally given to multiple applicants at the same time. Applicants are required to score at a certain level before they are eligible to continue in the hiring process.

d) *Background check and/or polygraph.* The background check process varies between agencies. Some agencies collect background information on the employment application, while other agencies keep the background process separate. Background checks may include a credit check, employment verification, education verification, and interviews with people known to the applicant who can attest to the applicant's character. Felony convictions will almost always eliminate a candidate from the hiring process. Misdemeanor convictions may be reviewed on a case-by-case basis depending upon individual department policy. Some departments require applicants to complete a polygraph examination, which is designed to detect deception about information provided to investigators during the hiring process.

e) *Psychological testing.* Psychological testing is designed to assist police departments with hiring people who will be the most successful as police officers. A variety of tests may be used, including personality tests and tests that may indicate if an applicant has attitudes that may impede him or her from fairly conducting police duties.

f) *Medical, vision, and hearing assessments.* Departments require that applicants submit to medical, vision, and hearing assessments. Applicants must meet the minimum standards set by each department to be eligible for the job of police officer.

g) *Drug testing.* Some departments require a drug test as part of the hiring process. Agency policy dictates whether prior drug use excludes a candidate from the hiring process. However, a current positive drug test for an illegal drug will likely disqualify a candidate from holding the job of police officer.

h) *Interview.* Applicants will be required to have an interview. The interview may be with the chief administrator of the department, or with a panel of representatives. The interview serves several purposes. An interview allows applicants to get acquainted with police leadership, and to demonstrate their skills under pressure. Panel interviews may include members of the community. The interview provides an opportunity for police representatives to assess the likelihood of an applicant being a good fit for the department. There are a variety of ways to prepare for the interview. Practicing answers to possible questions in front of others is helpful.

Spotlight: Police Training in West Virginia

The first training academy for city police officers was hosted by the WVSP in 1950 (Cole, 1998). Currently, all police officers in West Virginia are required to attend the basic police academy supervised by the West Virginia State Police. The minimum physical requirements to enter the police academy are the same for all candidates. Each candidate must complete at a minimum (WVDMAPS, 2018):

a) 28 sit-ups in one minute;
b) 18 push-ups in one minute; and
c) A 1.5 minute mile run within 14 minutes and 36 seconds.

The WVSP academy hosts three types of basic training classes. The Basic Police Officer Course trains recruits to become members of county and municipal agencies. This academy lasts 16 weeks, and the total training time is 800 hours. The goal of this training is to give all recruits basic knowledge of policing practices and tactics that assist officers is being effective and safe while executing their duties. Recruits are trained in a variety of topics including, but not limited to, criminal and constitutional law, emergency vehicle operation, firearms, defensive tactics, basic criminal investigations, and basic accident investigations. Because the basic academy is designed to be all-purpose and serve all departments in the state, each individual agency is responsible for providing more specific training to their recruits, such as city or county ordinances and standard operating procedures.

The second type of basic training academy is for those desiring to become members of the state police. The State Police Cadet Course lasts 24 weeks, extending the basic 800 hours of required training for all police officers in the state. State police recruits in the academy learn policies, procedures, and tactics specific to the state police. These additional topics include, but are not limited to public speaking, terrorism, and officer survivability training.

The third basic training academy is the Accelerated State Police Cadet Training Course (11 weeks), developed in conjunction with the Kentucky State Police. This academy course was offered in March 2014 for the first time. The Accelerated Cadet Course is for new West Virginia State Police Officers who have previously been academy trained.

The WVSP academy also hosts a variety of advanced training courses designed to enhance officer knowledge about a variety of topics. Examples of advanced training requirements are crash reconstruction, digital forensics, leadership, tactical training (e.g., handcuffing and weapons), and advanced investigations (West Virginia State Police Professional Development Center, 2018).

Field Officer Training Program

For most departments, additional training is completed after academy graduation as part of the ***Field Training Officer (FTO)*** program. FTO programs pair new officers with experienced officers for the first few weeks or months the new officers are on duty. FTO programs have several goals. One goal of an FTO program is to acclimate new officers to the policies and procedures of the department. While new officers are given a ***standard operating procedure*** manual, it is important for new officers to observe the implementation of these policies and procedures. The FTO program also gives new officers a chance to see policing in practice and apply what was learned in the academy to street performance under supervision and with backup. Another goal of the FTO program is to assist new officers in meeting the citizens they will be policing, and be given advice about how to handle specific situations.

Key Terms and Definitions

Alcohol Firearms Tobacco and Explosives, Bureau of (ATF): A federal agency responsible for investigating federal cases involving illegal activities with alcohol, firearms, tobacco, or explosives; has a presence in West Virginia.

Bicycle patrol: A police patrol tactic used as part of regular duties or to provide services for special events.

Bow Street Runners: Organized group of paid detectives founded by Henry Fielding in England; responsible for locating stolen property and apprehending wanted persons.

Central Intelligence Agency (CIA): A federal agency responsible for national security and gathering international intelligence; has a presence in West Virginia.

Clery Act: Federal legislation that requires institutions of higher learning to take several steps to maintain a safe learning environment for students. Campuses are required to maintain publicly available information about campus crime; to issue yearly crime and safety reports; and to document policies and procedures for reporting criminal activity to proper authorities.

Community Oriented Policing (COP): A policing philosophy that encourages partnerships with the community to identify needs and problems.

Community Oriented Policing Office (COPS): Formed in 1994 to assist departments with funding and resources related to Community Oriented Policing.

Community policing era: 1970s to present; efforts focus on connecting police to the community; concerted attention given to police relationships with minority communities.

Consent decrees: Agreement between a police agency and the federal government; goal is to change policies and practices that contribute to constitutional violations of citizen or employee rights.

Constable: Enforced the law and night watch after the frankpledge system dissolved.

Criminal Justice Information Services Division (CJIS): Division of the FBI located in Clarksburg, WV; administers the Uniform Crime Report, the National Instant Criminal Background Check System (NICS), the National Crime Information Center (NCIC), and the National Data Exchange (N-Dex).

Crime lab: Laboratory responsible for storing and processing evidence from criminal investigations.

Drug Enforcement Administration (DEA): The DEA is a federal agency with a presence in West Virginia. The focus of the DEA is narcotics enforcement.

Field Training Officer (FTO): A training program that familiarizes new officers with department policies, procedures, and practices.

Foot patrol: A police patrol tactic used in downtown areas or local events; allows police to easily interact with the public.

Formal social control: A legal means of encouraging people to conform to social norms.

Frankpledge system: Way of organizing the British population into manageable groups after the Norman invasion; made citizens responsible for reporting lawbreaking and apprehending criminals.

Hammurabi's Code: Identified prohibited behavior and assigned punishments for rule-breaking in ancient Mesopotamia; early type of formal social control.

Hue and cry: Required all men between the ages of 15 and 60 to assist the constable.

Informal social control: Encourages people to conform to social norms using socialization.

Justice of the peace: Early English judges who presided over criminal trials.

Law enforcement duties: Activities that may result in the arrest of a citizen.

***Lex talionis*:** "An eye for an eye," one way that early civilization obtained justice for wrongdoing.

London Metropolitan Police: Formed in 1829 and led by Sir Robert Peel; provided a model for developing American police departments.

National Crime Information Center (NCIC): Contains information about citizens' criminal histories; administered by the FBI and housed in Clarksburg, WV.

National Data Exchange (N-Dex): Links criminal cases across jurisdictions for easier information sharing between criminal justice agencies; administered by the FBI and housed in Clarksburg, WV.

National Instant Criminal Background Check System (NICS): Contains information used for firearms background checks; administered by the FBI and housed in Clarksburg, WV.

Night watch system: An early American practice that was responsible for general safety; eventually evolved to include response to criminal activity.

Order maintenance and peacekeeping: A form of policing that largely ensures that public disorder is kept to a minimum.

Political era of policing: 1840s to the early 1900s; characterized by corruption and misconduct.

Proactive policing: Officer-initiated activities, such as traffic stops.

Problem Oriented Policing (POP): A policing strategy that hinges on police identifying problems in the community and addressing these problems at their sources.

Reactive policing: Police activities initiated by a citizen.

Reform/professionalization era of policing: Early 1900s to 1950s; efforts focused on reducing corruption and making advances in police technology, training, and hiring practices; spearheaded by August Vollmer and O.W. Wilson.

Service duties: Police activities that provide community service outside of law enforcement and order maintenance; examples include funeral processions and event security; service duties rarely involve enforcement of the law.

Shire reeves: Oversaw the shires in England; precursor to modern sheriffs.

Slave patrols: A policing system used by southern states to maintain social control over slaves; regarded by some researchers as the precursor to modern American policing.

Social control: How society encourages people to adhere to social norms.

Standard operating procedures: Policies and procedures for a police department.

Uniform Crime Report (UCR): Official crime statistics from the Federal Bureau of Investigation; housed in Clarksburg, WV.

United States Customs and Border Protection (CBP): A federal agency responsible for investigating citizens who enter America without following appropriate procedure; has a presence in West Virginia.

United States Marshals Service: A federal agency responsible for fugitive apprehension and protection of the federal courts; has a presence in West Virginia.

Vehicle patrol: Police activity designed to deter and detect crime and make citizens feel safe.

West Virginia State Police: Formed in 1919; currently has approximately 630 sworn officers; responsible for providing all-purpose police services to the state; administers the police academy and the state crime lab.

Select Internet Sources

Criminal Justice Information Services (CJIS) [FBI]: https://www.fbi.gov/services/cjis.

West Virginia Sheriffs' Association: http://www.wvsheriff.org/.

West Virginia State Police: https://www.wvsp.gov.

West Virginia State Police Forensic Laboratory: https://www.wvsp.gov/about/Pages/CrimeLab.aspx.

Review and Critical Thinking Questions

1. What aspects of West Virginia's history and landscape shaped the way in which law enforcement evolved in the state? What factors and conditions influence how policing is carried out today?
2. Pretend you are the chief of police or sheriff of a department. How would you use today's social media, technology, and the Internet to keep citizens informed of your department's activities? Would the way you use these tools change based upon the size of your department and the population it serves?
3. What can police agencies in West Virginia do to encourage more women and minorities to seek careers in policing?
4. Review the minimum physical fitness requirements for being accepted into the police academy. Create a plan for reaching these physical fitness goals.
5. Research five police agencies in West Virginia of varying sizes. Which of these agencies do you believe would best fit your personality? Why?

References

Bailey, K. R. (2013, October). Battle of Blair Mountain. *e-WV: The West Virginia Encyclopedia.* Charleston, WV: West Virginia Humanities Council. Retrieved from https://www.wvencyclopedia.org/articles/532.

Bastress, R. M. (2011). *The West Virginia state constitution.* New York: Oxford University Press.

Bopp, W. J. (1975). *In quest of a police profession: A biography of Orlando W. Wilson* (Doctoral Dissertation). Retrieved from Florida Atlantic University Digital Collections, Legacy FAU Student Theses and Dissertations 1967–2006.

Brandl, S. G. (2018). *Policing in America.* Thousand Oaks, CA: Sage.

Brooks, L. W., & Piquero, L. N. (1998). Police stress: Does department size matter? *Policing: An International Journal of Police Strategies & Management, 21*(4), 600–617. doi:10.1108/13639519810241647.

Carte, G., Carte, E., & Robinson, J. H. (1983). *August Vollmer: Pioneer in police professionalism* (Vol. 2). Berkeley, CA: University of Berkeley Bancroft Library.

Center for Problem Oriented Policing. (2018). *Case studies.* Retrieved from http://www.popcenter.org/casestudies/.

Centers for Disease Control (CDC). (2017). *Drug overdose death data.* Retrieved from https://www.cdc.gov/drugoverdose/data/statedeaths.html.

Chriss, J. J. (2010). *Social control: Informal, legal, and medical.* United Kingdom: Emerald Group Publishing Limited.

Clery Center. (2018a). *Clery Act Policy: Compliance insights and resources for institutions of higher education.* Retrieved from https://clerycenter.org/policy-resources/.

Clery Center. (2018b). *Summary of the Jeanne Clery Act: A compliance and reporting overview* [Policy and resources page]. Retrieved from https://clerycenter.org/policy-resources/the-clery-act/.

Clery Center. (2018c). *What happened to Jeanne Clery was a tragedy* [About page]. Retrieved from https://clerycenter.org/about-page/.

Cole, M. T. (1998). *A comprehensive history of the West Virginia State Police, 1919–1979.* Retrieved from https://www.wvsp.gov/about/Pages/History.aspx.

Corbin, D. A. (2016, December). The mine wars. *e-WV: The West Virginia Encyclopedia.* Charleston, WV: West Virginia Humanities Council. Retrieved from https://www.wvencyclopedia.org/articles/1799.

Cox, D. J. (2008). Bow street 'Runners.' In T. Newburn, & P. Neyroud (Eds.), *Dictionary of policing.* Devon, UK: Willan Publishing. Retrieved from https://marshall.idm.oclc.org/login?url=https://search.credoreference.com/content/entry willanpolicing/bow_street_runners/0?institutionId=3309.

Federal Bureau of Investigation (FBI). (2016). *2016 Crime in the United States, Police employee data.* Retrieved from https://ucr.fbi.gov/crime-in-the-u.s/2016/crime-in-the-u.s.-2016/topic-pages/police-employees?.

Glenville State College. (2015–2016). *Public safety.* Retrieved from http://www.glenville.edu/life/public_safety.php.

Grant, H. B., & Terry, K. J. (2017). *Law enforcement in the 21st century.* Boston, MA: Pearson.

Hatfield-McCoy trails. (2016). Retrieved from http://www.trailsheaven.com/HatfieldAndMcCoyTrails/media/Brochure/2016-Hatfield-McCoy-Brochure_Updated.pdf.

Hessler, C., & Nash, B. (2016, September 13). Huntington Police: 65 percent of DUI arrest drug related. *The Herald-Dispatch.* Retrieved from www.herald-dispatch.com.

Huntington Police Department. (2016). *About the Huntington Police Department.* Retrieved from http://www.hpdwv.com/about.php.

Kelling, G. L., & Moore, M. H. (1988). *The evolving strategy of policing* (No. 4). Washington, DC: United States Department of Justice, National Institute of Justice. Retrieved from https://www.policefoundation.org/publication/perspectives-on-policing-the-evolving-strategy-of-policing/.

Musser, C. S. (1931). *Two hundred years' history of Shepherdstown.* Shepherdstown, WV: The Independent.

Nash, B. (2017, July 19). HPD officers treated after accidental drug exposure. *The Herald Dispatch*. Retrieved from www.herald-dispatch.com.

Oliver, W. M., & Hilgenberg, J. F. Jr. (2010). *A history of crime and justice in America*. Durham, NC: Carolina Academic Press.

Oliver, W. M., & Meier, C. (2004). Stress in small town and rural law enforcement: Testing the assumptions. *American Journal of Criminal Justice, 29*(1), 37–56. doi:10.1007/BF02885703.

Perkins Gilbert, W. (2012). Reform, police and enforcement. In W. R. Miller (Ed.), *The social history of crime and punishment* (Vol. 4, pp. 1509–1513). Thousand Oaks, CA: Sage Publications.

Sandy, J.P., & Devine, D.A. (1978). Four stress factors unique to rural patrol. *The Police Chief, 45*(9), 42–44.

Sealock, M. D. (2012). Professionalization of police. In W. R. Miller (Ed.), *The social history of crime and punishment* (Vol. 3, pp. 1440–1444). Thousand Oaks, CA: Sage Publications.

Shelden, R. G. (2001). *Controlling the dangerous classes*. Needham Heights, MA: Allyn & Bacon.

Uchida, C. (2015). The development of the American police: An historical overview. In R. G. Dunham & G. P. Alpert (Eds.), *Critical issues in policing: Contemporary readings* (pp. 11–30). Long Grove, IL: Waveland Press.

United States Department of Justice (USDOJ). (2012). *Equal access to education: 40 years of Title IX*. Retrieved from https://www.justice.gov/sites/default/files/crt/legacy/2012/06/20/titleixreport.pdf.

United States Department of Justice, Federal Bureau of Investigation (USDOJ/FBI). (2017, September). *Crime in the United States, 2016*. Retrieved from https://ucr.fbi.gov/crime-in-the-u.s/2016/crime-in-the-u.s.-2016/cius-2016.

Westfall, R. (2014). *History of the Charleston Police Department*. Retrieved from www.charlestonwvpolice.org/history.html.

West Virginia Department of Military Affairs & Public Safety, Division of Justice & Community Services (WVDMAPS). (2018). New standards for the P.A.T. (Physical Agility Test). Retrieved from https://djcs.wv.gov/law-enforcement-professional-standards/Documents/New%20Standards%20for%20the%20PAT.pdf.

West Virginia Division of Natural Resources (WVDNR). (2003). *About law enforcement*. South Charleston, WV: West Virginia Division of Natural Resources Law Enforcement Section. Retrieved from http://www.wvdnr.gov/lenforce/law.shtm.

West Virginia Division of Natural Resources (WVDNR). (2010). *Natural resources police officer job description*. South Charleston, WV: West Virginia

Division of Natural Resources Law Enforcement Section. Retrieved from http://www.wvdnr.gov/LEnforce/8550.shtm.

West Virginia Higher Education Policy Commission (WVHEPC). (2017). *West Virginia higher education report card.* Retrieved from http://www.wvhepc.edu/wp-content/uploads/2017/01/Report-Card.pdf.

West Virginia State Police (WVSP). (2016). *West Virginia State Police annual report 2015–2016.* Charleston, WV: author. Retrieved from https://www.wvsp.gov/about/Documents/AnnualReports/2016annualReport.pdf.

West Virginia State Police Professional Development Center. (2018). *2018 course training schedule.* Retrieved from https://www.wvsp.gov/academy/Documents/2018CourseCatalog.pdf.

West Virginia State Police, Crime lab. (2018). *West Virginia State Police forensic laboratory.* Retrieved from https://www.wvsp.gov/about/Pages/CrimeLab.aspx.

West Virginia State Police (WVSP). (2018). *West Virginia State Police.* Retrieved from http://www.wvsp.gov/Pages/default.aspx.

West Virginia State University (WVSU). (2018). *Public safety.* Retrieved from http://www.wvstateu.edu/About/Administration/Public-Safety.aspx.

West Virginia University (WVU). (2017). *Preparing right: Training for today's fast-paced, always on the go environment.* Retrieved from https://police.wvu.edu/training.

Williams, H., & Murphy, P. V. (1990). *The evolving strategy of police: A minority view.* (NCJ121019). Washington, DC: United States Department of Justice.

Legal References

Jeanne Clery Disclosure of Campus Security Policy and Campus Crime Statistics Act (Clery Act), 20 U.S.C. § 1092(f) (1990).

W. Va. Code § 8-14-3 (2017).

W. Va. Code § 15-2-12(a) (2017).

Chapter 5

The West Virginia Courts

West Virginia Supreme Court of Appeals. Courtesy of Sam Dameron.

Unlike the component of law enforcement, whose primary function is that of enforcing social control (i.e., criminal laws), the courts are responsible for enforcing both criminal and civil law.[1] While there are significant differences between these two types of cases, the court's role in either capacity is not that fundamentally different. Both types of cases involve some control of behavior, both impose some sort of sanction, and both use similar areas of legal action. In fact, when students attend law school, they initially are not trained to practice one type of law over another. They are taught the basics of processing a legal case, regardless of whether it is civil or criminal. It is not until later in their legal education that those students begin specializing in one form or the other. With this being said, the focus will be on the criminal aspects of the West Virginia court system. However, where overlap between criminal and civil functions is present, it will be mentioned.

In this chapter the following areas will be addressed: the key players in the court process, which are the judiciary, prosecution, and defense, as well as the

1. County sheriffs' offices do perform certain civil functions.

petit and grand juries; the current organization and structure of the court system; and a detailed look at the appellate, lower, and treatment courts. While the focus here is on the state courts, it must be noted that there are two federal district courts located in West Virginia. However, 98% of cases are handled at the state level (Smith, 2017a). Before the current status of the West Virginia courts is examined, a brief historical analysis is presented for a better understanding of the current system and its origins.

Historical Background

The establishment of the West Virginia court system dates back to 1863, when it was admitted to the United States as the 35th state. However, courts existed in the area prior to this time as a part of the Virginia court system, which in turn, was born during the establishment of the colonies under the control of the British. As is evident by now, as a British colony, Virginia was obligated to follow the English Common Law. Thus, the history of the American courts is closely aligned with the English court system. However, the problem was that the American colonies were vastly different from the mother country in terms of geography. Much of the area was still untamed wilderness and small villages were the norm. The very formal and complex British system did not translate well here (Neubauer & Fradella, 2011). The courts of the early American colonies were far from formal. An added obstacle was that there was variation in how each colony was founded. Some colonies were chartered, others were established as royal colonies, and still others were developed as proprietary colonies. These variations dictated how much control the English Crown had on the day-to-day operations of each colony. As such, Virginia was founded as a royal colony, which meant direct control by the King (Oliver & Hilgenberg, 2010). In short, these distinct differences in the formation of the colonies help to explain, in part, the differences that exist from state to state today in not only governmental authority, but the criminal justice system as well. However, one consistency throughout all 50 states is jurisdiction, and this is related to the concept of tiers of courts. Essentially, all states have three tiers, which are appellate jurisdiction (courts of last resort), general jurisdiction (trial courts), and limited jurisdiction (inferior trial courts).

After independence, the early Virginia courts were organized at the county level, as well as offices of the ***justice of the peace***, or "JPs" as they were commonly called. While a small number of cases were presided over by judges with some legal knowledge at the county level (mostly members of local government, such as county commissioners), the bulk of the caseload was handled by justices of the peace who had very little to no legal knowledge or training. In fact, the office of the justice of the peace was a carryover concept from England. These JPs were made up of people of noble stature and influence, who took on the responsibility more as a sign of prestige rather than knowledge of the law. Furthermore, in the colonies, many justices of the peace only worked on a part-time basis. The use of this office in the colonies, and after independence, made sense at the time because they could be easily scattered geographically, and it also limited the need for full-time judges. With such vast wilderness and open territory, it made practical sense (Rogers, 2013). However, these justice of the peace courts mostly handled minor civil controversies and for the most part "kept the peace."

After its separation from Virginia, it took nearly 100 years for West Virginia's court system to evolve into what it is today. The first thing the new state did was create its own Supreme Court of Appeals with three judges, later adding a fourth, and ultimately a fifth. It also established 11 circuit courts and several justice of the peace positions for every county (Smith, 2017b). These JPs had jurisdiction over misdemeanors and small civil suits, but more authority than their predecessors by having the power to set bail and conduct preliminary hearings in felony matters (Rogers, 2013). The problem with this office, however, was that these justices were not paid a fixed salary. Rather, they were paid based on financial judgments assessed against defendants. One can quickly see the potential for corruption here, as it would be in the best interest for JPs to always side with the plaintiff in a civil case, or to convict in a criminal case.

In 1976, the West Virginia Judicial Reorganization Amendment went into effect, which set the basis for the current structure and hierarchy of the West Virginia courts (Dameron, 2005). The Amendment effectively ended the justice of the peace system and created a structure of unification, with the Supreme Court of Appeals of West Virginia as the primary administrator of the appellate, general, and limited jurisdiction courts. The one exception is municipal courts, which are controlled at the local level. The Amendment also created magistrate courts to handle the tasks that were once delegated to JPs. A more detailed description of the structure and organization of the courts will be presented later in the chapter, but first a brief overview of the primary players in the court system is essential.

The Key Players in the Court Process

As is typical in the criminal justice system, the three key players in the courtroom workgroup are the judge, prosecutor, and the defense attorney. Ancillary support is provided by the Clerk of the Court, the bailiff, and the court reporter, to name just a few. Furthermore, juries also are considered part of this workgroup. The concept of a workgroup signifies the importance of cooperation between all the parties involved for efficient functioning of the court process and a timelier disposition of cases. This implies that courts should follow a "systems" approach to dispensing justice. However, some argue that the workgroup concept is contrary to the adversarial process, which should be the goal if we are to follow the "traditional" mission of the courts (Siegel & Senna, 2004). Nonetheless, we will explore the judiciary, prosecution, defense, as well as juries (both petit and grand) as they are reflected in West Virginia.

Judiciary

The judiciary represents objectivity in the court process. However, the responsibilities of judges vary by the courts over which they preside. In West Virginia, there are four types of judges: supreme court justices, circuit court judges, family court judges, and magistrates. All four types are determined by nonpartisan elections. There are five supreme court justices who hear appeals of both criminal and civil cases that are brought forth to the West Virginia Supreme Court of Appeals. They are elected to 12-year terms, and the minimum qualifications are that they be at least 30 years old, have practiced law for 10 years, and have lived in the state for at least five years as a resident (Cleckley & Palmer, 1994). Originally, these members of West Virginia's high court were simply referred to as judges, but with the termination of the justice of the peace system, the term justice is now reserved solely for this role.

Conversely, circuit court judges in West Virginia are trial judges who hear civil and criminal cases. Currently, there are 74 judges over 31 circuits. They are elected to serve eight-year terms and have the same age and residency requirement as supreme court justices; however, they need only to have practiced law for five years instead of 10. In addition, their elections are only determined by the voters within the circuit over which they preside. In the event there is a vacancy in between elections, the Governor appoints an individual to serve the remainder of the term. If an appointee wishes to remain in the position, he or she is required to run in the next scheduled election.

Next, there are family court judges. Unlike the other members of West Virginia's judiciary, these family court judges do not oversee criminal matters, but are limited to civil proceedings. Nonetheless, they are an important part of the overall court structure in the state. There are 47 family court judges within 27 circuits. These judges must meet the same minimum requirements as circuit court judges, but until 2002 were appointed by the Governor. Today, they are elected in nonpartisan elections just like all other members of West Virginia's judiciary. They each serve an initial six-year term, but upon reelection the term increases to eight years.

At the lowest level in the state structure are the magistrate courts, which are presided over by 158 magistrate judges. Unlike their counterparts mentioned above, these judges are not required by the state constitution to have a formal legal education. This means, they do not have to be lawyers, very much like the former justices of the peace. In fact, this position was created to replace JPs through the Judicial Reorganization Amendment. While magistrates in West Virginia are not required to be attorneys, after being selected, these individuals are required to complete certain basic courses of instruction in legal procedure and rules of evidence. Anyone can run for magistrate and, if elected, serve four-year terms. The only requirements to run for this office is that the candidate must be a resident of the state, be at least 21 years of age, have a high school or equivalent degree, and not convicted of a felony or misdemeanor "involving moral turpitude" (W. Va. §50-1-4). In the case of a vacancy during an unexpired term as magistrate, a circuit court judge from the same jurisdiction will name a replacement for the remainder of the term. If that appointed magistrate chooses to remain in office, he or she must run in the next scheduled election. Magistrates are salaried, unlike the historical JPs; thus, the impartiality of their decisions should not be questioned for financial reasons.

The final judicial component is the municipal court judges. However, they are not part of the state court structure and not all municipalities have them. They are all locally controlled. As such, there is variation on how these judicial officers are selected. Some are appointed, whereas others are elected. Just like magistrates, these judges do not have to be lawyers, but will have to undergo some legal coursework. These judges typically only handle violations of local ordinances and traffic-related offenses. In some instances, the city mayor or members of the city commission may fill this role if no municipal court has been established.

Prosecution

Courts are adversarial in nature, basically two sides competing against one another. In a criminal case, the state takes on the role of the injured party or the "symbolic" victim. As such, a prosecutor or state's attorney brings forth the case against the defendant, who is represented by a defense attorney. There are various types of state's attorneys in West Virginia. At the state level, there is the West Virginia Attorney General. This elected position of chief legal officer for the state is one of five constitutional officers that make up the executive branch within the government of West Virginia (Harris, 2013). Thus, all state agencies, including the Office of the Governor, will rely upon the Attorney General as the primary legal advisor. In addition, all suits in which the state is a party in the action will be handled by the Attorney General. A majority of the legal matters handled by this office involve cases regarding consumer protection, civil rights, tax and revenue, workers' compensation, and criminal appeals. The West Virginia Attorney General serves for four years and can be reelected with no term limit.

Arguably, the primary law "enforcer" is the county prosecutor.[2] All 55 counties in West Virginia elect a chief prosecutor to serve every four years. This office was constitutionally created through Article 9, Section 1 of the state constitution. The chief prosecutor then appoints assistant prosecutors, who are affirmed by the county commission. While the chief prosecutor will try high-profile cases, the bulk of everyday prosecutions are handled by assistant prosecutors. These prosecutors have a great deal of discretion to decide which cases to prosecute, plea bargain, and try in court (Neubauer & Fradella, 2011). Indeed, prosecutorial discretion is arguably second only to police discretion in the criminal justice system. ***Discretion*** is the ability to choose among alternatives. Police have the most discretionary authority in the criminal justice system, as they determine how to handle situations formally or informally on a daily basis. Prosecutors, on the other hand, determine what cases to prosecute, drop, plea bargain, as well as what type of sentences to recommend.

While the majority of criminal violations are prosecuted by a county prosecutor's office, state law does allow for the appointment of special prosecutors and private prosecutors, when necessary. Special prosecutors may be appointed by circuit court judges, in the event a prosecutor's office may be disqualified from acting in certain matters. For example, if a chief prosecutor is charged with domestic violence against his children, his office may not be allowed to handle similar cases until the ongoing investigation is concluded; thus, a special prosecutor may be hired to handle all domestic violence cases between parents and children. Conversely, a private prosecutor may be hired to provide assistance to a county prosecutor for a number of reasons. First, if the family of a victim wishes to achieve some satisfaction that their case is being vigorously prosecuted to the fullest extent, they may hire a private attorney to assist the prosecuting attorney. Second, if a public prosecutor needs assistance to carry out his or

2. Some states use the term District Attorney for this role.

her duties effectively, a private attorney may be hired to provide support. And last, in certain high-profile cases, the need to satisfy public concern may warrant additional support (Cleckley & Palmer, 1994).

Defense

If the prosecution represents the state's case against a criminal defendant in an adversarial contest, there must be someone to represent the best interests of the accused. This is the function of the defense counsel. The Sixth Amendment to the U.S. Constitution affords legal assistance to those who cannot provide it for themselves, and this is further supported by Section 3, Section 14 of the West Virginia state constitution. Without this protection, ***indigent defendants*** [those who are too poor to afford an attorney] could not be guaranteed due process and fairness in the adversarial process. Of course, defendants who can afford their own counsel are free to choose any lawyer they wish to retain. In this case, the attorney fees will be paid by the defendant. This discussion will center on the most common type of legal service in criminal cases, which is assigned counsel for those in need.

The key question regarding assistance of counsel, however, is determination of financial need. This is addressed in West Virginia Code § 29-21-16(e), which states:

> (e) The following factors shall be considered in determining eligibility for legal representation made available under the provisions of this article:
>
> (1) Current income prospects, taking into account seasonal variations in income;
>
> (2) Liquid assets, assets which may provide collateral to obtain funds to employ private counsel and other assets which may be liquidated to provide funds to employ private counsel;
>
> (3) Fixed debts and obligations, including federal, state and local taxes and medical expenses;
>
> (4) Child care, transportation and other expenses necessary for employment;
>
> (5) Age or physical infirmity of resident family members;
>
> (6) Whether the person seeking publicly funded legal representation has made reasonable and diligent efforts to obtain private legal representation, and the results of those efforts;
>
> (7) The cost of obtaining private legal representation with respect to the particular matter in which assistance is sought;

(8) Whether the person seeking publicly funded legal representation has posted a cash bond for bail or has obtained release on bond for bail through the services of a professional bondsman for compensation and the amount and source of the money provided for such bond;

(9) The consequences for the individual if legal assistance is denied.

The method by which indigent defendants are provided legal counsel when charged with a criminal act varies from state to state, and even within West Virginia, there is some variation at the county level. However, the basic structure is that there is one central body, which is the office of West Virginia Public Defender Services. This agency provides funding for legal services to each circuit based on two methods. The first method involves public defender corporations that have been established to serve 29 counties; however, these corporations are grouped by circuit, hence 18 of West Virginia's 31 circuits employ this method. Under this option, salaried attorneys work for these corporations as full-time public defenders to represent clients processed in their respective circuits. There is currently a proposal to establish public defender corporations in an additional 8 circuits, which serve 15 other counties. This leaves 5 circuits, which serve 11 counties (Summers, Monroe, Putnam, Pleasants, Ritchie, Doddridge, Lewis, Upshur, Tucker, Grant, and Mineral Counties), without a corporation. Hence, these circuits use a second method of assigning counsel based on private panel attorneys. This method utilizes volunteer attorneys who make themselves available for various types of cases based on their level of expertise. When it is time to assign counsel to an indigent defendant, a circuit judge will choose an attorney based on this list of volunteers. The costs associated with providing legal assistance via the public defender corporations and private panel attorneys will be paid by West Virginia Public Defender Services.

Juries

One of the fundamental rights we have as United States citizens is the right to a trial by jury of our peers. Each year about 50,000 people are randomly selected to be members of juries in West Virginia, although not that many will actually serve (Perry, Canterbury, & Sole, 2009). To be eligible to serve on a jury, one must be a U.S. citizen, 18 years old, and typically a resident of the county from which the summons was issued. However, there are two different types of juries that exist—the petit jury and the grand jury. Each is briefly examined below, and to what extent West Virginia uses them in the court process.

Petit Jury

A ***petit jury*** is also known as a trial jury. The common conception for the layperson regarding a jury is a panel of 12 people given the task of determining innocence or guilt of another person charged with a crime. There is no doubt that this image has been heavily depicted in the media (i.e., news, crime dramas, movies, novels, etc.). However, what most people do not realize is that while more formal trials are heard by juries, many defendants waive this right and opt for a ***bench trial***, where a judge will determine the final outcome. In fact, in courts of limited jurisdiction, where most criminal violations are heard, it is more likely that the judge makes the decision. Regardless, the jury trial is one of the hallmarks of our justice system, and it is a fundamental right afforded to us by the Sixth Amendment of the U.S. Constitution. Furthermore, while 12 jurors is a common notion in a jury trial, the Sixth Amendment does not specifically prescribe the number of jurors necessary; therefore, the state constitution is more specific that 12 individuals make up the jury in felony prosecutions and 6 individuals for trials held at magistrate courts (Cleckley & Palmer, 1994).

In West Virginia, Chapter 52, Section 1 of the state code describes all the elements of the petit jury, including prohibition of discrimination, jury selection, qualifications, disqualifications, and reimbursement. But, the basic tenets for disqualification according to §52-1-8 include:

> (1) Is not a citizen of the United States, at least eighteen years old and a resident of the county;
> (2) Is unable to read, speak and understand the English language. For the purposes of this section, the requirement of speaking and understanding the English language is met by the ability to communicate in American Sign Language or Signed English;
> (3) Is incapable, by reason of substantial physical or mental disability, of rendering satisfactory jury service. A person claiming this disqualification may be required to submit a physician's certificate as to the disability and the certifying physician is subject to inquiry by the court at its discretion;
> (4) Has, within the preceding two years, been summoned to serve as a petit juror, grand juror or magistrate court juror and has attended sessions of the magistrate or circuit court and been reimbursed for his or her expenses as a juror pursuant to the provisions of section twenty-one of this article, section thirteen, article two of this chapter, or pursuant to an applicable rule or regulation of the Supreme Court

> of Appeals promulgated pursuant to the provisions of section eight, article five, chapter fifty of this code;
> (5) Has lost the right to vote because of a criminal conviction; or
> (6) Has been convicted of perjury, false swearing or any crime punishable by imprisonment in excess of one year under the applicable law of this state, another state or the United States.

Once the circuit clerk's office randomly selects members from the community for jury service, these individuals will go through the ***voir dire*** process with which students of criminal justice should already be familiar. This involves a process of filtering out jurors who may not be able to render an impartial verdict. These people will be ***challenged for cause*** by the courts, and released from service. This means if the court determines a prospective juror harbors some bias toward one side or the other, he or she will be disqualified from serving on the petit jury. However, after individuals are eliminated for cause, both the prosecution and defense may still use ***peremptory challenges*** to release other jurors who they believe to be prejudicial to their side for an undisclosed reason. Unlike challenges for cause that are unlimited in number, in West Virginia, for felony matters where the punishment involves incarceration for more than one year, the prosecution is allowed two peremptory strikes, whereas the defense is given six strikes (Cleckley & Palmer, 1994).

Upon conclusion of the *voir dire* process, the 12 individuals who have been selected (six for magistrate court), plus alternates, make up the petit jury that is now ready to hear the case. The jury will be guided by the judge regarding the laws in question and requirements necessary for a guilty conviction. The jury will be led by a foreman, who the jury members will elect at the outset. The foreman will communicate between the jury and the court regarding clarification or further instruction that may be necessary. After all the evidence is heard, the jury will deliberate in private and, upon reaching a verdict, the foremen will convey to the bailiff that a decision has been reached unanimously by the jury. West Virginia rules of criminal procedure require that the jury be polled when a verdict is returned, and before it is officially recorded (Cleckley & Palmer, 1994). This poll will reflect whether each member of the jury agrees with the overall decision. If any member's answer is contrary to the majority, the court (i.e., the judge) may send the jury back to deliberate further. If the jury cannot come to a unanimous decision, a judge may have to render a mistrial. Furthermore, a verdict of guilty implies the prosecution was able to prove ***beyond a reasonable doubt*** each element of the criminal offense. "Proof beyond a reasonable doubt is proof that leaves a juror firmly convinced of the defendant's guilt" (Neubauer & Fradella, 2011, p. 349).

Grand Jury

While most Americans are familiar with juries by way of petit or trial juries, the concept of a ***grand jury*** may be foreign to them. The grand jury is made up of randomly selected members of the community, just like in a petit jury, but rather than determining guilt or innocence in a public forum, their task is to determine ***probable cause*** to merit a criminal trial. Probable cause can be defined as "a fair probability, under the totality of the facts and circumstances known, that the person arrested committed the crime(s) charged" (Neubauer & Fradella, 2011, p. 242). However, in the case of a grand jury, the suspect may or may not have been arrested yet.

Grand jury investigations are not open to the public and only involve the members of the grand jury and the prosecution. Part of the reason for the general public's unfamiliarity with grand juries is that not all states use this system. In fact, today only about half the states use it (Neubauer & Fradella, 2011). In reality, the use of the grand jury system has been declining since the mid-1960s. The favored alternative is to have a preliminary hearing to determine probable cause.[3] Much of the criticism surrounding the use of a grand jury centers on the fact that it is seen as a "rubber stamp" for the prosecutor, not to mention the secretive nature of the hearings. Nonetheless, the West Virginia constitution dictates that a grand jury must be used in felony prosecutions, thus it has been retained.

More specifically, Chapter 52, Section 2 of the West Virginia code spells out the terms of the grand jury, as well as selection process, duties, and length of service. As far as selection, the same process that is used by the circuit court clerk in selecting petit jurors is used for the grand jury as well. In fact, when the initial random summons is issued for jury service, those individuals can be selected to sit on either the petit or grand jury. In fact, the same disqualification criteria previously mentioned under the petit jury applies to the grand jury. However, two key differences are that the grand jury requires a 16-member panel, and they do not sit through a *voir dire* process, as does a trial jury.

Once a grand jury has been convened, they will hear evidence that the prosecutor has been collecting to demonstrate the state has enough probable cause to take a case to trial. However, it is not just one case the grand jury will investigate, but a large volume of cases that have been accumulating. They will examine each one carefully and then issue a ***presentment***, which is a report that contains the findings of their investigation as well as the recommendation

---

3. West Virginia uses both preliminary hearings and grand juries for prosecution.

to indict or not (Siegel & Senna, 2004). If the recommendation of the grand jury is to indict, then a "true bill" has been passed. If not, then it is referred to as a "no bill." An ***indictment*** means the grand jury has enough probable cause to believe a defendant should be prosecuted by the state. One point to be made here is that unlike the petit jury, whose verdict is required to be unanimous, the grand jury's decision to indict does not have to be so. In West Virginia, only 12 people are necessary to issue an indictment. Once an indictment has been issued, if the person who has been indicted is not already under arrest, then an arrest warrant will be issued.

While indictment by a grand jury for felony prosecutions is mandatory, the defendant does have the right to waive prosecution by indictment if not facing life imprisonment. Furthermore, West Virginia has two separate mechanisms to determine probable cause. One is the grand jury, and the other is a preliminary hearing. The preliminary hearing, unlike the grand jury, is open to the public and very much resembles an ordinary trial. The only difference is that the judge, prosecution, and defense will be present. But there is no jury. The judge will make the decision regarding probable cause. Moreover, the judge in this case may be a magistrate, as magistrate courts routinely conduct preliminary hearings for felony prosecutions. If the presiding judge finds sufficient probable cause that the defendant committed the alleged crime, the defendant will be bound over for trial and the prosecutor will file an ***information*** with the circuit court (Siegel & Senna, 2004). This information is a charging document similar to the indictment used by the grand jury.

Where the process can become confusing is if a defendant has already been arrested. If a defendant has not been arrested on the charge, the state can directly present a case to the grand jury, and initiate it there as described earlier. However, if a defendant has been arrested, that defendant will receive a preliminary hearing and grand jury presentment, with a few exceptions. First, if the defendant is indicted by the grand jury prior to a preliminary hearing, the defendant is no longer entitled to a preliminary hearing. In other words, there is no constitutional right to a preliminary hearing. Second, a defendant may waive his or her right to a grand jury presentment and allow the state to file an information, in lieu of an indictment. This can only be done with the defendant's affirmative waiver and is usually done only when there is already a plea agreement.

While there is much criticism of the grand jury system for its secretive nature, there is some merit in the argument that it can act as a sword and a shield. As a sword, the grand jury involves "investigating cases to bring to trial persons accused on just grounds, and as a shield, protecting citizens against unfounded malicious or frivolous prosecutions" (Cleckley & Palmer, 1994, p. 212). In fact, when grand juries were first developed under English Common

Law in the Magna Carta of 1215, it was formed under the premise that "they" would act as the "community's conscience" (Siegel & Senna, 2004, p. 266).

Organization and Structure of the Courts

On November 5, 1974, the voters of West Virginia ratified to reorganize the court structure, which had been in place since the birth of the state. Thus, the Judicial Reorganization Amendment took effect in 1976. The stimulus for the reorganization was rooted in a 1973 West Virginia Supreme Court of Appeals ruling (*State ex rel. Reece v. Giles, J.P.*) that the system of funding justices of the peace through the collection of fines was unconstitutional (Smith, 2017b).

The newly established court structure would resemble a pyramid with three levels. Later, a fourth level was added to account for family courts. Today, the top and smallest part represents the West Virginia Supreme Court of Appeals, the second smaller layer represents the circuit courts, the third and slightly larger layer are the family courts (this piece was added in 2000), and the bottom and largest layer would be the newly founded magistrate courts. The size of each layer of the pyramid also represents the caseload at each level, with the magistrate courts dealing with the most cases, followed by the family courts, then the circuit courts, and finally the supreme court with the fewest cases. Within this reorganization, the introduction of the magistrate courts to replace the previous justices of the peace is the most notable change. Moreover, the 1976 Amendment also opened the path for the creation of an intermediate appellate court between the circuit courts and supreme court if the legislature so chooses. At this point, they have not chosen to do so.

The Administrative Office of the Courts oversees the daily operations of the entire court system within West Virginia. These matters are related mostly to budgets and human resources. However, as stated earlier, the Supreme Court of Appeals of West Virginia is considered the primary supervisor of all courts within the state, with the exception of municipal courts (see Figure 5.1). A constitutionally created officer or administrative director is appointed by the Supreme Court of Appeals to manage this Administrative Office.

Supreme Court of Appeals

The West Virginia Supreme Court of Appeals is currently the only appellate level court in the state and serves as the court of last resort. Although this can be misleading as the United States Supreme Court can hear a state case, making it the ultimate court of last resort. However, a state case making it to the U.S.

Figure 5.1. West Virginia Judicial System

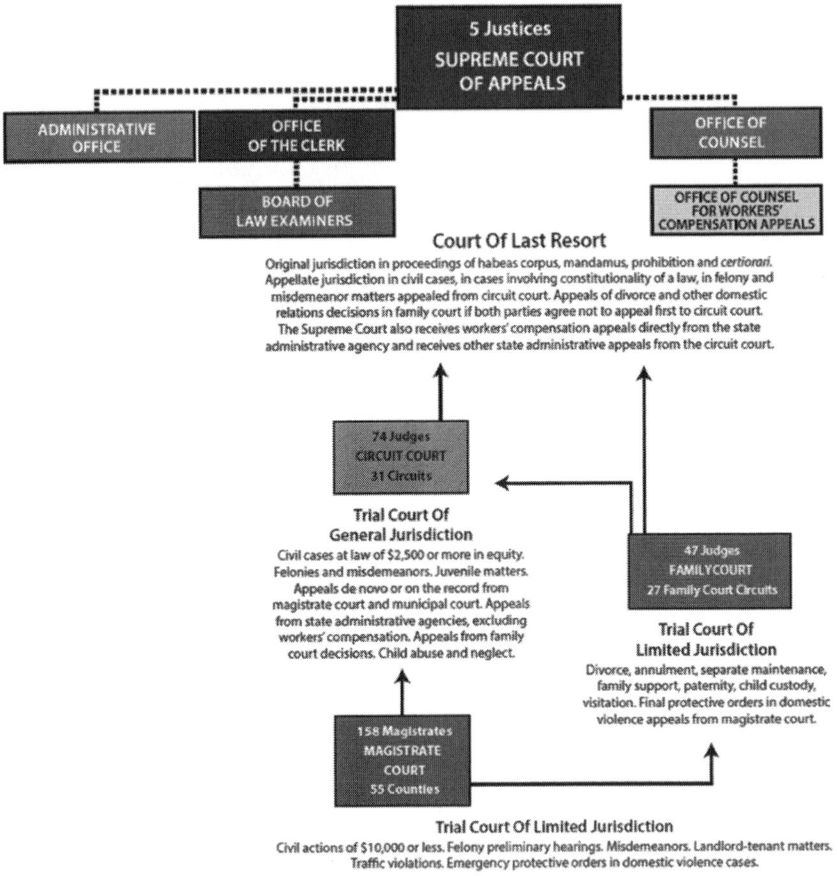

Source: Bundy, J., & Harless, A. (2017). *The Supreme Court of Appeals of West Virginia.* Charleston, WV: Administrative Office of The Supreme Court of Appeals of West Virginia. Retrieved from http://www.courtswv.gov/public-resources/press/Publications/2017SupremeCourtBrochure.pdf (figure modified from page 2).

Supreme Court is not a common occurrence. West Virginia is currently only one of 10 states where a case can go directly from the trial court to the supreme court level. In other words, there is no intermediate appellate court. As an appellate court, juries and witnesses are not present during hearings, and the court has a panel of five judges that preside over cases. Unlike the U.S. Supreme Court, whose justices are appointed for life, West Virginia's justices are elected by its voters for 12-year terms. Each year, the justices also select one member to serve as chief justice, making him or her the administrative head of the judicial branch of government for the state. Again, this varies from the U.S. Supreme Court, where the chief justice is nominated and confirmed into the position by the President and the U.S. Senate, and this justice can serve indefinitely in that role.

The West Virginia Supreme Court has the authority to review orders or judgments from a lower court, appeals from all 55 counties, and several state agencies. According to the annual brochure published yearly by the West Virginia Supreme Court of Appeals, it has:

- Original jurisdiction in proceedings of *habeas corpus*, *mandamus*, prohibition, and *certiorari*.
- Appellate jurisdiction in civil cases at law over $300 or in equity, in cases involving constitutionality of a law, in felony and misdemeanor matters appealed from circuit court.
- Appeals of divorce and other domestic relations decisions in family court if both parties agree not to appeal first to circuit court.
- The Supreme Court also receives workers' compensation appeals directly from the state administrative agency and receives other state administrative appeals from the circuit court (Bundy & Harless, 2017, p. 2).

A few terms above need to be quickly defined before moving forward. First, ***habeas corpus*** is a Latin term meaning "you have the body," which has evolved into a legal definition. When a prisoner files this legal petition, or "writ," with the supreme court, or any court for that matter, they are essentially arguing that they are being imprisoned unlawfully and their case must be brought in front of the courts or a judge. A writ of ***mandamus*** is also a Latin term, and it means "we command." When this petition is filed, it is simply an order from a higher court to a lower body of authority to perform a specific action. Conversely, a ***prohibition*** petition is a command from a superior court to refrain from doing something. And last, a writ of ***certiorari*** (Latin) means "to be informed of," which in a legal context simply implies an appeal to a higher court for review of a lower court's decision.

The West Virginia Supreme Court of Appeals has changed dramatically since its founding in 1863. Initially, the members of the court were called judges, but now are called justices. There were originally three members, with a fourth added in 1872, and then a fifth justice added in 1903. The original court was located in Wheeling, which was also the state's first capital. Over the course of its existence, the court would move six different times before finding its current home on the east wing of the third floor in Charleston's state capitol building (Perry, Canterbury, & Sole, 2009).

Cases typically make their way to the Supreme Court of Appeals when someone loses a criminal or civil case in circuit court. An appeal is a request for the state's highest court to review the case. However, the trial court transcripts and documents make up the basis for the review, nothing more. The Supreme Court of West Virginia typically receives around 3,000 cases a year, although the number has been declining in recent years. But not every case will be formally heard by the court. Each one is thoroughly reviewed by the justices and their law clerks, and if the court agrees with the lower court's decision, then the appeal is refused and the lower court's decision is allowed to stand. Upon completion of this initial review, if the appeal is granted, the lawyers for both sides of the original case will be called on to provide oral arguments in front of the justices. If it is a criminal case, there will be a representative from the prosecutor's office and the defense counsel for the convicted offender. In a civil case, it will be the plaintiff's attorney and the defendant's attorney. These oral arguments are meant to provide justification for why the case should be overturned, sustained, or remanded for a new trial.[4] The arguments only last about 20 minutes, unlike in the original trial where the presentation by the attorneys can last from a few hours to a few months. Furthermore, neither the defendant nor any witnesses are present for this hearing. The rationale for even allowing the oral arguments to supplement the original court transcripts is because the justices were not present at the original trial. Therefore, it is the lawyer's job to educate the justices well enough so that they can decide the case based on the review of the cold record (i.e., transcripts) of the trial (Perry, Canterbury, & Sole, 2009).

Attorneys working on an appeal to the state's highest court can spend up to six months preparing the petition for appeal, writing briefs, and getting ready for the oral arguments. Likewise, when the justices are not hearing arguments, their time may be spent reviewing other cases, conducting research, and writing opinions. When justices finally make a decision, in most cases, a formal written opinion is issued. An ***opinion*** is simply a written explanation of the decisions of the court. Every opinion also must contain a syllabus, which consists of numbered paragraphs that contain the new points of law or old points of law that were discussed in the opinion itself. A syllabus is a requirement of the state constitution (Perry, Canterbury, & Sole, 2009). Once an opinion is issued by the state's highest court, its rulings become applicable to all the

4. When a case is overturned, the court disagrees with the verdict of the lower court, and in a criminal case exonerates the defendant. If the case is sustained, the court agrees with the lower court's verdict. And, when a case is remanded for a new trial, the court is sending the case back to the lower courts for a retrial with any problematic elements of the original case removed (e.g., certain pieces of evidence that were collected in violation of the defendant's constitutional rights).

Hampshire County Courthouse. Courtesy of Silling Associates.

courts within the state. This is similar to landmark decisions by the U.S. Supreme Court, whose rulings may be applicable to the entire country. This concept of precedent within the courts is known as ***stare decisis***, which is Latin for "to stand by things decided."

The West Virginia Supreme Court of Appeals has issued more than 20,000 opinions that are recorded in more than 220 volumes of the West Virginia Reports. Together, these reports comprise the book of law in West Virginia. These decisions, along with legislative statutes and administrative regulations, make up the sum of West Virginia law (Perry, Canterbury, & Sole, 2009). If either side of an appeal is not satisfied with the decision of the state's supreme court, there is one final option. These cases can be appealed to the Supreme Court of the United States, which is the final court of last resort. However, there is no guarantee the highest court in the land will hear the appeal.

Lower Courts

Circuit Courts

The circuit courts in West Virginia are the trial courts of general jurisdiction. They are the only general jurisdiction trial courts of record and handle criminal cases, both adult and juvenile, as well as all civil cases totaling more than $2,500. These civil cases usually involve private property rights, not criminal activity. The circuit courts also can serve an appellate function for magistrate and municipal courts, as well as administrative agencies (Dameron, 2005). Their official jurisdiction is:

- civil cases at law of $2,500 or more in equity;
- felonies and misdemeanors;
- juvenile matters;
- appeals *de novo* or on the record from magistrate court and municipal court;
- appeals from state administrative agencies, excluding workers' compensation;
- appeals from family court decisions;
- and child abuse and neglect (Bundy & Harless, 2017, p. 2).

One point that should be clarified from the passage above is that circuit courts in West Virginia have authority over misdemeanors. Even though, as we will soon see with our discussion of magistrate courts, primary jurisdiction lies there. Magistrate courts, like all courts of limited jurisdiction in other states, generally handle misdemeanors. However, in West Virginia there is an overlap in jurisdiction with circuit courts. This is manifested on two levels. The first is transference to circuit court as an appeal from magistrate courts (or municipal courts), which is referred to as ***appeal de novo***, or simply a new trial. The reason for this is that courts of limited jurisdiction are not "courts of record," because its proceedings are not required to be transcribed. This does not mean that there are no records of the business conducted by these courts, but these records do not qualify "as a transcription of proceedings for court of record purposes" (Cleckley & Palmer, 1994, p. 150). So, unlike the Supreme Court of Appeals that has trial court transcripts to use as the basis for the review, the circuit court is left lacking. Thus, the case is retried as a new one.

The second area of overlap in regard to misdemeanors is a bit more complicated. The circuit court can initiate a misdemeanor indictment, but only if the "initial charging document" was not "rendered by the magistrate court" (Cleckley & Palmer, 1994, p. 146). This effectively means that circuit courts can try a misdemeanor violation as an original case if the indictment was initiated at that level, but this only happens in less than 10% of criminal cases that the circuit courts hear. Ultimately, magistrate courts handle almost all misdemeanor violations.

West Virginia is divided into 31 circuits with 74 presiding judges. Each circuit has between one and seven judges, based on the population of each circuit. And, each circuit contains between one to four of the 55 counties that make up the state (see Table 5.1). However, there is one courthouse for each

Table 5.1. Circuit Courts

Judicial Circuit	Counties	# of Judges	Judicial Circuit	Counties	# of Judges
1st	Hancock Brooke Ohio	4	17th	Monongalia	3
2nd	Marshall Wetzel Tyler	2	18th	Preston	1
3rd	Pleasants Ritchie Doddridge	1	19th	Taylor Barbour	1
4th	Wood Wirt	3	20th	Randolph	1
5th	Mason Jackson Calhoun Roane	3	21st	Tucker Grant Mineral	2
6th	Cabell	4	22nd	Pendleton Hardy Hampshire	2
7th	Logan	2	23rd	Morgan Berkeley	6
8th	McDowell	2	24th	Wayne	2
9th	Mercer	3	25th	Lincoln Boone	2
10th	Raleigh	4	26th	Lewis Upshur	2
11th	Greenbrier Pocahontas	2	27th	Wyoming	1
12th	Fayette	2	28th	Nicholas	1
13th	Kanawha	7	29th	Putnam	2
14th	Clay Braxton Webster Gilmer	2	30th	Mingo	1
15th	Harrison	3	31st	Summers Monroe	1
16th	Marion	2			

Source: Bundy, J., & Harless, A. (2017). *The Supreme Court of Appeals of West Virginia*. Charleston, WV: Administrative Office of the Supreme Court of Appeals of West Virginia. Retrieved from http://www.courtswv.gov/public resources/press/Publications/2017SupremeCourtBrochure.pdf.

county, so residents do not necessarily have to travel longer distances for their cases. Rather, the judges will come to them. Furthermore, in circuits that have more than one judge, a chief judge is chosen for that circuit.

Cases heard in the circuit courts are what the layperson commonly thinks of when they hear the words "criminal trial." A trial conjures up the image of two attorneys battling it out in front of a jury, with a judge that serves as a referee. Each side of this adversarial process presents witnesses and evidence indicating guilt or innocence of the defendant. Often, the mental image of this trial involves some act of personal violence, such as murder, rape, or robbery. In reality, an overwhelming number of the criminal cases heard at the circuit courts are nonviolent in nature, such as burglaries and thefts. The other misconception is that all cases go to trial, when in fact, much of the business conducted in the circuit courts actually involves sentencing of a convicted defendant, and not just because they have been found guilty in a trial, but because 90% of criminal convictions are a result of a negotiated plea (i.e., ***plea bargain***). One final misconception, though certainly not the only one, is that all the cases heard in circuit court are criminal in nature. However, the majority of cases with which these courts deal are civil in nature (Neubauer & Fradella, 2011). In fact, in 2016, of the 44,889 cases filed in the West Virginia's circuit courts, 25,821 (57.5%) were civil, 11,240 (25%) criminal, and 7,828 (17.4%) juvenile. In examining only the criminal cases, 6,792 were felonies, 794 misdemeanors, 182 appeals from magistrate courts, and 3,472 classified as "other" (Chapman, Blevins, Jones, & Walsh, 2016).

Family Courts

While family courts are not part of the criminal justice process, they are still part of the state pyramid as described earlier. There are 27 circuits that make up the family courts in West Virginia, which contain 47 judges. Family courts are considered trial courts of limited jurisdiction and primarily handle disputes related to children and families. More specifically, its jurisdiction is limited to:

- Divorce, annulment, separate maintenance, paternity, grandparent visitation, name change, infant guardianship, child custody, and family support proceedings, except those incidental to child abuse and neglect proceedings.
- Family court judges also conduct final hearings in civil domestic violence protective order proceedings and may perform marriages (Bundy & Harless, 2017, p. 6).

Cases from family court can be appealed to circuit court or the state supreme court, depending on the type of case. As the third layer in the pyramid, these courts hear the second highest number of cases. In 2016, West Virginia's family courts had 39,466 new cases filed. More specifically, 11,492 were domestic violence, 9,496 were divorces, and 5,699 were other domestic cases. On top of that, there "were 12,779 modification and contempt proceedings in cases reopened during the year, which were not counted as new cases filed" (Chapman et al., 2016, p. 8).

Magistrate Courts

With West Virginia's ending of the justice of the peace courts, the door was opened for the establishment of the magistrate courts. Again, these courts are considered trial courts of limited jurisdiction. This is the level of the pyramid that hears the greatest number of cases. However, they are usually small claims and misdemeanors. This also is the court that has the most contact with the public; therefore, they are considered the "people's court." In West Virginia, we have 158 magistrates statewide. With 55 counties in the state, this equals two to 10 magistrates per county. This is obviously based on the county's geographical and population size. Each county also has a chief magistrate who is selected by the circuit court judge or chief judge, and this chief magistrate serves as a liaison between the magistrate level courts and the circuit courts as well as carrying out other administrative functions as defined by state statutes and regulations (W. Va. Code §50-1-7).

The jurisdiction of the magistrate courts in regard to criminal trials is limited to misdemeanor cases. However, they can conduct preliminary hearings for felony cases (to determine probable cause) that will ultimately be tried at the circuit court level. Moreover, magistrate courts also hear civil matters involving $10,000 or less in dispute, landlord-tenant matters, traffic violations, and emergency protective orders in domestic violence cases (Bundy, & Harless, 2017). Cases lost at the magistrate courts can be appealed to circuit court, as discussed earlier; however, not as a true appeal, but rather appeal *de novo*.

The magistrate courts are without a doubt one of the busiest entities within the state court system in West Virginia. In 2017, there were 224,316 cases heard by the magistrate courts. And this number does not include day-to-day activities, such as issuing and recording affidavits, complaints, arrest and search warrants (for felonies and misdemeanors), as well as setting bail and making decisions concerning proposed plea agreements, the collection of court costs, cash bonds, and fines (Chapman et al., 2016).

In conclusion, one very important point about magistrate courts must be made. These courts are not physical buildings, per se. Rather, magistrate courts are a collection of people, with the magistrate being at the center of the circle, and then his/her clerks and assistants around the perimeter. These personnel have distinct roles that are defined by the state constitution, statutes, and rules

(Cleckley & Palmer, 1994). Regardless of where the business of the magistrate takes place, it is considered to have been conducted in magistrate court. This is different from the circuit courts, which refer to both personnel and physical locations (i.e., circuit courthouses). However, each magistrate does have a central location from which they conduct daily operations. And, while these locations will have specific working hours throughout the week, magistrate functions revolve around a 24-hour on-call role (Cleckley & Palmer, 1994).

Municipal Courts

The final, and lowest, level of courts in West Virginia, although not part of the state structure (and therefore not included in Figure 5.1), are the municipal courts. However, the Judicial Reorganization Amendment gave the legislature the power to create municipal courts based on the same power it has to create municipalities (i.e., cities, towns, and villages). This was done more specifically through Section 8, Section 11 of the state constitution, which states: "The legislature may provide for the establishment in incorporated cities, towns or villages of municipal, police or mayor's courts, and may also provide the manner of selection of judges of such courts" (W. Va. Const. art. 8, §11). Thus, all municipal courts are locally controlled rather than state controlled. Their only link to the state court structure is that cases from these courts can be appealed to circuit courts, but similar to appeals from magistrate court, they are appeals *de novo*.

The decision to call them municipal, police, or mayor's courts is solely based on the physical location of the court. In other words, if it is housed in a police station it would be called police court, and if it is housed within city hall it would be called mayor's court. However, the term *municipal court* is generally used to refer to the entire grouping. It is important to note here that not all municipalities in West Virginia have them. In the event a municipal court has not been established, other members of the local government (e.g., the mayor) may oversee ordinance violations.

Municipal courts do not have a significant role as a criminal court as they are constitutionally limited to traffic and city/municipal ordinances. However, where a municipal ordinance implies a criminal offense, such as carrying a weapon on or near a city building without a proper permit, the municipal courts have the power to arrest and provide an appropriate sanction, even incarceration for a limited time.

Treatment Courts and Systems

In addition to the courts mentioned above, West Virginia has devoted the past several years to developing premier diversion alternatives to assist individuals who are afflicted with substance abuse or mental health issues. Two of these efforts are briefly examined, which are drug courts and a mental health and hygiene system.

Drug Courts

The increased number of drug-related offenses in the mid-1980s served as a catalyst for establishing drug courts across the nation. With the "War on Drugs" at the forefront for most police departments, drug violations and arrests dominated most of their time, thereby increasing drug abuse caseloads. Ultimately, the result of this "war" was prison and jail overcrowding. One solution was to treat drug offenders as addicts instead of criminals. Hence, the drug court concept was created where low-risk offenders could be identified and diverted into a treatment program instead of incarcerated.

West Virginia's adult and juvenile drug courts were established well after the 1980s. The first adult drug court appeared in 2005 in the Northern Panhandle with the First Circuit serving Brooke, Hancock, and Ohio Counties (Bundy, 2013). Today, there are 26 other adult drug courts serving either a single county or an entire county circuit. Sole drug courts function in Cabell, Wayne, Putnam, Logan, Mason, Kanawha, McDowell, Mercer, Raleigh, Fayette, Nicholas, Randolph, Harrison, Marion, Monongalia, and Preston counties. The remaining 10 courts are divided among 27 counties, leaving nine counties without a court (Taylor, Barbour, Tucker, Grant, Mineral, Gilmer, Braxton, Clay, and Webster). Between 2013 and 2018, the number of adult drug courts more than doubled due to a rise in opioid abuse and a concerted effort by the West Virginia Supreme Court to expand treatment courts in the state. Conversely, the number of juvenile drug courts have actually declined, and there are currently only 14 in the state; whereas, there were 16 in 2013 (Bundy, 2013). More attention is given to juvenile drug courts in Chapter 7.

In lieu of a prison or jail sentence, in the adult drug courts, offenders must plead guilty to the charges and drugs must have played a significant role in the offense. Again, not all drug offenders qualify for drug court. The West Virginia code specifies how drug offenders are ineligible for the program, especially if they have committed a violent offense, sex offense, or have a prior felony record. Specifically, the criteria that exclude a person from drug court eligibility are:

> (1) The underlying offense involves a felony crime of violence, unless there is a specific treatment program available designed to address violent offenders;

(2) The underlying offense involves an offense that requires registration as a sex offender pursuant to the article twelve, chapter fifteen of this Code;
(3) The drug offender has a prior felony conviction in this state or another state for a felony crime of violence; or
(4) The drug offender has a prior conviction in this state or another state for a crime that requires registration as a sex offender pursuant to article twelve, chapter fifteen of this Code (W. Va. Code §62-15-6).

In an effort to reduce recidivism and substance abuse, the adult drug court model incorporates both alcohol and drug treatment services that are in line with evidence-based practice. The process is one that uses a nonadversarial approach where a coordinated strategy is employed by a multidisciplinary team, consisting of a member of law enforcement, prosecutor, defense counsel, judge, probation officers, and treatment professionals (Gebelein, 2000). For a minimum of one year, and over a series of phases, the drug court participant is supervised closely by a probation officer and is subject to frequent and random drug testing. Plus, there is ongoing judicial contact and status updates about the offender's progress throughout the process.

Mental Health and Hygiene System

In West Virginia there are 31 mental hygiene circuits with at least one commissioner per circuit. The respective chief circuit court judge appoints these commissioners. While they do not play a direct role in criminal justice proceedings, indirectly they are responsible in questions relating to determining probable cause in cases of involuntary commitments. More extensive details about the role of the mental hygiene commissioner and mental health hearings can be found in the statutory code (W. Va. Code §27-5-1).

Federal Courts

As stated in the opening of this chapter, more than 98% of cases are handled at the state level, but a handful of federal matters are handled within the borders of West Virginia through two federal district courts, which are the trial courts for the federal system. West Virginia's Northern Federal Judicial District is currently headquartered out of Wheeling,[5] but there are additional courthouses in Clarksburg, Elkins, and Martinsburg. This district comprises 32 counties.

---

5. The location of the headquarters is based on whoever is serving as chief district court judge at the time.

The remaining 23 counties are served by the Southern Federal Judicial District headquartered in Charleston, with courthouses also in Bluefield, Huntington, and Beckley. Any individual in violation of a federal offense while in the state of West Virginia would have his or her case tried in one of these two districts, based on location of the county in which the violation occurred.

Unlike the state court structure, which has a multilevel trial court structure, and only one appellate level, the federal courts are comprised of only one trial level court (i.e., U.S. District Courts), but two appellate levels. A case appealed from either the northern or southern districts would be heard at the Fourth Circuit Court of Appeals, which includes the states of West Virginia, Virginia, Maryland, North Carolina, and South Carolina. The physical location of the court is in Richmond, Virginia. The final appellate level for a case, after it has reached the Fourth Circuit, is the U.S. Supreme Court in Washington, D.C., although a case can be appealed directly to the U.S. Supreme Court and bypass the Fourth Circuit. Not only is the U.S. Supreme Court the court of last resort for federal cases, but as mentioned earlier, state matters as well.

Spotlight: The Need for an Intermediate Court of Appeals

While the Judicial Reorganization Amendment allows for the creation of an intermediate appellate court (IAC) in West Virginia, the state legislature has not done so. However, there has been a call for such a court. In fact, an Internet search on the topic yields numerous debates regarding whether West Virginia could use one. There have been a number of unsuccessful attempts to get a bill passed through the West Virginia legislature with the earliest bid in 1999 and the latest in February 2018 (which was still pending at the time of this writing).

There are more than 90 intermediate appellate courts nationwide, as some states have multiple courts. The primary reason for their adoption was to alleviate the workload of the states' highest courts, thus improving efficiency and allowing cases to be heard in a timely manner. Of the nine states[6] that do not currently have one, West Virginia is the most populated. Moreover, West Virginia is slowly becoming a member of a very exclusive minority. In fact,

6. The other states include Delaware, Maine, Montana, New Hampshire, Rhode Island, South Dakota, Vermont, and Wyoming. While North Dakota is not included in this list, it has a temporary IAC made up of rotating and retiring judges and cases are assigned to it by the North Dakota Supreme Court as needed (in some years no cases are assigned).

Nevada was the latest to adopt an intermediate appellate court in November 2014. The argument for adding such a court is not simply because most other states have one, but the West Virginia Supreme Court of Appeals caseload dictates strong consideration of the addition of another appellate court. As the court's brochure states, it "is one of the busiest appellate courts of its type in the United States" (Bundy & Harless, 2017, p. 4). In 2007, the court's caseload reached an all-time high, with 3,594 cases being filed. However, a vast majority were in the area of workers' compensation claims as a result of administrative changes in the system. Once the privatization of the compensation system was fully implemented, the number of cases filed dropped dramatically. In fact, the very next year the number of cases filed dipped below 2,500 and by 2016 the number was close to 1,300.

While the caseload for the Supreme Court of Appeals has declined over the last several years, it is not due to a lack of activity. In fact, a number of other diversionary programs as well as improved case management have assisted in the reduction of case filings. Moreover, as of 2011, because of changes to court rules that govern appeals, "appeal by right" is now guaranteed. As a result, the Supreme Court has not declined to hear a single appeal. Thus, the number of decisions made by the court increased by more than 700% from 2011 to 2015. This, combined with increasing incarceration rates in West Virginia, makes it presumable that *habeas corpus* petitions to the state supreme court will increase, and the court's caseload will once again rise. So, perhaps creation of an intermediate appellate court in West Virginia is necessary at this time?

Key Terms and Definitions

Appeal *de novo*: A review of a case for the second time, but with no regard to the prior decision.

Bench trial: The type of trial where a judge determines the final outcome of a case instead of a jury.

Beyond a reasonable doubt: Proof that leaves a juror firmly convinced of the defendant's guilt.

Certiorari (Latin): A legal petition to remove a case from a lower court to a higher court.

Challenged for cause: When the court determines a prospective juror to harbor some bias toward one side or the other; he or she will be disqualified from serving on the petit jury.

Discretion: The ability to choose among alternatives.

Grand jury: Randomly selected members of the community, just like in a petit jury, but rather than determining guilt or innocence in a public forum, their task is to determine probable cause to merit a criminal trial.

Habeas corpus **(Latin):** A legal petition for relief from unconstitutional confinement, mainly used by inmates.

Indictment: A formal accusation where the grand jury has concluded that there is enough probable cause to believe a defendant should be prosecuted by the state.

Indigent defendant: An individual who does not possess sufficient income to afford a lawyer for defense in a criminal case.

Information: A charging document filed by the prosecutor, after a preliminary hearing that is similar to the indictment used by the grand jury.

Justice of the peace: Officers of the court, often of nobility or influence, who handled minor civil controversies.

Mandamus **(Latin):** A legal petition for a superior court to require a public body, inferior court, or public official to perform a required duty.

Opinion: A written explanation of the decisions of the appellate court.

Peremptory challenge: Releasing jurors that either the prosecution or defense believe to be prejudicial to their side, but for an undisclosed reason.

Petit jury: A trial jury comprised of 12 people (or six people in magistrate court) who are given the task of determining innocence or guilt of another person charged with a crime.

Plea bargain: A negotiated deal in a criminal case between the prosecutor and defendant where the defendant agrees to plead guilty to a particular charge in return for some concession from the prosecutor.

Presentment: A report that contains the findings of the grand jury investigation as well as the recommendation to indict or not.

Probable cause: A fair probability, under the totality of the facts and circumstances known, that the person arrested committed the crime(s) charged.

Prohibition: A legal petition for a superior court to halt the performance of a particular act by an inferior court, state agency, or public official.

Stare decisis **(Latin):** A concept of precedent within the courts that means "to stand by things decided."

Voir dire **(French):** The process of filtering out petit jurors who may not be able to render an impartial verdict.

Select Internet Sources

e-WV: The West Virginia Encyclopedia: http://www.wvencyclopedia.org.
West Virginia Judiciary: http://www.courtswv.gov/.
West Virginia Public Defender Services: http://www.pds.wv.gov/Pages/default.aspx.
U.S. Northern District Court of West Virginia: http://www.wvnd.uscourts.gov/.
U.S. Southern District Court of West Virginia: http://www.wvsd.uscourts.gov/.

Review and Critical Thinking Questions

1. In addition to the fact that magistrates are salaried, are there fundamental differences between them and the previously used justices of the peace?
2. Because potential petit jurors may be biased, what pros and cons would there be if we used a system of professional jurors instead of laypeople?
3. What could be the underlying reason grand jury investigations are closed to the public and grand jurors are forbidden to communicate their investigation to anyone outside the grand jury itself?
4. In what situations would a defendant choose to waive their right to a preliminary hearing or grand jury indictment?
5. What would be the pros and cons of developing an intermediate appellate court in West Virginia?

References

Bundy, J. (2013). *West Virginia court system: 2013 annual report.* Charleston, WV: Administrative Office of the Supreme Court of Appeals of West Virginia. Retrieved from http://www.courtswv.gov/public-resources/press/Publications/2013AnnualReport.pdf.

Bundy, J., & Harless, A. (2017, July). *The Supreme Court of Appeals of West Virginia.* Charleston, WV: Administrative Office of the Supreme Court of Appeals of West Virginia. Retrieved from http://www.courtswv.gov/public-resources/press/Publications/2017SupremeCourtBrochure.pdf.

Chapman, C., Blevins, T., Jones, A., & Walsh, L. (2016). *The annual statistical report on circuit, family and magistrate courts: The West Virginia court system 2016 data.* Charleston, WV: Administrative Office of the Supreme Court of Appeals of West Virginia. Retrieved from http://www.courtswv.gov/public-resources/press/Publications/2016AnnualReportData.pdf.

Cleckley, F. D., & Palmer, L. J. Jr. (1994). *Introduction to the West Virginia criminal justice system and its laws.* Dubuque, IA: Kendall/Hunt Publishing.

Dameron, S. (2005). *Criminal justice in West Virginia (2004–2005 Update).* Boston, MA: Pearson Education.

Gebelein, R. S. (2000). *The rebirth of rehabilitation: Promise and perils of drug courts.* U.S. Department of Justice, Office of Justice Programs, National Institute of Justice. Retrieved from https://www.ncjrs.gov/pdffiles1/nij/181412.pdf.

Harris, E. L. (2013, August). Attorney General. *e-WV: The West Virginia Encyclopedia.* Charleston, WV: West Virginia Humanities Council. Retrieved from http://www.wvencyclopedia.org/articles/309.

Neubauer, D. W., & Fradella, H. F. (2011). *America's courts and the criminal justice system* (10th ed.). Belmont, CA: Wadsworth Publishing.

Oliver, W. M., & Hilgenberg, J. F. Jr. (2010). *A history of crime and criminal justice in America* (2nd ed.). Durham, NC: Carolina Academic Press.

Perry, R., Canterbury, S., & Sole, D. (Producers). (2009). *The foundation of justice: Supreme Court of Appeals of West Virginia* [DVD]. Available from http://www.state.wv.us/wvsca.

Rogers, H. J. (2013, August). Justice of the peace. *e-WV: The West Virginia Encyclopedia.* Charleston, WV: West Virginia Humanities Council. Retrieved from http://www.wvencyclopedia.org/articles/1084.

Siegel, L. J., & Senna, J. J. (2004). *Essentials of criminal justice* (4th ed.). Belmont, CA: Thompson/Wadsworth Publishing.

Smith, C. (2017a, April). The courts. *e-WV: The West Virginia Encyclopedia.* Charleston, WV: West Virginia Humanities Council. Retrieved from http://www.wvencyclopedia.org/articles/1655.

Smith, C. (2017b, April). Judicial branch. *e-WV: The West Virginia Encyclopedia.* Charleston, WV: West Virginia Humanities Council. Retrieved from http://www.wvencyclopedia.org/articles/1073.

Legal References

W. Va. Code §27-5-1 (2017).

W. Va. Code §29-21-16 (2017).

W. Va. Code §50-1-4 (2017).

W. Va. Code §50-1-7 (2017).

W. Va. Code §52-1-8 (2017).

W. Va. Code §62-15-6 (2017).
West Virginia Const. art. 8, §11.
West Virginia Const. art. 9, §1.

Chapter 6

Adult Corrections

Moundsville State Penitentiary.
Courtesy of the West Virginia Archives, Katy Wells Collection.

Over the past century, the state of West Virginia has seen a significant amount of change in correctional programming and practice. Like many states, it has had to embrace reform and strengthen community corrections alternatives as crime and incarceration rates have continued to climb. The state now boasts a correctional system that provides humane and safe state prisons, a model regional jail system, and one of the lowest recidivism rates in the country. In order to better address the state's rurality and the number of people who are plagued by poverty and drug addiction, the system is devoted to various correctional treatment programs to facilitate a more fruitful reintegration process for inmates returning to society. In addition, the state is among a few in the country that has a prison nursery program for female offenders. On the other hand, while the state was moving forward with the widespread adoption of a risk and needs assessment in corrections, probation, and day report centers to reduce the prison population and link offenders to the most appropriate treatment services, this is no longer the case for probation. Such a move puts the state's justice reinvestment strategies into question (see Council of State Governments, 2013).

Organizational Structure of Corrections in West Virginia

The organizational structure of the adult correctional system in West Virginia is quite decentralized. Two major agencies, the West Virginia Division of Corrections (WVDOC) and the West Virginia Regional Jail and Correctional Facility Authority, are housed under the Department of Military Affairs and Public Safety (DMAPS). Like other states, the WVDOC is led by administrative staff that includes a commissioner, deputy commissioner, assistant commissioner, and a chief of staff. The WVDOC oversees a number of correctional services and programs that include: state prisons, parole services, victim services, and offender programs related to drug and alcohol education, anger management, addiction issues faced by women, crime victim awareness, and domestic violence. Note that among those services and programs listed, jails are not included. Instead, jails are administered separately by the West Virginia Regional Jail and Correctional Facility Authority. Another important aspect of corrections-probation is administered by the West Virginia Supreme Court of Appeals in the Division of Probation Services. Each of these aspects of the correctional system is described in more detail below, except for victim services, which is presented in Chapter 8.

The West Virginia Division of Corrections

According to the WVDOC (2017b), the mission is "to enhance public safety by providing safe, secure, and humane correctional facilities, operating an effective system of offender re-entry and community supervision, reducing offender recidivism, and assisting victims of crime" (p. 7). It is clear from this statement that the mission of the WVDOC is in line with several correctional philosophies. One of the more explicit philosophies mentioned in this statement is ***incapacitation***. Here, the goal is to protect the community by preventing violent offenders from having the chance to commit new crimes by removing them from society. This is especially effective for the career or habitual criminal. Nevertheless, there are a few drawbacks to this philosophy. For instance, in many states across the country, a large number of non-violent offenders are incarcerated. The bulk of inmates are drug offenders and property offenders—many of whom would not be a risk to the community. As a consequence, our country, and even the State of West Virginia, has been overwhelmed with prison and jail overcrowding.

Mt. Olive Correctional Complex. Courtesy of Silling Associates, Inc.

With an emphasis on re-entry in the mission statement, it is clear that the WVDOC supports the philosophy of ***reintegration***, which became more popular across the country in the 1970s and 1980s. This approach is one that is very forward-thinking as nearly 90% of offenders will return to society. Returning offenders need skills as they segue from institutional life back to the "real world." This is not an easy process and, sadly, the research shows that many will reoffend in the first few months after release, especially those who have been incarcerated for longer periods. Yet, as will be discussed subsequently in this chapter, fewer offenders return to prison in the Mountain State compared to other states, suggesting that West Virginia's prison reintegration and reentry efforts may be more efficient.

There are additional correctional philosophies that are applicable to the WVDOC's mission statement, namely rehabilitation. While this philosophy is implied, it still encompasses correctional practice as it is embedded in most of the correctional programs and connected to the notion of reintegration. The philosophy of ***rehabilitation*** is one that is based on the medical model and assumes that criminal behavior is influenced by factors such as poverty, drug/alcohol abuse, discrimination, or psychological problems, and that people can, in fact, change. The goal is to reduce future crime by providing assistance through treatment or education so the individual will not reoffend. Treatment focuses more exclusively on the individual offender (e.g., counseling, drug and alcohol treatment, vocational education, or remedial education). The philosophical system of rehabilitation was very prominent from the 1950s to the 1970s, but fell out of vogue after the release of Martinson's (1974) "What Works" study, indicating that most correctional treatment programs were inefficient. Even today, some have argued that inmate programming is a waste of state finances and taxpayers' dollars. Despite Martinson's study, and his findings, there has been a resurgence in providing quality correctional programs and treatment for inmates.

In terms of state ***prisons*** under the tutelage of the WVDOC, there are 16 correctional facilities, two of which are characterized as minimum-security work camps, and four of these minimum-security facilities contain work release units (see Table 6.1). Aside from security level, the table also depicts the types of correctional centers and work camps by gender and capacity. In the last column of the table, correctional centers that house a residential substance abuse treatment (RSAT) program are noted. Last, it is important to note one exception [not shown on Table 6.1]. The Anthony Correctional Center differs from the other adult prisons in that it houses 18–24 year old men and women (WVDOC, 2017b). The young adult offenders who are placed there may serve a sentence as little as six months or as long as two years. "Each offender is sentenced to the facility with a suspended original sentence for their felony conviction" (WVDOC, 2017b, p. 26).

The information in Table 6.1 shows that three facilities are classified as ***multi-security prisons***, which are technically maximum-security institutions. These facilities house inmates on the same grounds, but in the proper security environment whether it is minimum, medium, or maximum security. For example, Lakin Correctional Center houses female inmates and has this security designation; it is a common feature for a female facility to cover a range of custody levels given the fact that there are typically fewer females who are incarcerated as a whole. Last, Huttonsville Correctional Center, located in Randolph County, bears this designation and also has an intake unit.

A ***maximum-security prison*** contains individual cells with doors that are controlled remotely from a secure control station and a narrow slot in the cell door, otherwise known as a "bean shoot" from which inmates can receive food and medicine. Inmates are confined to their cells for 23 hours per day. These units typically house the most violent and dangerous inmates who pose a threat to public safety as well as correctional staff and other inmates. Most prisons refer to these areas of the prison as restricted housing units (RHUs). Inmates are confined almost 23 hours a day but are permitted to shower and receive exercise time in a secure location within the facility. Mount Olive Correctional Center in Fayette County is well known in the state as a maximum-security institution. Opened in 1994, the prison, like most maximum-security facilities, is noted by its one-mile-long perimeter fence and state-of-the-art electronic security controls.

Unlike the maximum security prison, a ***medium security prison*** may have a dormitory environment that can provide housing for several inmates. Dor-

Table 6.1. Overview of West Virginia Correctional Institutions

Institution	Security Level	Gender	Capacity	RSAT Capacity
Anthony Correctional Center	Minimum	Male/Female	220	
Beckley Correctional Center	Minimum/ Work release unit	Male/Female	137	59 (RSAT males)
Charleston Correctional Center	Minimum/ Work release unit	Male/Female	96	32 (RSAT (females)
Denmar Correctional Center	Medium	Male	232	
Huttonsville Correctional Center	Maximum/Multi	Male	1135	80 RSAT
Huttonsville Work Camp	Work Camp	Male	48	
Lakin Correctional Center	Maximum/Multi	Female	543	RSAT
Martinsburg Correctional Center	Multi/Intake	Male	120	
Mount Olive Correctional Complex	Maximum	Male	1030	
Slayton Work Camp	Work Camp	Male	48	
Northern Correctional Center	Maximum/Multi	Male	253	
Ohio County Correctional Center	Minimum/ Work release unit	Male	67	
Parkersburg Correctional Center	Minimum/ Work release unit	Male	186	RSAT
Pruntytown Correctional Center	Minimum/ Medium	Male	369	RSAT
Saint Marys Correctional Center	Medium	Male	554	108 RSAT
Salem Correctional Center	Minimum/ Medium	Male	388	64 RSAT

Source: West Virginia Division of Corrections (WVDOC) (2017b). West Virginia Division of Corrections, *Annual report: FY 2017*. Charleston, WV: Office of Research and Planning. Retrieved from http://www.wvdoc.com/wvdoc/Portals/0/documents/2017-Annual-Report.pdf.

* McDowell County Correctional Center was included in the 2017 report but shortly thereafter the facility's operating status changed and it is now privately owned.

mitories are monitored by correctional staff and locked at night. In some cases, the cells are dry cells, which means that they do not contain a toilet or sink. Instead, there is a shared restroom with a shower area and sinks. The exterior of these facilities usually has a single- or a double-fence perimeter with armed watchtowers or armed roving patrols. What distinguishes medium-level facilities from the others is the fact that there is less supervision and control over the internal movement of the inmate, so that inmates can attend programs or complete various work assignments throughout the prison. In West Virginia, there are two facilities that are exclusively designated as medium-security—the Denmar Correctional Center in Pocahontas County and St. Marys Correctional Center in Pleasants County. Interestingly, Denmar was once a state mental hospital that treated patients with tuberculosis.

Minimum-security prisons are more relaxed and comprised of non-secure dormitories, which are routinely patrolled by correctional officers. Like the medium-security dorm, it has a group restroom and shower area often adjacent to the sleeping quarters that contain double bunk beds and lockers. It is important to remember that inmates who are assigned to a minimum-security prison generally pose the least amount of risk to public safety. Some prisons may contain a single perimeter fence for monitoring the grounds, but will not usually have armed officers on roving patrol. Because of this security classification, it is not unusual for these inmates to participate in community-based work assignments. In West Virginia, most of the minimum-security institutions also have work release units or are designed as prison work camps.

Prison work camps serve a variety of purposes and can be defined as minimum-security facilities for nonviolent, low-risk offenders that offer community work and treatment programs in an effort to prepare inmates for re-entry into society. Prison work camps are a necessity as they alleviate prison overcrowding and assist inmates who may be transitioning from a high-level security environment to a minimum-security environment. Both the Slayton Work Camp (SWC) and the Huttonsville Work Camp (HWC) offer inmates the opportunity to perform a variety of tasks in the community while under supervision. For example, work camp inmates may take part in volunteering for the Division of Highways, the West Virginia Farm Commission, and additional special projects based on the community's needs (i.e., schools, nonprofit organizations, local charities, or government buildings). In addition to serving the community, work camp inmates are provided with educational programming (WVDOC, 2017b).

Last, there are a few facilities in the state that operate a work release unit. ***Work release,*** or ***community corrections centers,*** house nonviolent offenders, provide programming and a therapeutic living environment, and often require steady employment, so that inmates will have the financial resources as they transition back to society. A work release center typically consists of dormitory-style living quarters. The Charleston Correctional Center (previously referred to as the Charleston Work Release Center) is designed as a minimum-security facility that houses 96 males and 32 females in the RSAT. To qualify, the inmate must have been treated successfully in one of the WVDOC's facilities' drug treatment units, plus they must be employed full-time, maintain good behavior, and continue their substance abuse treatment at the center, especially if they are part of the RSAT. Furthermore, they are obligated to make service contributions to the community and the facility. Even though the residents of the facility are able to leave for their jobs during the day, they are required to return to the center at the end of the work day. In order to successfully reintegrate back into society, inmates must also save a portion of their earnings, and while they are employed, they are expected to pay taxes, child support, rent at the facility, etc. (WVDOC, 2017b).

State Prison Data

Recent estimates across the country show that nearly 6.8 million offenders were under some form of correctional supervision in 2014 (Kaeble, Glaze, Tsoutis, & Minton, 2016). Put another way, 1 in 36 adults in the United States is in a state or federal prison, jail, or placed on probation or parole. According to 2017 estimates, West Virginia prisons housed approximately 5,867 inmates. The majority of inmates were male (90%) as opposed to female (10%). Furthermore, inmates were primarily white (86.26%) followed by black (12.51%). There were very small percentages of inmates who were classified as multi-racial/other (.68%), Hispanic (.33%), American Indian (.11%), or Asian (.10%). In terms of expense, the average daily cost per inmate was $71.45. This equals approximately $26,081 per inmate per year (WVDOC, 2017b).

In terms of age, most inmates in state prison facilities were 30 to 39 years of age (33.15%), 20 to 29 years of age (25.12%), or 40 to 49 years of age (20.98%) (WVDOC, 2017b). The remaining inmates were 50–59 years of age (12.99%). Clearly, the very old and the very young made up the least amount of those committed to WVDOC custody. That is, there were 11 inmates 80 years of age and older (.19%) and only eight inmates under 20 years of age (.14%). When it comes to education levels, very few state prisoners had a high school diploma (33.37%) and more than half did not graduate from high school (59.14%). Even fewer (7.21%) had an education beyond high school.

Ohio County Correctional Center. Courtesy of Nicole Myers White.

In 2017, the West Virginia state prison population data revealed that most inmates were incarcerated for violent crimes such as forcible sex offenses (15%), followed by homicide (13.8%), and burglary/breaking and entering (13.2%) (WVDOC, 2017b). The next largest offense type for which inmates were imprisoned consisted of drug/narcotic crimes (11.4%). Some inmates were incarcerated for crimes like conspiracy to commit a felony, failure to register as a sexual predator, or fleeing from an officer, among others. These offenses were categorized as "other" and made up 8.7% of all offenses total. Robbery (9.8%), larceny (6.1%), and assault (4.7%) comprised additional offenses for which inmates served time. As for sentence type, very few inmates were serving life with mercy (4.8%) or life without mercy (4.05%).

On a different note, clearly one of the most damaging or collateral consequences of incarceration is its impact on families and children. According to recent estimates, about two million children in the United States have a parent in prison. Sadly, about half of these children are likely to follow in their parent's footsteps. This concept is known as the ***intergenerational cycle of incarceration***. In 2008, the WVDOC Office of Research and Planning conducted a survey to determine the number of inmates who have children (Douglas, 2008). Approximately 4,690 surveys were collected among inmates who were currently in the custody of WVDOC at the start of the 2008 fiscal year. Results indicated that 67.1% of female inmates reported having children, whereas a little more than half of male inmates (50.7%) reported having a child or children. In total, the 2,498 inmates were parents to 4,902 children. Almost equally these children were male or female. Twenty percent of the children were reported as being between the ages of seven to nine years of age, followed by 19% who were reported to be between four to six years of age.

In many states, it would be common to discuss death penalty statistics and data about inmates who are on death row. Since West Virginia abolished the death penalty in 1965 there are no relevant data to present. Executions were conducted publicly before 1899, but after the construction of the West Virginia State Penitentiary, all other executions of male inmates were conducted there, mostly by hanging (Death Penalty Information Center, 2014). The electric chair was used in 1951, and the last execution took place in 1959. Since then, bills to reinstate the death penalty have failed before the state legislature several times; the most recent attempt was in 2011. West Virginia is one of 19 states that does not have the death penalty as well as the District of Columbia.

Recidivism in West Virginia

One of the most important aspects of corrections, as mentioned earlier, is the successful reintegration of the inmate, which coincides with reducing the likelihood of future offending. Most correctional facilities across the country monitor recidivism rates. Similar to the definition used by the WVDOC, the Pew Center (2011) states that "***recidivism*** is the act of reengaging in criminal offending despite having been punished ... the recidivism rate ... is the proportion of persons released from prison who are rearrested, reconvicted or returned to custody within a specific time period" (p. 7). According to a recent Pew Center Study (2011), the average recidivism rate in the country from 2004–2007 was 43.3%. However, about nine states did not provide data, so some caution must be used in interpreting this figure. Nonetheless, the rate in West Virginia in 2007 was 26.8%, which was the third lowest rate among states that reported data. Only Oregon and Wyoming reported lower recidivism rates, with rates of 22.8%, and 24.8%, respectively. Minnesota had the highest reported recidivism rate of 61.2%, followed by California at 57.8%.

In 2013, the recidivism rate in West Virginia was 25% among those inmates who were released, which was very similar to what was reported in 2007 (WVDOC, 2017c). Upon further inspection, 15.4% of those who recidivated were returned as a result of revocation of parole, and 9.7% of those who recidivated were returned with a new crime conviction. Recidivism data is computed by the WVDOC's office of research and planning, and due to the complexity of measuring recidivism, data are only compiled every three to four years.

Correctional Officer Training and Duties in West Virginia

Both correctional officers and parole officers undergo basic training and also complete specialized training as prescribed by their assigned job duties, whether they will be employed at a regional jail, state prison, or with parole services, etc. The WVDOC requires that all staff remain informed and knowledgeable of current practice by completing continued education courses throughout their time of employment. Also, aside from training, employees are encouraged to earn an associate's degree through a partnership with Glenville State College.

Correctional Officers (COs) are trained at the Public Safety Professional Development Center in Glenville, West Virginia. The training program is divided into two main phases. The first phase, or Basic Training, takes place over a period of three weeks at the place of employment. Here, the trainee receives typical classroom and computer-based instruction. After this phase, for another three weeks, or phase two, the trainee completes a residential course. An Academy Platoon Sergeant provides the training, which is carried out in a paramilitary fashion where officers learn discipline, teamwork, compliance with rules and regulations, along with how to follow the proper chain of command. Furthermore, trainees receive firearms instruction or re-certification, first aid, Community Emergency Response Team (CERT) training, and cell extraction training, among other types of training.

As firearms training is an additional component of the training, it is important to note that correctional officers, namely those who work in jails or in probation, are granted the privilege of carrying a firearm, concealing a firearm while on duty, and having arrest powers similar to those of a sheriff, so long as they have successfully completed the firearms certification program. The powers for jail staff are stipulated in the West Virginia Code §31-20-27(a)(b) as follows:

> (b) Persons employed by the Regional Jail Authority as correctional officers are hereby authorized and empowered to make arrests of persons already charged with a violation of law who surrender themselves to such correctional officer, to arrest persons already in the custody of the Regional Jail Authority for violations of law occurring in the officer's presence, to detain persons for violations of state law committed on the property of any regional jail, and to conduct investigations, pursue and apprehend escapees from the custody of regional jail.

Aside from the standard training that is required of corrections personnel, West Virginia is home to the Mock Prison Riot, which is held at the retired state penitentiary in Moundsville. The first mock prison riot was held in 1997 under the direction of a federal program called the Office of Law Enforcement Technology Commercialization (OLETC), which at the time was part of the United States Department of Justice (DOJ) and the National Institute of Justice (NIJ) (Barone, Goudy, & Fialkoff, 2009). With funding eliminated by NIJ for the mock prison riot, the WVDOC and a non-profit agency, known as the West Virginia Corrections Training Foundation, have assumed control and responsibility of the training activities since 2011 (WVDOC, 2017b). Today, the training program is comprised of a four-day tactical and technological showcase. Correctional staff take part in various competitions, workshops, and training scenarios to better prepare themselves for a potential crisis or threatening incident in prison. In 2017, the event was attended by more than 25 states; representatives from countries such as Belize, Columbia, Haiti, and Senegal also were in attendance (WVDOC, 2017b).

Inmate Programs

Nearly all correctional institutions in the state offer some type of educational (i.e., GED), substance abuse treatment, anger management, and/or victim awareness programming. Vocational or trade skills also are offered in a variety of prisons ranging from auto mechanics, welding, and carpentry, which are offered at Huttonsville Correctional Center, to culinary arts, life skills, and cosmetology, which are offered exclusively at the Lakin Correctional Center for women, for example. Moreover, several prisons as shown earlier in Table 6.1 have a ***Residential Substance Abuse Treatment Unit (RSAT)***. Some of these facilities include the Beckley Correctional Center, the Huttonsville Correctional Center, and the Parkersburg Correctional Center, just to name a few. Inmates who qualify for the residential substance abuse program are housed in a separate part of the prison with anywhere from 30 to 80 beds. They receive intensive substance abuse counseling and are subject to periodic and random drug testing. The ultimate goal of the program is to take a comprehensive approach in addressing the inmate's substance abuse issues in context with their cognitive, behavioral, social, and vocational skills so that they will be able to succeed upon reentry to society. Most RSAT programs also function as a "therapeutic community." These are social living environments where inmates take part in actively changing their behavior through peer-led intervention and positive reinforcement. Moreover, they "self-govern" their living space with additional rules and regulations that must be followed and reject the influences of the traditional inmate culture in order to be productive "citizens" of the prison community.

Figure 6.1. The West Virginia Penitentiary

One of the most iconic buildings in the state is the West Virginia penitentiary (known as the "old pen"), located in Moundsville. Shortly after West Virginia became a state in 1863 and with no adequate resources for the state to house inmates of its own since its separation from the state of Virginia, a new facility to house inmates was sorely needed. The original structure was designed with gothic revival architecture including turrets for the guards, resembling what most would consider a medieval prison. Given its remarkable and fortress-like appearance, it is on the United States National Register of Historic Places, and it is well known not just locally but internationally. Today, prison tours are given on almost a daily basis.

The prison was officially opened in 1876, nearly half a century after the Eastern State Penitentiary was opened in Philadelphia, Pennsylvania. Despite the best efforts of those who designed the prison and carried out the daily operations of the facility, it has a very tumultuous history and was deemed by the United States Department of Justice as one of the most violent prisons in the country. Approximately 94 executions, either by electric chair or hanging, took place at the institution. In addition, two famous riots took place, one in 1973 and another in 1986. The latter riot, which is more famously known, took place on New Year's Day by a group of inmates who referred to themselves as the "Avengers." Six guards were taken hostage as well as a member of the food service staff. In total, three inmates were killed by other inmates. The riot lasted for two days until Governor Arch Moore intervened.

The impetus for the closure of the penitentiary was a habeas corpus petition filed in 1981 (*Crain v. Bordenkircher,* 1986). Robert Crain, an inmate of the WVP, alleged that conditions were unconstitutional and violated the Eighth Amendment by being cruel and unusual punishment. Other petitions were gathered similar to Crain's and an investigation of the prison confirmed the deplorable living conditions. Since the prison was built in the late 1800s, providing heat in the wintertime was difficult, summers were extremely hot, rodents infested the grounds, the plumbing and sanitation system was faulty, and the 5 x 7 cells were well below standard regulation, especially for as many as three inmates in a cell at a time (Cleckley & Palmer, 1994). Even with attempts to improve prison conditions, it was difficult and costly. Further complaints ensued, such as the food was often contaminated and rotten, and the law library was not only inadequate, but inmates had limited access to it. In addition, there were limited recreational activities to reduce idleness and no continuous educational or vocational programming made available to the inmates. With the prison declared a violation of human rights by the West Virginia Supreme Court, it was closed in 1995. Inmates were transferred to the new maximum-security facility, the Mt. Olive Correctional Complex, which is located in Fayette County.

Other unique programs include Paws-4-People, which is offered at Lakin Correctional Center, Pruntytown Correctional Center, and St. Marys Correctional Center. In addition, federal institutions, FPC Alderson and USP Hazelton's Secure Female Facility (SFF) have similar "paws" programs, while an Appalachian Bible College program is offered at Mt. Olive Correctional Complex. Lakin Correctional Center for women also has a Keeping Infant Development Successful (KIDS) program. More attention is given to the KIDS program later in this chapter. In the Paws-4-People program, inmates are paired with a shelter-rescue dog to provide obedience training, so that the dog can assist a juvenile or adult who is impaired or has a mental or physical disability. In some cases, dogs are trained to learn more than 100 commands. The training program for the inmate is quite rigorous as they receive extensive academic training in order to learn how dogs "learn," the relationship between trainers and dogs, training challenges, and canine behavior, among other subjects. The benefits are clearly tremendous, especially to the inmates, who by way of the program, also learn how to be accountable for their crime and how to make a positive impact on the community. As for the Bible College program, it is a Christian-based program for inmates who are serving either life in prison or a lengthy prison sentence. Upon successful program completion, inmates receive a bachelor of arts degree in Bible and theology provided at no cost by Catalyst Ministries.

Last, and one of the oldest types of program, is the prison industry. Prison industries were established in West Virginia in 1939, and are described in Chapter 25, article 7, §25-7-1 of the state code (aka Correctional Industries Act of 2009). To date, Denmar, Huttonsville, Lakin, Mt. Olive, and Pruntytown have prison industry. Similar to other states, the West Virginia correctional industries is a state-use-only system that provides all goods and services to state agencies and county schools. By way of revenues, items like clothing, janitorial supplies, printing, furniture, and linens, are manufactured for the correctional system, thereby reducing costs to taxpayers. From another standpoint, inmates gain important job skills that are necessary for them to obtain successful employment when they reenter society. These programs also are a great asset as they have been known to reduce recidivism, and while the inmate is in prison, they reduce idleness. Typically, correctional industry inmates must possess a high school diploma or demonstrate progress toward earning a GED, plus they must maintain regular work hours.

Federal Institutions in West Virginia

Across the nation in the post-Civil War era, federal prison facilities were in demand as state facilities became largely overcrowded with prisoners of war and other federal inmates. In 1930, Congress created the Federal Bureau of Prisons (FBOP) within the Department of Justice under President Hoover in order to create a more centralized administration of federal prisons, to provide progressive and humane care of federal inmates, while maintaining the utmost professionalism among the federal prison complex. Today, federal institutions house inmates sentenced for federal crimes and detain individuals awaiting trial or sentencing in federal court. Federal prisoners are incarcerated for interstate commerce violations, certain serious felonies such as bank robbery, violations of federal law specified in Title 18 of the U.S. Code (e.g., racketeering offenses—obtain money illegally through bootlegging or fraud, tax evasion, interstate kidnapping), and crimes committed on federal property, just to name a few.

Of the 122 federal correctional institutions in the country, West Virginia, which is part of the Mid-Atlantic region of the bureau, has six main facilities. They are: the Federal Correctional Institution (FCI) Gilmer, United States Penitentiary (USP) and Federal Correctional Complex (FCC) Hazelton, FCI Morgantown, FCI Beckley, FCI McDowell, and Federal Prison Camp (FPC) Alderson, plus the Bureau of Prisons has a medium Secure Female Facility (SFF) at USP Hazelton. Overall, the FBOP manages more than 180,000 federal offenders in the country; approximately 9,000–10,000 federal offenders are housed in federal facilities in West Virginia on any given day.

Also, shown in Table 6.2, the majority of satellite institutions are classified as minimum security, which includes the federal prison camp for women at Alderson and the camps at Beckley, Gilmer, McDowell, and Hazelton. There are four medium-security facilities, including FCI Beckley, FCI Gilmer, FCI McDowell, and FCI Hazleton with separate units for male and female inmates. USP Hazelton houses more dangerous inmate populations. As shown in the table, the majority of federal prisons can hold inmate populations of more

Figure 6.2. Kathleen Hawk Sawyer

One notable aspect about the Federal Bureau of Prisons is Kathleen Hawk Sawyer, a native of West Virginia, who served as the Federal Bureau of Prisons Sixth director from 1992–2003 (ASCA, 2003). Dr. Hawk Sawyer is the only female to serve in this capacity. Her career with the Bureau began in 1976 at FCI Morgantown. Over the years, her career unfolded as she took on additional roles such as Chief of Psychology Services in 1983 at FCI Morgantown and Senior Instructor for the Staff Training Academy that same year. She was employed as the Associate Warden for Programs at FCI Fort Worth, Texas, while in 1986 she became the Chief Staff of Training. She transferred to FCI Butner in North Carolina in 1987, where she served as Warden. Moreover, she was named the Assistant Director for the Program Review Division at the Bureau's Central Office. Dr. Hawk Sawyer received a number of awards and accolades for her contributions to the federal correctional system. She was recognized by the U.S. Surgeon General, the American Correctional Association, and President of the United States, among others. Dr. Hawk Sawyer retired in 2003.

Table 6.2. Overview of West Virginia Correctional Institutions

Institution	Security Level	Inmate Population	Gender	County
Alderson FPC	Minimum	959	Female	Greenbrier
Beckley FCI	Medium	1511	Male	Raleigh
Beckley camp	Minimum	159	Male	Raleigh
Gilmer FCI	Medium	1325	Male	Gilmer
Gilmer camp	Minimum	94	Male	Gilmer
Hazelton FCI (SFF)	Medium	571	Female	Preston
Hazelton FCI	Medium	1394	Male	Preston
Hazelton USP	High	1337	Male	Preston
Hazelton camp	Minimum	113	Male	Preston
McDowell FCI	Medium	1138	Male	McDowell
McDowell camp	Minimum	74	Male	McDowell
Morgantown FCI	Minimum	952	Male	Monongalia
Total		9667		

Source: Federal Bureau of Prisons (FBOP). *Inmate population report*. Retrieved from https://www.bop.gov/about/statistics/population_statistics.jsp.

Note: The FBOP's inmate population figures are "live" and calculated daily. The figures presented above were compiled at the time this table was produced.

than 1,000, while the prison camps and the secure female institution at Hazelton house fewer federal inmates.

Not surprisingly, most federal institutions in the state house male inmates as opposed to female inmates. A notable feature to mention is that West Virginia was home to the first female federal prison for women, FPC Alderson, located in Greenbrier County. The other federal minimum-security female prison in the country is located in Texas (FPC Bryan). FPC Alderson was opened in 1927, just a few years before the Federal Bureau of Prisons was created in 1930. It is also famously known for when Martha Stewart served time for insider trade fraud from October 2004 to March 2005. She was charged with violating the Securities Act of 1933 and the Securities Exchange Act of 1934.

FPC Alderson is also home to one of the most famous research studies about female offenders and the notion of the pseudo-family. Rose Giallombardo

(1986) examined the female prison experience, and how females deal with the pains of imprisonment, including the deprivations of heterosexual relationships. Her research took place from 1962–1963. She concluded that because females are assigned cultural roles of "wife" and "mother," it was not uncommon for them to continue to adopt these roles in prison, perhaps as a coping mechanism. With these roles, she found that kinship groups or ***pseudo-families*** were created by inmates taking on the role of husband, wife, uncle, cousin, etc. Even today, correctional staff will attest that these kinship groups exist in most female correctional institutions.

The West Virginia Regional Jail and Correctional Facility Authority

As mentioned earlier, the West Virginia Regional Jail Authority is housed within the Department of Military Affairs and Public Safety. The West Virginia Regional Jail and Prison Authority was created by the state legislature in 1985 (WVRJA & CFA, 2017). Prior to this, the stated depended largely on its county jails, many of which were deemed unfit for humans. Given the deteriorating and poor living conditions of the county jails, litigation ensued. Even with Law Enforcement Administration Association monies, improvements still fell below the standards to ensure quality living space for jailed offenders. In tandem with the impact of the West Virginia Supreme Court of Appeals decision in the *Crain v. Bordenkircher* (1986) case, the authority was renamed the West Virginia Regional Jail and Correctional Facility Authority so as not to exclude prisons from the authority's direction.

Today, the mission of the Regional Jail and Correctional Facility Authority "is to ensure the safety of the public, staff and inmates by maintaining a safe, secure and humane system of regional jails, and to provide incarcerated persons with the opportunities for self-improvement and rehabilitation by participating in educational programs" (WVRJA & CFA, 2017, p. 11). In total, there are 10 regional jails, serving multiple counties. The first facility to open was the Eastern Regional Jail (ERJ) in Martinsburg in 1989 (see Table 6.3).

The cooperative, or ***regional jail*** concept, is a multi-county effort where inmates are housed on a per diem basis. Kentucky, Virginia, North Dakota, South Dakota, and Kansas employ this regional jail model as well (Siegel & Bartollas, 2014). In the state, each regional jail was based on a prototypical design that was modified or adjusted depending on the characteristics and needs of the community it served and a bond system. ***Jails*** in comparison to prisons, are short-term facilities that house inmates for less than one year. Typically, there are a myriad of different populations housed within the jail.

Table 6.3. West Virginia Regional Jails and Inmate Population Data

Facility	Opened	Average Daily Total	Admissions Total
Central Regional Jail	1993	308	3066
Eastern Regional Jail	1989/1999	475	5507
North Central Regional Jail	2001	658	6187
Northern Regional Jail	1994	307	3053
Potomac Highlands Regional Jail	2000	295	2402
South Central Regional Jail	1993	532	7233
Southern Regional Jail	1994	555	6786
Southwestern Regional Jail	1998	444	3159
Tygart Valley Regional Jail	2005	500	3250
Western Regional Jail	2003	611	6685
Total		4,685	47,328

Source: West Virginia Regional Jail and Correctional Facility Authority (WVRJA & CFA). (2017). *Annual report FY 2017*. Retrieved from http://rja.wv.gov/Documents/Annual%20Reports%20and%20Inmate%20Resources/RJA%20Annual%20Report%20FY%202017.pdf.

Note: The Eastern Regional Jail was first opened in 1989, but the new facility was opened in 1999.

For instance, there are some inmates awaiting WVDOC placement or federal prison transfer, while there also are pretrial misdemeanants and pre-trial felons. And last, there are those who are serving a jail sentence. More specifically, among the jail population, about 30% were awaiting transfer to a WVDOC facility or transfer to a federal prison (3%) (WVRJA & CFA, 2017).

More than 700,000 people are jailed on any one day in the United States (Minton & Zeng, 2016). This equals a rate of 230 individuals per 100,000 in the population. West Virginia's jail admissions for 2017 reached more than 47,000 inmates. In 2017, the majority of inmates were male (74.7%) versus female (25.2%). In comparison to national data from 2015, about 85.7% of jailed inmates were male (Minton & Zeng, 2016). If the national percentage remained steady, this suggests that West Virginia's regional jails were occupied by more females in comparison to the percentage of females jailed nationally.

Moreover, most were white (86.7%) followed by black (10.8%) (WVRJA & CFA, 2017). Nationally, there were fewer white inmates in jails (48.3%) and a larger percentage of black inmates (35.1%) and Hispanic inmates (14.3%), yet these numbers are problematic as comparisons because they reflect the 2015 calendar year (Minton & Zeng, 2016). Again, these figures have to be placed into context, and given that West Virginia's racial demographic is largely comprised of whites as discussed in Chapter 2, these results are not surprising. More importantly, there are a disproportionate number of minorities who are jailed in proportion to their population in the State of West Virginia (e.g., 3.6% of people in the population in West Virginia are African American, compared to 10.8% who are in regional jails). Smaller percentages of inmates were classified as Asian, Hispanic, and Native American. Among those housed in jails, most were committed for domestic battery, capias (arrest warrants), possession of a controlled substance, obstructing, DUI, fugitive from justice, grand larceny, possession with intent, probation violation, and driving revoked for DUI. Also, as depicted in Table 6.3, on a daily basis most jailed inmates were housed in the Western Regional Jail, followed by the North Central Regional Jail, and the Southern Regional Jail.

Some programming is available to jailed inmates, but inmates are responsible for paying a fee of $25 for each class session (WVRJA & CFA, 2017). One major incentive is that inmates who have a jail sentence of six or more months are eligible to receive five days of "good time" for successful program completion. Over the 2016–2017 fiscal year, the most successfully completed programs included parenting classes (356 inmates) and life skills classes (348 inmates), followed by substance abuse classes (348 inmates). However, when examining the volume of inmates taking part in these programs (1,881 inmates were enrolled), the percentage of completion is very small (56%). Programs in the jail system are complicated by the fact that the inmate often has a shorter length of stay.

Community-Based Corrections

The "get-tough" rhetoric of the 1980s led to an unprecedented influx of people committed to prison throughout our country. With limited budgets to construct and operate more prisons, many states were faced with the crisis of prison overcrowding. In turn, states have had to rely on intermediate sanctions. ***Intermediate sanctions*** are alternative forms of punishment that provide graduated levels of supervision in the community (Siegel & Bartollas, 2014).

These community-based alternatives are not always the most favorable to the general public, criminal justice professionals, or legislators; however, they represent a necessity as we continue to incarcerate more and more people in our country than in any other country in the world. West Virginia employs intermediate sanctions such as home confinement, electronic monitoring, drug courts, day report centers, as well as probation and parole. In this section, more attention will be given to day report centers, probation, and parole, whereas drug courts are covered in Chapter 5.

Day Report Centers

One of the most cost-effective intermediate sanctions is a day report center. In the state of West Virginia, there are 30 centers that serve 51 of the 55 counties (Messina, 2017); these centers are funded by the state through the Community Corrections Subcommittee of the Governor's Committee on Crime, Delinquency, and Corrections, and in part by a 30% match from each county. The grants are administered by the West Virginia Division of Justice and Community Services. A ***Day Report Center (DRC)*** refers to a facility where an offender must report every day and where they receive counseling, life skills, battering intervention, and/or drug and alcohol treatment programs. The overarching philosophy of most of these centers is community ***restorative justice***. For instance, the Western Regional DRC (2018) in Wayne County defines community restorative justice as a mechanism "to provide a means by which victim, offender, and community address the problem of crime" (para. 3). In order for restorative justice to be effective, all three components are necessary. The offender has to take responsibility for his/her actions, the community has to be invested in working with the offender to address the harm caused by the crime, and the victim has to have an opportunity for redress.

It is important to note that not all DRCs operate in the same capacity throughout the state, so a few generalizations have been made here. For example, not all DRCs have clients who report to them daily. At other DRCs, some clients may report every 30, 60, or 90 days; or, in some cases, up to six months, depending on their sentence. The DRCs in the state assist nonviolent offenders, mainly those who have committed a misdemeanor or felony offense sentenced by the judge or as a condition of home confinement or probation. The WVDOC also refers inmates to the DRC to coincide with the reentry process. With this said, it is clear that this type of intermediate sanction is less stigmatizing; however, the outcome as to their effectiveness in reducing recidivism is still debatable (Siegel & Bartollas, 2014).

Parole

One of the most important distinctions that must be made when speaking of corrections is the difference between probation and parole. ***Parole*** is the conditional release of an inmate from prison after they have served a portion of their imposed sentence. In contrast, ***probation*** is a form of punishment where the convicted offender remains in the community under supervision of a probation officer. Parole is not guaranteed but based on the discretionary powers of a parole board. Research has shown that over the past several years as many as 1,500 inmates were denied parole each year (Bauer-Leffler & Haas, 2014).

Parole Services in West Virginia is divided into two primary districts—the northern district and the southern district, both with a supervisor. These districts are further divided into eight regions. They are: Northern, Northcentral, Northeastern, Northwestern, Southern, Southcentral, Southeastern, and Southwestern. Each region has a regional supervisor along with six to seven parole officers per region. Not unlike the mission of the WVDOC,

> parole services is dedicated to enhancing public safety, remediating the behavior of criminal offenders to acceptable community standards, protecting the interests of the victims of crime and sustaining a secure environment for all people in the State of West Virginia through active supervision techniques and the effective use of evidence-based, re-entry programming and treatment practices (WVDOC, 2017a, para. 1).

In West Virginia, the parole board consists of nine members, who are eligible to serve a term of six years. Parole board members must be a resident of West Virginia or have lived in West Virginia for five consecutive years. Furthermore, parole board members must possess a college degree or five years of experience in corrections, law enforcement, law, social work, sociology, education, or medicine, or a combination of these fields. The West Virginia Code §62-12-13 stipulates the eligibility criteria for inmates seeking parole as well as the obligations, powers, and duties of the parole board as follows:

> (a) The Parole Board, whenever it is of the opinion that the best interests of the state and of the inmate will be served, and subject to the limitations provided in this section, shall release any inmate on parole for terms and upon conditions provided by this article.
> (b) Any inmate of a state correctional institution is eligible for parole if he or she:

(1)(A) Has served the minimum term of his or her indeterminate sentence or has served one fourth of his or her definite term sentence, as the case may be; or

(B) He or she:

(i) Has applied for and been accepted by the Commissioner of Corrections into an accelerated parole program;

(ii) Does not have a prior criminal conviction for a felony crime of violence against the person, a felony offense involving the use of a firearm or a felony offense where the victim was a minor child;

(iii) Is not serving a sentence for a crime of violence against the person, or more than one felony for a controlled substance offense for which the inmate is serving a consecutive sentence, a felony offense involving the use of a firearm or a felony offense where the victim was a minor child; and

(iv) Has successfully completed a rehabilitation treatment program created with the assistance of a standardized risk and needs assessment.

About one month prior to the inmate being paroled, the parole officer will review the inmate's home plan. This entails investigating the inmate's new residence to ensure that it is safe, adequate to fit their needs (e.g., running water, electricity, sleep space), free of weapons and firearms, and that there are no other felons in the dwelling. It is imperative that when granted parole, the parolee follow the prescribed conditions, shown in Figure 6.3. While these conditions are applicable to most parolees, there are certain cases that warrant additional or special conditions. In other words, given the circumstances of the parolee, a parole officer may enhance or alter the conditions as he or she sees fit. Regardless, the parole officer spends an ample amount of time in the field, making home checks and employment contacts, plus they will conduct drug screenings. Parole officers are trained for a period of six weeks and may be certified to carry a weapon upon successful completion of the firearms training at the academy.

According to the WVDOC (2017b), there were 3,310 people supervised by Parole Services. Interestingly, not all of those who comprise a parole officer's caseload are from West Virginia. Of those 3,310 parolees, 1,139 were out-of-state parolees, and 190 were out-of-state probationers. Around 58% of these cases were for West Virginia parolees. Evidently, parole officers in the state carry a complex caseload that involves not just parolees who are residents of the state, but parolees/probationers who are out of state and part of the interstate compact. Kanawha County (326 parolees) had the largest number of parolees.

Figure 6.3. West Virginia Conditions of Parole

- Must report within 24 hours.
- Stay within a certain area.
- Obtain permission before changing residence or employment.
- Obtain and maintain employment.
- Maintain acceptable, non-threatening behavior.
- Must not possess firearms or weapons.
- Report any arrest within 24 hours.
- Complete monthly written report.
- Report as instructed.
- Must not use drugs or alcohol or enter drinking establishments.
- Must not break any state or local laws.
- Abide by other written requirements.
- Pay $40 supervision fee monthly.
- Sex Offenders of children cannot live with anyone under 18.
- Sex Offenders must register with WV State Police within 3 days.
- Allow contacts at home or employment without obstruction.
- Submit to search of person, residence or motor vehicle at any time by Parole Officers.

Source: West Virginia Division of Corrections (WVDOC). (2017a). *Standard conditions for parole.* Retrieved from http://www.wvdoc.com/wvdoc/ParoleServicesResources/StandardConditionsofParole/tabid/143/Default.aspx.

The other counties with a large number of parolees in 2017 included: Mercer County (317 parolees), Berkeley County (258 parolees), and Cabell County (240 parolees). Population size may be a factor for some counties like Kanawha county, but counties that border other states may have a higher caseload given the parolees who are part of the interstate compact.

Probation

As stated earlier, the state judiciary administers probation in West Virginia. Thus, probation officers are considered "officers of the court" and serve at the will and pleasure of the West Virginia Supreme Court of Appeals. The two major functions of the probation officer include investigation and supervision. As part of their duties, they are required to prepare a ***Pre-Sentence Report*** (PSR) (or Pre-Sentence Investigation), which is a standardized and comprehensive document prepared before sentencing that contains summary information about the offender. This report aids the court in making decisions about the offender's sentence length and potential for community placement. Typically, the PSR contains a court data summary about the current charges, a criminal history summary, adult arrest history, family history, marital status and dependents, education background, military history, employment history, economic status, and the defendant's health and habits (i.e., alcohol and drug use, mental health, etc.), in addition to recommended sentencing options.[1]

Probation officers perform supervisory functions similar to that of a parole officer, although a larger portion of their time is devoted to the court or office rather than the field. Home checks, drug screenings, case plan management, and employment visits, as necessary, are important assigned duties. The probation officer, who is also licensed to carry a firearm, has the power to arrest (with or without an order or warrant) any probationer who has violated their conditions, when there is reasonable cause (see Powers and Duties of Probation Officers, W. Va. Code §62-12-6). Recently, special conditions of probation have extended to several of the state's drug court programs, which are discussed in more detail in Chapters 5 and 7.

State prison data presented earlier in this chapter showed that a large percentage of inmates in the state are serving time for a sex offense. Sex offenses range from forcible rape to sexual assault and to other sex crimes such as molestation, prostitution, and possession or manufacturing of child pornography, just to name a few. With the growing need to ensure the safety of children and to provide a more stringent monitoring system of convicted sex offenders, the West Virginia legislature passed the Child Protection Act in 2006. Within two years after the act was passed, the Division of Probation Services established a specialized sex offender intensive supervision unit. Six sex offender supervision regions were created within the state to serve all 55 counties. However, this specialized probation unit was abolished in September of 2017 due to the fact that the actual number of sex offenders requiring supervision had decreased in the state from 14,000 to 10,000 (Hessler, 2017). The other reason for dissolving the unit was the fact that the probation officers were at a disadvantage of covering multiple counties at one time to supervise offenders. Currently, sex offenders have been added to all county probation officers' regular caseload.

1. For a few years the PSR also included the results of the Level of Service/Case Management Inventory (LS/CMI), which is the risk and needs assessment that was adopted by the Supreme Court of Appeals of West Virginia upon the adoption of West Virginia Senate Bill 371 (discussed later in this chapter). The LS/CMI identifies areas (risks) that need attention for supervision and programming (needs) that if properly addressed will reduce the offender's likelihood of recidivating. The LS/CMI may be used again by probation officers throughout the state at some point in the future.

To supervise this population effectively requires what is known as ***intensive supervision probation***, which is an enhanced set of conditions where the probationer is under strict surveillance by a certified probation officer while living in the community. In these cases, the probationer must complete additional weekly meetings, additional drug screenings, regularly attend school or treatment programs, and undergo additional employment checks. As a high-risk population, and since they are under more scrutiny, their lives are more regulated by a refined set of probation conditions when it comes to curfew, substance use, and living conditions, especially within the proximity of schools or child care facilities (see W. Va. Code §62-12-26). Because of the intensive and time-consuming nature of this type of probation, adult probation officers manage a demanding caseload. One sex offender on a caseload is equivalent to 3.2 regular probationers. Since a significant amount of time involves working with the judge in the courtroom and compiling PSRs, it can be challenging to balance the amount of work that is expected to be completed in the courtroom with effectively supervising sex offenders in the community.

Twenty-First-Century Challenges

As mentioned earlier, West Virginia has rather low recidivism rates compared to other states in the country; however, the state's Office of Research and Strategic Planning has predicted that the state's prison population is projected to increase by 24% from 2012 to 2018 (CSG Justice Center, 2013). Such a sobering and rising trend has been causing more concern for West Virginia's financial future, leaving little room for celebration. Additional data analyses showed that from 2005 to 2011, there was a 47% increase in the number of offenders who were returned to prison as a result of having their community service revoked. In other words, offenders, whether they were in a community corrections facility, probation, parole, or home confinement, violated their conditions and were sent back to prison. These alarming trends, coupled with the continued use of jail or prison time for low-risk offenders, comes at a cost. The bottom line is that the state is looking at a price tag of $200 million to construct new prisons and more than $140 million to operate these facilities during this time of exponential growth unless a new framework is implemented.

Given these glaring and daunting statistics, the state took part in a bipartisan and multiagency effort to develop a data-driven justice investment strategy in 2012 (CSG Justice Center, 2013) that is now reflected in Senate Bill 371. The framework called for three main improvement policies that included: (1) improving the supervision of those who are on probation, parole, home confinement, or in a day report center, (2) improving inmate accountability, and (3) reducing substance abuse by investing in community-based treatment programs and in programs for those who are incarcerated in state prison. One of the underlying ways to increase the effectiveness of community supervision and to reduce recidivism is by using a standardized and objective risk/needs assessment instrument, such as the Level of Service/Case Management Inventory (LS/CMI). The LS/CMI is based not only on assessing and predicting the offender's level of risk as either low, medium, or high (whether to themselves or the community), but their criminogenic (e.g., criminal associates, antisocial values, educational success, and skills deficiencies), and non-criminogenic needs (e.g., career issues, job skills, and employment opportunities). When these needs are adequately addressed, the likelihood of recidivism may be reduced by nearly 30%. In a study by Orsini, Haas, and Spence (2015), using LS/CMI data from 1,288 offenders under WDOC custody, they found that a high-risk score from the LS/CMI was predictive of higher rates of recidivism (51%). In addition, younger offenders (28.8%) were more likely to recidivate than older offenders (44.5%) and those who stayed incarcerated for longer periods were more likely to recidivate as well. Today, WVDOC prison staff, parole officers, and day report center staff have been trained to administer the LS/CMI. In time, it is hoped that these reinvestment strategies will prove beneficial for the state, the taxpayer, and those who struggle with a criminal lifestyle.

Spotlight: Lakin's Prison Nursery Program

Given that a large number of children are raised in single-female headed households, a larger burden is placed on women to care for their children. This issue is compounded by the growing number of mothers who are incarcerated. In addition to the children who are left behind, there are pregnant inmates who are essentially bringing their child with them to prison. Estimates have shown that nearly 2,000 babies are born each year in prisons (Rowland & Watts, 2007). In most states, these children are either placed in foster care or placed in the custody of a kinship relative.

Aside from the prison philosophies mentioned earlier, some prisons across the country have established prison nursery programs based on the notion that a child's first few years of life are most critical in their development, and that the separation of mother and child can be very damaging. According to DeBoer (2012), there are 10 prison nursery programs in the country (see

Table 6.4); the first program was opened at Bedford Hills Correctional Facility in New York in 1901. West Virginia's prison nursery program (Keeping Infant Development Successful-KIDS) was created at the female prison, Lakin Correctional Center, in West Columbia, in 2009 (Nohe, 2014). The nursery program is similar to others around the nation. In order to qualify for the program, the female inmate must be pregnant before entering prison, she must have been charged with a nonviolent offense with no prior record of child abuse, and she must be serving no longer than 18 months from the time the child is born. As part of the application process, a review is conducted to also determine if the mother is physically and mentally sound and able to care for her infant.

Many people question the safety of an infant or toddler in prison, yet these children are not in harm's way. For instance, infants and toddlers are kept with their mothers in a confined area of the prison, free from violent or dangerous offenders. At Lakin, the prison nursery unit is located outside of the main prison facility in a separate, four-bedroom modular home, with routine staff supervision (Nohe, 2014). Cameras and closed circuit television are equipped throughout the unit to monitor the inmates. Non-routine visits are made to ensure the safety of the infants. Across the country, prison nursery programs have been known to have extraordinary benefits. The chief strength of these programs is lower recidivism rates among women who have their children with them for a prescribed amount of time in prison (Smith Goshin, & Woods Byrne, 2009).

Table 6.4. United States Prison Nursery Programs

State/Facility	Program Start	Capacity	Eligibility/Length of Child's Stay
California Institution for Women, Corona	2009	16 women—10 with infants and 6 who are pregnant	Up to 18 months
Illinois, Decatur Correctional Center	2007	8 mother/ infant pairs	Mother must have two years or less from time of birth until discharge and not have a history of violent crimes or child abuse; mother and child must be healthy; Up to 18 months
Indiana Women's Prison, Indianapolis	2008	10 mother/ infant pairs and 4 nannies	Mother must be pregnant at the time of entering custody, never have been convicted of a violent crime, have 18 months or less from time of birth until discharge, read at an eighth grade level, and pass screenings based on medical and mental health; Up to 18 months
Ohio Reformatory for Women, Marysville	2001	20 mothers and up to 21 infants	Mother must be pregnant at the time of entering custody, serving for nonviolent crimes, have 18 months or less from time of birth until discharge, and pass screenings based on medical and mental health and family history; Up to 18 months
Nebraska Correctional Center for Women	1994	15 mother/ infant pairs	Mother generally must have 18 months or less until discharge from time of birth until discharge and not have a violent history or convictions of serious child abuse; 18 months; can be extended at staff discretion
Bedford Hills Correctional Facility, Bedford Hills, New York	1901	29 mother/ infant pairs	Mother must be physically fit to care for the child and pass evaluation based on parenting abilities and criminal record (N.Y. Correct. Law §611). The child can stay for up to 18 months if the mother will be paroled by then, otherwise the child must leave the facility at 12 months of age.

Table 6.4. *Continued*

State/Facility	Program Start	Capacity	Eligibility/Length of Child's Stay
Taconic Correctional Facility Bedford Hills, New York	1990	15 mother/ infant pairs	12–18 months depending on the mother's program.
South Dakota Women's Prison Pierre	1998	No limit	Mothers must be pregnant at the time of entering custody; 30 Days
Washington Correctional Center for Women Gig Harbor	1999	20 mother/ infant pairs	Mother must be pregnant at the time of entering custody; have 30 months or less from time of birth until discharge; and pass screenings based on type of offense, family history, and behavior; Up to 36 months
Lakin Correctional Center for Women, West Virginia	2009	5 mother/ infant pairs	Mother must be pregnant at the time of entering custody; have 18 months or less from time of birth until discharge; pass evaluation based on medical and mental health, and have no history of child abuse; Up to 18 months

Source: Adapted from DeBoer, H. (2012, March). *Prison nursery programs in other states.* Retrieved from http://www.cga.ct.gov/2012/rpt/2012-R-0157.htm and from Kring Villanueva, C., From, S. B., & Lerner, G. (2009, May). *Mothers, Infants and Imprisonment: A national look at prison nurseries and community-based alternatives.* New York: Women's Prison Association.

Note: Additional information regarding a child's length of stay for the California Institution for Women, Corona, and the Taconic Correctional Facility, Bedford Hills, New York, could not be found.

Key Terms and Definitions

Day Report Center (DRC): A facility where an offender must report every day and where they receive counseling, life skills, battering intervention, and/or drug and alcohol treatment programs.

Incapacitation: A correctional philosophy that refers to the goal of protecting the community by removing violent offenders from society as a way to prevent them from having the chance to commit new crimes.

Intensive supervision probation: An enhanced set of conditions where the probationer is under strict surveillance by a certified probation officer while living in the community.

Intergenerational cycle of incarceration: A concept that children who have a parent(s) incarcerated have a higher likelihood or are at risk themselves of becoming delinquent.

Intermediate sanctions: Alternative forms of punishment that provide graduated levels of supervision in the community.

Jail: A facility that houses individuals who are charged with a misdemeanor offense and serving less than one year. Also, the facilities house individuals who are awaiting transfer to a state or federal prison, pre-trial misdemeanants, and felony misdemeanants.

Maximum-security prison: A hardware secure facility or designated area of a prison where violent and dangerous inmates are confined to their cells for 23 hours per day.

Medium-security prison: A security classification of a correctional institution that houses inmates in a more relaxed security setting, often comprised of dormitory-style living quarters. The exterior conditions may be marked by a single or double security fence perimeter.

Minimum-security prison: A security classification for prison facilities that are more relaxed and comprised of non-secure dormitories, which are routinely patrolled by correctional officers.

Multi-security prison: A security classification of a correctional institution that houses inmates on the same grounds, but in the proper security environment whether it is minimum, medium, or maximum security.

Parole: The conditional release of an inmate from prison after they have served a portion of their imposed sentence.

Pre-Sentence Report/Investigation (PSR): A standardized and comprehensive document prepared before sentencing that contains summary information about the offender, which aids the court in making decisions about the offender's sentence length and potential for community placement.

Prison: A facility that houses individuals, who are charged with a felony crime, serving more than one year.

Prison work camp: Minimum-security facilities for nonviolent, low-risk offenders that offer community work and treatment programs in an effort to prepare inmates for reentry into society.

Probation: A form of punishment where the convicted offender remains in the community under supervision of a probation officer.

Pseudo-families: Kinship groups that are often formed in female facilities.

Recidivism: The act of reengaging in criminal offending after one has been released from state custody. This includes being rearrested, reconvicted, or returned to custody within a specific period for an additional offense.

Regional jail: A multi-county effort where inmates are housed on a per diem basis.

Rehabilitation: A correctional philosophy that assumes that criminal behavior is influenced by factors such as poverty, drug/alcohol abuse, discrimination, or psychological problems, and treatment is needed in order to reduce future offending.

Reintegration: A correctional philosophy that refers to providing inmates with important education, vocational, and society skills prior to release so that they will be able to reenter society successfully.

Residential Substance Abuse Treatment (RSAT): A specialized program that houses inmates in a separate part of the prison in order to receive intensive substance abuse counseling and random drug screenings. The ultimate goal of these programs is to take a comprehensive approach in addressing the inmate's substance abuse issues in context with their cognitive, behavioral, social, and vocational skills so that they will be able to succeed upon reentry to society.

Restorative justice: A philosophy and practice where the victim, offender, and community work together to address and repair the harms caused by a crime.

Work release/community corrections center: A community correctional facility that houses non-violent offenders, provides programming and a therapeutic living environment, and often requires steady employment to support inmates as they transition back to society.

Select Internet Sources

American Correctional Association: http://www.aca.org/.

Federal Bureau of Prisons: http://www.bop.gov/.

West Virginia Correctional Industries: http://wvcorrectionalindustries.com/.

West Virginia Division of Corrections: http://www.wvdoc.com/wvdoc/.

West Virginia Regional Jail and Correctional Facility Authority: http://www.rja.wv.gov/Pages/default.aspx.

Review and Critical Thinking Questions

1. Which prison philosophies guide correctional practice in the state? Why are they important and how are they related to each institution's mission statement?

2. What are the most common types of offenses among those who are committed in state prisons? How do they differ from jails?

3. What are intermediate sanctions? What types of intermediate sanctions exist in the state?

4. What is recidivism? What efforts has the state taken to reduce recidivism? What other approaches do you think would be effective?

5. How are children impacted when a parent(s) is incarcerated? What are the benefits of prison nursery programs?

References

Association of State Correctional Administrators (ASCA). (2003, January/February). *Corrections directions, 19*(1), 1–13.

Barone, C. R., Goudy, S., & Fialkoff, D. (2009, February). Mock prison riot prepares corrections staff for potential incidents. *Corrections Today, 71*(1), 64–65.

Bauer-Leffler, S. C., & Haas, S. M. (2013, February). *West Virginia correctional population forecast 2012–2022: A study of the state's prison population.* Charleston, WV: Office of Research and Strategic Planning, Division of Justice and Community Services, Department of Military Affairs and Public Safety.

Cleckley, F. D., & Palmer, L. J. Jr. (1994). *Introduction to the West Virginia criminal justice system and its laws.* Dubuque, IA: Kendall Hunt Publishing Company.

Council of State Governments (CSG) Justice Center. (2013, January). *Justice reinvestment in WV: Analyses and policy options to reduce spending on corrections and reinvest in strategies to increase public safety.* New York: Author. Retrieved from https://csgjusticecenter.org/wp-content/uploads/2013/06/BJA.JR-West-Virginia_v5.pdf.

Death Penalty Information Center (DPIC). (2014). *West Virginia: General information.* Retrieved from http://www.deathpenaltyinfo.org/west-virginia-0.

DeBoer, H. (2012, March). *Prison nursery programs in other states.* Retrieved from http://www.cga.ct.gov/2012/rpt/2012-R-0157.htm.

Douglas, B. (2008). *Children of incarcerated parents.* Charleston, WV: West Virginia Division of Corrections: Office of Research & Planning. Retrieved from http://www.wvdoc.com/wvdoc/Portals/0/documents/children08.pdf.

Federal Bureau of Prisons (FBOP). *Inmate population report.* (n.d.) Retrieved from: http://www.bop.gov/about/statistics/population_statistics.jsp.

Giallombardo, R. (1986). *Society of women: A study of a women's prison.* Boston, MA: Allyn and Bacon.

Hessler, C. (2017, August). Sex offender supervision unit ending in WV. *The Herald Dispatch.* Retrieved from http://www.herald-dispatch.com/news/sex-offender-supervision-unit-ending-in-wv/article_c3b671a6-e81e-56da-9fd2-85c611cb28fa.html.

Kaeble, D., Glaze, L. Tsoutis, A., & Minton, T. (2016, January). *Correctional populations in the United States, 2014* (NCJ 249513). Washington, DC: United States Department of Justice, Bureau of Justice Statistics. Retrieved from https://www.bjs.gov/content/pub/pdf/cpus14.pdf.

Kring Villanueva, C., From, S. B., & Lerner, G. (2009, May). *Mothers, infants and imprisonment: A national look at prison nurseries and community-based alternatives.* New York: Women's Prison Association.

Martinson, R. (1974). What works? Questions and answers about prison reform. *The Public Interest, 35*, 22–54.

Messina, L. (2017, September). *West Virginia bolsters community corrections panel.* West Virginia Department of Military Affairs and Public Safety: Charleston, WV. Retrieved from http://dmaps.wv.gov/News-Announcements/Pages/WV-bolsters-Community-Corrections-panel.aspx.

Minton, T. D, & Zeng, Z. (2016, December). *Jail inmates in 2015* (NCJ 250394). Washington, DC: United States Department of Justice, Bureau of Justice Statistics. Retrieved from https://www.bjs.gov/content/pub/pdf/ji15.pdf.

Nohe, L. A. (2014, January/February). West Virginia's premier program for incarcerated mothers. *Corrections Today, 76*(1), 42–45.

Orsini, M. M., Haas, S. M., & Spence, D. H. (2015, September). *Predicting recidivism of offenders released from the West Virginia division of corrections: Validation of the level of service/case management inventory.* Charleston, WV: Office of Research and Strategic Planning, Criminal Justice Statistical Analysis Center. Retrieved from http://djcs.wv.gov/ORSP/SAC/Documents/JCEBP%20LSCMI%20Validation%20DOC%202015.pdf.

Rowland, M., & Watts, A. (2007, August). Washington state's effort to the generational impact on crime. *Corrections Today, 69*(4), 34–37, 42.

Siegel, L. J., & Bartollas, C. (2014). *Corrections today* (2nd ed.). Belmont, CA: Cengage Learning.

Smith Goshin, L., & Woods Byrne, M. (2009, April). Converging streams of opportunity for prison nursery programs in the United States. *Journal of Offender Rehabilitation, 48*, 271–295. doi: 10.1080/10509670902848972.

The Pew Center. (2011, April). *State of recidivism: The revolving door of America's prisons.* Washington, DC: The Pew Charitable Trusts. Retrieved from http://www.pewtrusts.org/uploadedFiles/wwwpewtrustsorg/Reports/sentencing_and_corrections/State_Recidivism_Revolving_Door_America_Prisons%20.pdf.

Western Regional DRC. (2018). *Welcome, philosophical foundation.* Retrieved from http://wrdrc.net/wayne/index.html.

West Virginia Division of Corrections (WVDOC). (2017a). *Parole services mission and duty.* Retrieved from http://www.wvdoc.com/wvdoc/ParoleServicesResources/ParoleServicesMissionandDuty/tabid/72/Default.aspx.

West Virginia Division of Corrections (WVDOC). (2017b). *West Virginia Division of Corrections, Annual report: FY 2017.* Charleston, WV: Office of Research and Planning. Retrieved from http://www.wvdoc.com/wvdoc/Portals/0/documents/2017-Annual-Report.pdf.

West Virginia Division of Corrections (WVDOC). (2017c, July). *West Virginia Division of Corrections, Recidivism ... inmates released in 2013.* Charleston, WV: Office of Research and Planning. Retrieved from http://www.wvdoc.com/wvdoc/Portals/0/documents/Recidivism2013.pdf.

West Virginia Regional Jail and Correctional Facility Authority (WVRJA & CFA). (2017). *Annual report FY 2017.* Retrieved from http://www.rja.wv.gov/Documents/Annual%20Reports%20and%20Meeting%20Minutes/RJA%20Annual%20Report%20FY%202013.pdf.

Legal References

Crain v. Bordenkircher, 176 W. Va. 338 (1986).

W. Va. Code §25-7-1 (2017).

W. Va. Code §31-20-27(a)(b) (2017).

W. Va. Code §62-12-6 (2017).

W. Va. Code §62-12-13 (2017).

W. Va. Code §62-12-26 (2017).

Chapter 7

The Juvenile Justice System

Group of buildings at Pruntytown. Courtesy of the West Virginia Archives.

The juvenile system in the state of West Virginia embodies the notion of treatment and rehabilitation while maintaining public safety, thereby recognizing the distinct differences between children and adults. Over the years, the system has not been impervious to change. Advancements have been made so that juveniles are ensured their rights and are provided with evidence-based programs and treatment. For instance, juvenile drug courts exist in at least one-third of the counties in the state, and the use of community-based alternatives such as juvenile day report centers have become even more widespread. While professionals and practitioners within the state have initiated most of the change, some change has been spurred by legal action. In 2012, the state was confronted with a lawsuit, prompting the transfer of the Industrial Home for Youth in Salem from the Division of Juvenile Services to the Division of Corrections, which now serves adult offenders instead (W. Va. Code §28-3-1). This legal action also was the catalyst for reclassifying some of the state's juvenile centers and served as a reminder that juveniles cannot be physically punished, deprived of physical exercise, nutritious food, educational services, or placed in solitary confinement (W. Va. Code §45-5-16(a)). Despite such challenges, the men and women who serve the juvenile population are passionate about their work and, without a doubt, seek to make a difference in the lives of young people who are often plagued by poverty, family discord, and substance abuse. Like other states, there are several avenues for juveniles to be diverted from the formal trappings of the system and to avoid the stigma that the label "delinquent" can provide. In brief, it is a system of "second chances."

The West Virginia Juvenile Court and Its Jurisdiction

Juvenile matters and jurisdiction in the state involve multiple institutions to ensure the fair and humane treatment of youth. Although there are many parties entrenched in juvenile matters, the administration of juvenile justice is carried out by two main entities of government in the State of West Virginia. First, the Judicial Services branch of the Supreme Court of Appeals oversees the courts as well as the Division of Probation Services, and second, the Division of Juvenile Services (DJS) is housed within the Department of Military Affairs and Public Safety. It is important to note that while there are cases that involve handling and processing juveniles in a "criminal" sense, there also are cases that require the assistance of the Department of Health and Human Resources (DHHR). That is, cases involving abused and/or neglected youth as well as status offenders are placed in DHHR custody.[1] Some emphasis is given to DHHR in this chapter, but more is addressed in Chapter 8.

In our nation, a great deal of the legacy of the juvenile court, and the juvenile system as a whole, is attributed to the Illinois Juvenile Court Act of 1899. It was here that the first separate court for juveniles was created. By 1917, all but three states had a court for juveniles (Hess, Orthmann, & Wright, 2013). The act marked a significant turning point in our country's history as it held that not only must a separate court be established for juveniles, but also that decisions must be made in the best interests of the child, among other directives.

Similar to other states in the country, West Virginia's juvenile system is predicated on the concept of ***parens patriae***, which is Latin for "father of his country" and has been inferred to mean that the state is the parent, or that the government

1. The differences between status offenders and juvenile delinquents is not always black and white. There are many cases when a juvenile delinquent will be placed in a residential facility under DHHR custody in the event that such a placement is in the best interests of the child and is the least restrictive alternative.

Figure 7.1. The West Virginia State Code: Child Welfare

§49-1-1. Purpose.
(a) The purpose of this chapter is to provide a coordinated system of child welfare and juvenile justice for the children of this state that has goals to:

(1) Assure each child care, safety and guidance;
(2) Serve the mental and physical welfare of the child;
(3) Preserve and strengthen the child's family ties;
(4) Recognize the fundamental rights of children and parents;
(5) Adopt procedures and establish programs that are family-focused rather than focused on specific family members, except where the best interests of the child or the safety of the community are at risk;
(6) Involve the child and his or her family or caregiver in the planning and delivery of programs and services;
(7) Provide services that are community-based, in the least restrictive settings that are consonant with the needs and potentials of the child and his or her family;
(8) Provide for early identification of the problems of children and their families, and respond appropriately with measures and services to prevent abuse and neglect or delinquency;
(9) Provide a system for the rehabilitation of status offenders and juvenile delinquents;
(10) Provide a system for the secure detention of certain juveniles alleged or adjudicated delinquent;
(11) Provide a system for the secure incarceration of juveniles adjudicated delinquent and committed to the custody of the director of the division of juvenile services; and
(12) Protect the welfare of the general public.

is the ultimate guardian, especially for children (Whitehead & Lab, 2013). As can be seen in Figure 7.1, Article 1 §49-1-1 of the West Virginia Code stipulates the importance of creating a child welfare and juvenile justice system that takes into consideration a youth's safety, mental and physical welfare, as well as a family and community-centered approach to resolve juvenile concerns. The language used here is a great departure from what is specified in the criminal code as it pertains to adults.

In the state system, a juvenile or child is defined as:

> any person under eighteen years of age. Once a juvenile or child is transferred to a court with criminal jurisdiction pursuant to section ten, article five of this chapter, he or she nevertheless remains a juvenile or child for the purposes of the applicability of the provisions of this chapter with the exception of sections one through seventeen of article five of this chapter, unless otherwise stated therein (W. Va. Code §49-1-2).

While there is no specified lower age of jurisdiction, the upper age of jurisdiction in juvenile delinquency cases in the state is 17 as stated above. This is a common upper age limit for most states. However, delinquent youth up to age 21 can be monitored. That is, the courts have the power to extend jurisdiction by providing what is in the best interest of the child in terms of either sanctions and/or services beyond the upper age limit. Additional exceptions are made in cases that involve juveniles who have been adjudicated for truancy. In such cases, jurisdiction may extend to the age of 21 or the case will be deemed complete should the juvenile graduate from high school (West Virginia Judiciary, 2016).

Delinquency proceedings are handled throughout the state by the West Virginia magistrate courts and the 31 judicial circuit courts (Chapman, Blevins, Jones, & Walsh, 2016). However, it is important to note that the West Virginia Code §49-5-2 describes explicitly how juvenile cases are handled by the circuit court as this is deemed the court of original jurisdiction. Magistrate courts have what is called ***concurrent juvenile court jurisdiction.*** This means that magistrate courts are afforded some powers to sanction juveniles, but only for the violation of municipal offenses, such as public intoxication, possession of alcohol or tobacco, or a misdemeanor traffic violation. In other situations involving juveniles, the magistrate has the authority to place the youth on an improvement period or dismiss the charges, if necessary. However, "magistrate courts have no jurisdiction to impose a sentence of incarceration for the violation of these laws" (W. Va. Code §49-5-2). In other words, the magistrate cannot adjudicate a juvenile (i.e., find the youth "guilty" of the charge).

Juvenile Delinquents and Status Offenders

One of the most important distinctions in discussing the juvenile justice system is the difference between status offenders and juvenile delinquents. As stated in the West Virginia Code, a ***juvenile delinquent*** refers to "a juvenile who has been adjudicated as one who commits an act which would be a crime under state law or a municipal ordinance if committed by an adult" (W. Va. Code §49-1-4). In contrast, the state defines a ***status offender*** in Article II of Chapter 49, as "a person found to have committed an offense that would not be a criminal offense if committed by an adult." In terms of the latter, it is important to note that once a status offender has been taken into custody, the Department of Health and Human Resources must be notified. Because a status offender has not committed an adult crime per se, every effort is made to keep the youth out of placement. However, should pre-adjudicatory placement be warranted, according to state law, the status offender can only be detained if "(A) circumstances present an immediate threat of serious bodily harm to the juvenile if released" or if "(B) no responsible adult can be found into whose custody the juvenile can be delivered" (W. Va. Code §49-5-8), but only in a "nonsecure or staff-secure facility." The only other exception that may arise are those youth who fall under the jurisdiction of the Interstate Compact for Juveniles *(W. Va. Code* §49-7-301).

Like other states, a juvenile can be adjudicated for a few status offenses. These include incorrigibility, truancy, running away, and underage offenses such as smoking or drinking underage. The West Virginia Code defines ***incorrigibility*** as an adjudicated status offender "who habitually and continually refuses to respond to the lawful supervision by his or her parents, guardian or legal custodian such that the child's behavior substantially endangers the health, safety or welfare of the juvenile or any other person" (W. Va. Code §49-1-4(15)(A)). Adjudicated status offenders who have committed ***truancy*** are deemed to be "habitually absent from school without good cause" (W. Va. Code §49-1-4(15)(C)), and an adjudicated status offender deemed a ***runaway*** signals that the juvenile is one "who has left the care of his or her parents, guardian or custodian without the consent of such person or without good cause" (W. Va. Code §49-1-4(15)(B)). Offenses such as smoking tobacco while underage and the consumption of alcohol underage are self-explanatory.

In order to place these offenses into context, it is helpful to examine some of the national and state-level data. According to the most recent annual report, there were a total of 7,828 cases filed with the circuit courts (Chapman et al., 2016). Of these, there were 1,817 juvenile delinquency cases filed, and 1,302 status offense cases filed, while the remaining 4,709 cases involved abuse and neglect. To put this in perspective, the United States as a whole processes close to one million delinquency cases each year (Hockenberry & Puzzanchera, 2017).

Regarding status offenses, public state data is limited, but in 2009 most minors were charged with truancy (46.9%), followed by incorrigibility (32.3%) (Supreme Court of Appeals of West Virginia, 2009). There were fewer charged with running away (7.2%), and consumption/possession of alcohol or tobacco (9.6%). The remaining number of charges was attributed to a probation violation (2.7%) or violation of an improvement period (1.3%). Given the large percentage of truants, the state made concerted efforts to increase the penalties for truancy in 2010. Instead of 10 unexcused absences, youth who had five unexcused absences for the school year went before a magistrate and faced time in detention (Gately, 2015). The American Civil Liberties Union of West Virginia challenged these efforts, citing that bringing a youth into the juvenile justice system for the status offense of truancy invited collateral consequences that would potentially lead a youth to crime into adulthood. The state returned to 10 unexcused absences in 2015 and uses alternatives such as youth reporting centers or home visits instead of placement in juvenile detention.

Again, current data is not available, but according to data from 2009, most delinquent offenses involved property crimes (29.8%), assault/battery (22%), and substance/drug offenses (12.4%) (Supreme Court of Appeals of West Virginia, 2009). Only .02% of the cases involved a homicide charge or kidnapping. Delinquent youth also committed offenses such as burglary/robbery (7.1%), followed by obstructing justice (6%), which means that the youth may have fled from an officer, provided false information, resisted arrest, etc. Traffic offenses accounted for 4.1% of all delinquency charges, and arson accounted for 3.5% of all delinquency charges. Last, there were 130 delinquents charged with sex offenses (2.5% of all charges).

The Juvenile Court System and Process

Taking a Juvenile into Custody

As most know, the first point of contact typically involves law enforcement. Clearly, police officers have a great deal of discretion when dealing with juveniles, especially since many of them involve minor offenses. Recalling that the system is one of "second chances," a number of youth who come into contact with law enforcement are returned to a parent or guardian's custody with or without a warning (Hess et al., 2013). Nonetheless, in matters that are more serious or when the child is known to be harmful to him/herself or others, the police officer can take the child into custody.

To some, the phrase "***taken into custody***" is equivalent to an arrest in the criminal or adult system. According to the West Virginia Code §49-5-8(a), a juvenile may be taken into custody prior to adjudication when a petition has been filed and if there is probable cause in the event that one of the following situations is presented:

> (1) The petition shows that grounds exist for the arrest of an adult in identical circumstances; (2) the health, safety and welfare of the juvenile demand such custody; (3) the juvenile is a fugitive from a lawful custody or commitment order of a juvenile court; or (4) the juvenile is alleged to be a juvenile delinquent with a record of willful failure to

appear at juvenile proceedings and custody is necessary to assure his or her presence before the court (W. Va. Code §49-5-8(a)).

Without a court order, police officers are only subject to taking a juvenile into custody if the youth has committed an offense similar to that of an adult, if the juvenile is a danger to him- or herself or others, if the juvenile is found to have fled the custody of the state or is a fugitive, if it is reasonably suspected that the juvenile was drinking and driving, or if "the juvenile is the named respondent in an emergency protective order" (W. Va. Code §49-5-8(b)(6)).

Petitions

A juvenile case is handled by the court when a juvenile ***petition*** is filed alleging that the person is a juvenile delinquent or status offender (W. Va. Code §49-4-704(a)(1)). In some counties, juvenile matters are started by filing what is known as an informal complaint instead. In this case, a juvenile probation officer, magistrate, or prosecutor may serve as an intake officer to decide the best course of action. Upon reviewing the complaint, the intake officer may decide to divert the case or file a formal petition. Or, in some jurisdictions, the intake officer may place the juvenile on what is known as an improvement plan, which is described later.

Unlike the adult criminal system, the juvenile system is known for its mechanisms and processes to divert youth away from the formal trappings of the system. This is evident with the West Virginia juvenile justice system, as it affords certain juveniles what is known as a prepetition diversion agreement (W. Va. Code §49-4-702). This occurs when a case is brought to a prosecuting attorney, and it is commonly used for cases that involve status offenses and nonviolent delinquent offenses where a misdemeanor crime has been committed. A courtroom workgroup consisting of caseworkers, a probation officer, and a truancy diversion specialist (if necessary) are brought together to determine the diversion agreement conditions. With consent of the juvenile and the parent or guardian, the agreement is initiated (W. Va. Code §49-4-702(d)(1)). If the conditions are followed successfully, no petition is subsequently filed. Should the juvenile's parents or guardians deny the diversion agreement conditions, a petition could be issued to start the formal legal process (W. Va. Code §49-4-702(d)(4) (West Virginia Judiciary, 2016).

The Detention Hearing

Even though the system for juveniles is separate and distinct from the adult system, a youth who is taken into custody is granted many of the same constitutional rights as adults. Thus, if holding the youth is necessary, a detention hearing must occur within 24 hours. As stipulated in the code, a judge, juvenile referee, or magistrate is authorized to preside over the hearing (W. Va. Code §49-5-8). As of now and in practice, magistrates are used in this capacity as there are no juvenile referees in the state. Unlike the adult system, this process also involves notifying the child's parent(s) or legal guardian. If a parent/guardian cannot be reached, efforts are made to notify a kinship relative. At the hearing, the juvenile is informed of his/her rights, can choose counsel, or have counsel appointed to them, if needed. Ultimately, the main purpose of the hearing is to determine whether detention is required prior to court.

One of the outcomes of the detention hearing is to release the youth back to the parent/guardian or relative, whereas other youth may be detained if they are a threat to themselves or others. The latter refers to a concept known as ***pretrial*** or ***preventive detention*** (see *Shall v. Martin*, 1984). Moreover, additional possible outcomes of the detention hearing are to detain the youth if they have committed a delinquent offense in which being placed in a secure facility is warranted, or to detain the youth if there is no adult to be found to be responsible for the youth. In cases involving a status offender, DHHR is notified immediately, and the youth is placed in their custody. The only exception for status offenders to be placed in a nonsecure or staff secure facility is when the juvenile poses a risk to himself/herself or others, or if no suitable guardian can be found (W. Va. Code §49-4-706(a)(3)).

The Preliminary Hearing

Preliminary hearings are held within 10 days from the time the juvenile is placed in detention. Sometimes these hearings are held at the same time as the detention hearing. At this stage, too, the Circuit Court judge will ensure that the juvenile is represented by counsel or appointed counsel. However, the main objective is to examine the facts of the petition in order to determine if there was probable cause that the youth committed a delinquent act or status offense. There are additional outcomes possible here. First, if probable cause is found, the case is moved to circuit court and an adjudication hearing will take place. Then, a decision is made whether to release the youth to a parent/guardian or to detain the youth prior to their court hearing. The code stipulates that if the child is to be detained, his/her stay cannot exceed 30 days unless a continuance is granted or in the event of a jury trial. Second, if it is in the best interest of the child, the magistrate may place the youth on an ***improvement period*** (W. Va. Code §49-5-9). An improvement period entails a set of specified conditions (overseen by a probation officer) that must be met by the juvenile, not to exceed one year. If the juvenile meets these conditions, the facts stated in the petition are dismissed. Conversely, if the juvenile fails to meet these conditions, the case proceeds to an adjudication hearing. It is important to note that the improvement period is commonly used in juvenile proceedings in tandem with the probation office. Again, efforts are made to divert the youth from the formal system as much as possible given their lack of maturity and dependent status, and with the assumption that a juvenile's behavior is more malleable. Last, the preliminary hearing is where the juvenile is informed that they have a right to a jury trial[2] (W. Va. Code §49-5-9). In practice, however, this is not a common occurrence. Bench trials, where the judge presides over the case, versus a jury, is a more likely possibility, but still, even these are rare.

The Adjudication Hearing

Like many states, the adjudication and disposition stages involve separate hearings or bifurcated hearings. ***Adjudication*** is the trial stage of juvenile court proceedings, and essentially, it means that the juvenile will be judged or convicted of the offense (Hess et al., 2013). The adjudication hearing or trial involves determining whether the allegations of the petition are supported by evidence beyond a reasonable doubt (W. Va. Code §49-5-11). It is here that the juvenile (called the petitioner instead of a defendant) admits or denies the charges.

There are several outcomes at the adjudication stage. First, the judge may decide that there is insufficient evidence to allege that the youth is a delinquent or status offender. Second, the judge may conclude that the allegations of the petition are true and that the youth requires supervision. Last, the judge may dismiss the case because of a lack of sufficient or faulty evidence. Nonetheless, if the allegations stated in the petition are found to be to be true, meaning that the youth is adjudicated a delinquent or status offender, a date is set for a disposition hearing. Again, in practice, the disposition hearing may occur immediately after the adjudication hearing in order to expedite the case. Nonetheless, this involves the judge ordering the probation officer to compile a predisposition report, nearly identical to the pre-sentence report described in Chapter 6 with adults.

---

2. Status offenders do not have the right to a jury trial (W. Va. Code §49-4-709(b); West Virginia Judiciary, 2016).

The Disposition Hearing

If the juvenile has been adjudicated or formally charged, a disposition hearing will take place. Again, the term ***disposition***[3] refers to the process of determining the appropriate sanction or sentence for the youth, which takes into consideration both the best interests of the child and the general safety and welfare of the public (W. Va. Code §49-5-13). At this time, a number of individuals may be present in the court such as a social worker, probation officer, parent/guardian, as well as the defense counsel and prosecutor.

As stated earlier, the role of the probation officer is an important one (W. Va. Code §49-5-15). The pre-disposition report contains information that is gathered about the youth's psychological and medical condition, family status, and a recommendation of the appropriate sanction (W. Va. Code §49-5-13). In addition, more exclusive details and information related to the youth's performance and behavior in school, as opposed to their employment status, is included. This document is critical in assisting the judge in making decisions about what disposition is best for the adjudicated youth. In most cases, with reliable and accurate assessments from the probation officer, the judge will base their disposition on this recommendation. Keeping the juvenile's rights in mind, it is at this stage that the juvenile also is given the right to appeal.

Similar to other states, there are several possible dispositions contingent on whether the juvenile was charged with a delinquent or status offense, and the types of resources that exist within the county or jurisdiction, among other factors. A few possible options of the disposition hearing include: (1) dismissing the petition, (2) placing the youth in the parent's or guardian's custody, (3) placing the youth on probation, (4) committing the juvenile to the custody of the Division of Juvenile Services, which entails placing the youth in a juvenile center for treatment, school instruction, and 24-hour supervision, and (5) placing the youth in a mental health facility given their treatment needs (W. Va. Code §49-5-13).

In West Virginia, current information about youth dispositions has not been made publicly available for a few years. As of the latest report, published in 2009, the most common disposition for delinquent offenders was probation, followed by dismissal of the case, placement in DHHR custody and probation, or an improvement period (Supreme Court of Appeals of West Virginia, 2009). Among status offenders, the most common disposition was a referral to DHHR,

---

3. Prior to disposition, the court may order that the youth receive a specialized risk and needs assessment (W. Va. Code §49-4-724) and/or be required to fulfill a diagnostic examination at a secure juvenile diagnostic center (W. Va. Code §49-2-907(a)).

followed by probation, an improvement period, and placement in DHHR custody. Home confinement, placement in DJS custody, community service, and fines were used as well but less frequently, according to the 2009 report. However, since the 2009 report, it is important to recognize that changes have been made to managing status offenders and the state has moved away from placing status offenders in detention and in DJS custody.

Juvenile Specialty Courts

Juvenile Drug Court

With the unprecedented increase in the number of drug-related offenses in the 1980s and its impact on the court system, alternative strategies were needed to address the complexity of drug crime and addiction among both adult and juvenile populations. According to the National Institute of Justice (2017), there are more than 3,100 drug courts in the country, and about half of these were for juveniles. In West Virginia, the juvenile drug court movement began in Cabell County in 1999. The impetus was an examination of court data revealing that drug violations accounted for the third most common offense among juveniles (West Virginia Judiciary, 2017). The pilot project in Cabell County was funded in part by the U.S. Department of Justice as well as U.S. Substance Abuse and Mental Health Service Administration grant funding. Wayne County's juvenile drug court became operational in 2007, followed by Logan and Mercer Counties in 2009. Today, there are 14 juvenile drug courts in the state that serve 19 counties. Most of the drug court participants are enrolled in the program for approximately 8.5 months.

Essentially, the juvenile drug court is both a diversion program and a program based on intensive supervision probation. To qualify for the program, the juvenile must be 10 to 17 years of age with no prior sex offense charges, have a clinical assessment that demonstrates a history of substance abuse and dependency, and have committed a nonviolent felony or misdemeanor offense. More specifically, youth cannot participate in drug court if they committed an offense that involved the use of a firearm or deadly weapon or caused bodily injury to a person(s) that warranted medical attention. The juvenile drug court involves a "team" of individuals, which is often comprised of the judge, a case coordinator, prosecutor, defense attorney, probation officer, a member from law enforcement, a DHHR representative, a member of the school board, and a treatment specialist. The program hinges on three rigorous phases involving strict probation supervision, random drug screenings, treatment, and counseling. Comparable to a restorative justice approach, juvenile offenders are encouraged to take ownership of their actions and behaviors (i.e., accountability). By completing these three phases successfully, the juvenile will reach the final phase, which is graduation. Since the inception of drug courts in the state, results have been positive. National research also has shown a reduction in recidivism rates among juvenile drug court participants (Stein, Deberard, & Homan, 2013).

Teen Court

According to the West Virginia Teen Court Association (n.d.), about 10 counties in the state employ a teen court program and several more are under development. The program mainly serves status offenders, youth who have violated a municipal ordinance, or youth who have committed a delinquent act that would be classified as a misdemeanor if committed by an adult (W. Va. Code §49-5-13(d). In turn, youth opt for the teen court program in lieu of a formal petition being filed. Teen court participants are given a copy of the procedures and agree to community service, as well as any fines that may be applied.

The West Virginia Code outlines the protocol for teen courts as follows:

> (1) The judge for each teen court proceeding shall be an acting or retired circuit court judge or an active member of the West Virginia State Bar, who serves on a voluntary basis.
> (2) Any juvenile who selects the teen court program as an alternative disposition shall agree to serve thereafter on at least two occasions as a teen court juror.
> (3) Volunteer students from grades seven through twelve of the schools within the county shall be selected to serve as defense attorney, prosecuting attorney, court clerk, bailiff and jurors for each proceeding.
> (4) Disposition in a teen court proceeding shall consist of requiring the juvenile to perform sixteen to forty hours of community service, the duration and type of which shall be determined by the teen court jury from a standard list of available community service programs provided by the county juvenile probation system and a standard list of alternative consequences that are consistent with the purposes of this article. The performance of the juvenile shall be monitored by the county juvenile probation system for cases originating in the circuit court's jurisdiction, or municipal teen court coordinator or other designee for cases originating in the municipal court's

jurisdiction. The juvenile shall also perform at least two sessions of teen court jury service and, if considered appropriate by the circuit court judge or teen court judge, participate in an education program. Nothing in this section may be construed so as to deny availability of the services provided under section eleven-a of this article to juveniles who are otherwise eligible for such service (W. Va. Code §49-5-13(d)(b).

Confidentiality Rights of Juveniles

It is quite commonly known that juvenile proceedings and records are kept confidential and closed to the public or the press. These details are expressed in §49-5-18 and §49-5-101 of the West Virginia Code. The law stipulates that a juvenile's file and records, one year beyond their 18th birthday or after they are no longer in custody, should be kept in a secure and confidential location, and that those who wish to access the files must have an order from the circuit court. It is through this process of marking the records as confidential that, in essence, the youth's records have been sealed. Moreover, if the juvenile's case is transferred to adult or criminal court, these same conditions generally apply.

The Division of Juvenile Services

In October 1996, the state held a Summit on Juvenile Justice where recommendations were provided regarding juvenile detention, prevention, intervention, and training. The outcome of the summit was the creation of the Division of Juvenile Services (DJS), under the authority of the Department of Military Affairs and Public Safety (House bill 2680) in 1997. Prior to this, five juvenile detention facilities were under DHHR and the two juvenile prisons were under the WVDOC. This was certainly a step in the right direction, as juvenile delinquents are a special population, who require different standards of care in the eyes of the law. Today, the mission of DJS reads that they are: "committed to providing effective, beneficial services to youth in the Juvenile Justice System that promote positive development and accountability, while preserving community safety, and sustaining a work environment predicated upon principles of professionalism, with dignity and respect for all" (WVDJS, 2017, p. 6).

In 2012 and as stated in the beginning of this chapter, a dark shadow was cast on the Division of Juvenile Services after the filing of the lawsuit, *State of West Virginia ex rel. D.L. and K.P. v. Dale Humphreys, Division of Juvenile Services, et al.* (West Virginia Supreme Court of Appeals, 2013). Efforts were being made by the Adjudicated Juvenile Rehabilitation Review Commission, which was formed in 2011 by Justice Margaret Workman to examine and assess all operating procedures and programs at the Industrial Home for Youth and the Kenneth "Honey" Rubenstein Center. With the lawsuit and additional legal concerns mounting, the review was extended to include all DJS facilities. This was carried out by appointing Juvenile Justice Monitors to examine each facility, to serve as an advocate for juvenile rights, and as a liaison between the courts and DJS. Upon review of the juvenile court system, as well as the operations, treatment programs, and compliance of polices in each juvenile facility, etc., further corrective and legislative action was deemed necessary. As a result, the Industrial Home was renamed the Salem Correctional Center to house adult offenders, and the juveniles were relocated to different facilities (W. Va. Code §28-3-1). Eight out of the 10 DJS juvenile centers (see Table 7.1) were reclassified and had to change their mission based on the type of youth that they now must serve. Although the impact of these drastic changes are still being felt, and with the reputation of juvenile services tarnished, many would agree that the system is better off adopting a unified and comprehensive approach that involves all branches of government to ensure that juvenile services in the State of West Virginia continue to be progressive and humane.

Juvenile Detention and Diagnostic Centers

Currently, the state has 10 residential juvenile centers as shown in Table 7.1. Nine of the centers are operated by DJS, while one facility, the Ronald C. Mulholland Juvenile Center (formerly the Northern Regional Juvenile Detention Center) is under private contract. The largest facility, the Kenneth "Honey" Rubenstein Juvenile Center, is designated as a minimum-security facility that houses up to 70 males. The center is known for its Leadership Academy, which provides youth called "cadets" with a paramilitary (i.e., boot camp) and rehabilitative setting. Seven of the facilities in the state are ***hardware secure*** (see Table 7.1). As a residential facility, this means that juveniles are monitored in their movement and activity throughout the facility. Plus, it "limits its residents' access to the surrounding community, but is not characterized by construction fixtures designed to physically restrict the movements and activities of residents" (W.Va. §49-1-4(13)). The J.M. "Tiger" Morton Juvenile Center has both a hardware secure and a staff secure section, and the Robert L. Shell Juvenile

Table 7.1. West Virginia Juvenile Facilities

Juvenile Center	County/Description	Custody Level/Security	Gender	Capacity
Kenneth "Honey" Rubenstein Juvenile Center	Tucker County; Houses a Leadership Academy, based on a military style program where cadets have five phases to complete. Houses non-violent youthful offenders.	Minimum secure	Male	70
Gene Spadaro Juvenile Center	Fayette County; Houses males (ages 10–21) and high-risk females (ages 12–21), who have misdemeanor or felony charges.	Hardware secure	Males and females	23
Robert L. Shell Juvenile Center	Cabell County; Contains the Diagnostic and Intake/Assessment Center for the entire state; Consists of 13 beds for diagnostics, 5 beds for intake, and 5 beds for youth awaiting transfer to other DJS facilities.	Staff secure	Males and females	23
Donald R. Kuhn Juvenile Center	Boone County; Houses high-risk males (ages 10–21) and high-risk females (ages 12–21).	Hardware secure	Male	48
James H. "Tiger" Morton Juvenile Center	Kanawha County; Part of the center includes a hardware secure facility and a wellness unit.	Staff and hardware secure	Males and females	23
J. M. "Chick" Buckbee Juvenile Center	Hampshire County; Houses medium-risk juveniles for commitment or detention purposes.	Hardware secure	Male	24
Lorrie Yeager Jr. Juvenile Center	Wood County; Houses male and female juvenile delinquents.	Hardware secure	Males and females	24

Center is a ***staff secure*** and diagnostic/intake facility. One notable distinction is that a staff secure center does not have cell doors with locking mechanisms.

Table 7.1. *Continued*

Juvenile Center	County/Description	Custody Level/Security	Gender	Capacity
Northern Regional Juvenile Center	Ohio County; Private/ contracted facility operated by Youth Services System, Inc.; consists of a co-ed juvenile detention facility (14 beds) and Treatment Center (12 beds) for female offenders only	Hardware secure	Males and females	19
Sam Perdue Juvenile Center	Mercer County; Houses the Gateway Treatment Program for adjudicated juvenile sex offenders.	Hardware secure	Males	20
Vicki V. Douglas Juvenile Center	Berkley and Jefferson County; Houses pre-adjudicated male and female youth, ages 10–21.	Hardware secure	Males and females	23

Note: Information for this table was found using the West Virginia Division of Juvenile Services website and from the Division of Justice Services. (2017). *Division of juvenile services annual report for fiscal year 2016*. Retrieved from http://djs.wv.gov/annualreport/Documents/Annual%20Report%202016.pdf.

Also, the Shell Juvenile Center is unique in that it contains a diagnostic program (see Table 7.1). Youth who are court-ordered receive a medical exam, educational assessment, IQ testing, personality test, substance abuse screening, and an overall assessment by administering the Youth LS/CMI. All of the youth placed there are adjudicated delinquents, in the custody of DJS, and undergo a 30-day assessment with an average stay of 45 to 50 days. Upon completion of the assessment, referrals are made to assist the youth with additional placements or services based on their needs.

In 2016, juvenile delinquents in residential facilities could be characterized as primarily male (75%) versus female (25.8%) as well as predominantly white, non-Hispanic (77.4%) (WVDJS, 2017). In comparison to state data, a disproportionate number of youth in residential facilities as a whole were African American (12%). Very few were classified by race as Asian/Pacific Islander (0.5%) or American Indian (0.4%). Around half (50.2%) were 17–18 years of age and around 41.2% were 13–16 years of age. Among those who were received at residential intake in 2016, 32.3% were charged with a crime against a person, while 18% were charged with a property crime, and 27.3% were

Robert L. Shell Juvenile Center.
Courtesy of the Robert L. Shell Juvenile Center.

charged with a court recruitment violation (27.3%). Kanawha County had the most residential intakes in the state (14.4%), followed by Cabell County (11.9%), and Berkley County (7%). Upon being discharged from the facility, most juveniles (50.4%) return home and approximately a third (32.9%) enter a DHHR placement.

Youth Reporting Centers

One important aspect of the juvenile system is to reduce stigma and to keep young people integrated into the community. Juvenile Day Report Centers (referred to as Youth Reporting Centers) are an alternative to detention, treatment oriented, and cost effective. In West Virginia, there are a total of 13 Youth Reporting Centers (YRC) spanning 15 counties (WVDJS, 2017). To be eligible for YRC, the youth must be between the ages of 12 and 18, and be ordered to the program by a circuit court judge, referred by a magistrate or, oftentimes, a juvenile probation officer (WVDJS, 2018). These youth could be fulfilling the conditions for an improvement period, the conditions for probation, conditions based on their concurrent participation in the juvenile drug court program, or a prepetition diversion condition. Largely, youth who attend day report are either classified as pre-adjudicated, adjudicated, or a status offender. The program operates daily, and youth are expected to check in and attend support group counseling, plus individual counseling. Educational support of the youth are met with tutoring and homework supervision. Youth are also administered the Juvenile Automated Substance Abuse Evaluation (JASAE), the Youth Level of Service/Case Management Inventory (YLS/CMI), and a psychological assessment to determine treatment needs. Given the individual needs of the youth, a variety of programs are provided that may cover anger management, life skills, substance abuse and education, in addition to programs that address school bullying and violence prevention. Last, youth reporting centers provide transportation to and from the youth's home, which ensures program attendance and supervision.

In 2016, these nonresidential facilities served primarily white (83%) and male (64%) youth (WVDJS, 2017). A little over half of youth were ages 13–16 (53%), followed by those ages 17–18 (43%). Primarily, youth in day report centers as a whole were charged with a status offense (37.2%), a crime against a person (16.7%), a drug/alcohol crime (15.1%), or a crime against property (14.1%). Some of the centers with the most successful rates of program completion included: Harrison County YRC (71% completion rate), Putnam County YRC (66% completion rate), and Mason County YRC (58% completion rate).

Non-Secure Residential Programs

For troubled and wayward youth who have serious impairments, coupled with a history of status offenses (and a possible delinquent history), different options are available. Numerous non-secure residential programs exist throughout the state, many of which are nonprofit, but accredited and licensed. They also are referred to as group homes, as they are small, family-like facilities that provide intensive therapy, education, and job training. Many of these facilities are state licensed by DHHR. A few of these group homes from various parts of the state are described next.

The Youth Academy is a therapeutic residential program located in Fairmont, West Virginia, which serves youth from ages 12 to 17 (Youth Academy, 2018). Here, youth receive intensive treatment in a community and family-centered environment. The residents of this home may have clinical diagnoses such as ADHD, depression, conduct disorder, and oppositional defiance disorder, just to name a few. Similarly, the Cammack Children's Center is a therapeutic group home in Huntington, West Virginia, that houses youth who have been placed in DHHR custody (Cammack Children's Center, 2018). To qualify, youth must be in need of multidisciplinary treatment and be 12 to 17 years of age. Last, Falling Waters, located in Martinsburg, serves the youth population from ages 12 to 21 (Board of Child Care, 2017). However, they provide a more structured therapeutic living environment for as many as 50 youth who require behavioral and emotional treatment. Again, youth can only be admitted with a court order and they must be in the custody of DHHR.

There are also a number of emergency shelters in the state, which primarily house youth who are abused and neglected, but may also house status offenders and juvenile delinquents. For example, the Children's Home Society operates nine shelters in the state in the following cities: Charleston, Huntington, Lewisburg, Logan, Martinsburg, Norfolk, Parkersburg, Romney, and Summersville. These shelters are often actual houses/residences that typically hold a small number of youth (10–15) ranging in ages from 2 to 18. Emergency shelters provide a safe place where the youth can also receive the appropriate support and care while allowing DHHR staff the time to assess the needs of the youth and how best those needs can be met after shelter placement.

Spotlight: Waiver to Adult Court

The 1990s marked a significant period of concern and uncertainty for the juvenile system as young offenders who committed violent crimes gained more attention. With increasing pressure from the public, predictions of continued youth violence among researchers, and the influence of the media magnifying violent juvenile crimes, many were led to believe that our country was facing an epidemic of youth violence.

Naturally, the public policy response to the concerns raised about these violent young people was to enact statutes that would allow states to sanction youth at a certain age with an "adult" sentence and an "adult" punishment. While it may seem that there is a growing number of violent youth offenders given how they are portrayed by the media, research indicates that of the 974,900 delinquency cases brought to the courts nationwide in 2014, around 542,500 (56%) resulted in the filing of a formal petition (Hockenberry & Puzzanchera, 2017). Only 4,200 cases were transferred to criminal court.

West Virginia has the same type of legislation to waive or transfer certain felony juvenile cases to criminal court. *Waiver* refers to the process by which a juvenile over whom the juvenile court has original jurisdiction is transferred to adult court (Cox, Allen, Hanser, & Conrad, 2014). There are two types of waiver or transfer laws in the state-discretionary judicial waiver and mandatory waiver (West Virginia Judiciary, 2016). Regardless of the type of transfer requested, according to the West Virginia Code §49-4-710, the process begins with a transfer motion filed by the prosecuting attorney eight days before the adjudication hearing. Then, a waiver hearing is held within seven days to determine if the case is to be transferred to adult criminal court. Several conditions apply in order for the case to be waived to criminal court, but one of the most important is that there has to be probable cause. Clear and convincing evidence is a must in such cases.

Regarding a mandatory transfer, a hearing is held for the juvenile, who is at least 14 years old. The case is reviewed to determine if there was probable cause that the juvenile committed:

1. Treason, murder, armed robbery, kidnapping, first-degree arson or sexual assault in the first degree. W. Va. Code §49-4-710(d)(1);
2. An offense that would be a felony offense of violence against another person if the juvenile had been an adult, provided that the juvenile has a prior delinquency adjudication of a felony offense of violence against another person. W. Va. Code §49-4-710(d)(2); or
3. An offense that would be a felony offense if the juvenile had been an adult, and the juvenile has two prior delinquency adjudications for felony offenses. W. Va. Code §49-4-710(d)(3) (West Virginia Judiciary, 2016).

Discretionary transfer is possible should probable cause be established and in the event that the juvenile is under 14 years of age and committed:

1. Treason, murder, armed robbery, first-degree arson, kidnapping or first-degree sexual assault. W. Va. Code §49-4-710(e);
2. What would be for an adult a felony offense of violence against another person, and the juvenile has a prior delinquency adjudication for a felony offense of violence against another person, after considering personal factors of the juvenile, such as mental and physical condition or maturity. W. Va. Code §49-4-710(f); or
3. What would be for an adult a felony, and the juvenile has two prior delinquency adjudications for a felony, after a consideration of personal factors of the juvenile. W. Va. Code §49-4-710(f) (West Virginia Judiciary, 2016).

Other state provisions exist for a discretionary transfer in the event that probable cause has been established for a juvenile who is at least 14 years of age, who has committed a felony crime of violence involving another person, or any felony offense for which the youth had been adjudicated delinquent, or the youth used or presented a deadly weapon or firearm while committing a felony crime, or the youth committed second degree arson (West Virginia Judiciary, 2016).

Waiving juvenile cases to criminal court and sanctioning juveniles to adult time remains controversial and without a lot of promise as a deterrent. Since the 1980s, when most transfer laws were implemented, more research has been conducted in which a bigger picture has emerged. Namely, the desired effects of transfer policies are not quite evident. In fact, those youth who are transferred to adult court have higher conviction rates, higher rates of incarceration, and a higher rate of being victimized as most are placed in medium- to maximum-security adult facilities (Hess et al., 2013). Moreover, research indicates a modest deterrent effect; that is, youth sentenced as adults have higher rates of recidivism.

Key Terms and Definitions

Adjudication: The trial stage of juvenile court proceedings where the juvenile will be judged or convicted of the offense; the hearing or trial involves determining whether the allegations of the petition are supported by evidence beyond a reasonable doubt.

Concurrent juvenile court jurisdiction: The powers afforded to the magistrate court to preside over juvenile offenses that involve the violation of municipal offenses such as public intoxication or possession of alcohol or tobacco; this court cannot impose a sentence of incarceration. Additional powers are stipulated in the state code.

Disposition: The process of determining the appropriate sanction or sentence for a youth, which takes place during a disposition hearing.

Hardware secure: A juvenile residential facility where the residents' movement and activity is restricted throughout the facility but is not characterized by construction fixtures designed to physically restrict the movements and activities of residents.

Improvement period: A set of specified conditions that must be met by the juvenile, not to exceed one year.

Incorrigibility: A type of status offense that involves the habitual and continual refusal to respond to the lawful supervision by a parent, guardian, or legal custodian such that the behavior substantially endangers the health, safety, or welfare of the juvenile or any other person.

Juvenile delinquent: A juvenile who has been adjudicated as one who commits an act that would be a crime under state law or a municipal ordinance if committed by an adult.

Parens patriae: The "father of his country"; a term that indicates the state is the parent or that the government is the ultimate guardian, especially for children.

Petition: Filed charges alleging that the person is a juvenile delinquent or status offender.

Pretrial/Preventive detention: The concept that a youth may be detained if they are a threat to themselves or others in order to prevent additional offending.

Runaway: A type of status offense that involves leaving the care of parent, guardian, or custodian without the consent or without good cause.

Staff secure: A juvenile residential facility that typically houses low-level offenders and does not have cell doors with locking mechanisms.

Status offender: A person found to have committed an offense that would not be a criminal offense if committed by an adult.

Taken into custody: A term used in juvenile matters that is equivalent to making an arrest in the criminal or adult system.

Truancy: A type of status offense that involves habitual absence from school without good cause.

Waiver: The process by which a juvenile over whom the juvenile court has original jurisdiction is transferred to adult court.

Select Internet Sources

National Center for Juvenile Justice (NCJJ): http://www.ncjj.org/default.aspx.

Office of Juvenile Justice and Delinquency Prevention (OJJDP): http://www.ojjdp.gov/.

West Virginia Division of Juvenile Services: http://djs.wv.gov/Pages/default.aspx/.

Review and Critical Thinking Questions

1. How does the juvenile justice system differ from the adult system? Why?

2. What happens at each stage of the court process starting from when a youth is taken into custody?

3. What is the difference between a status offender and a juvenile delinquent? Why is this distinction necessary?

4. What types of dispositions exist? Which ones reduce stigma or are the most cost-effective?

5. What does the process for waiving a juvenile case to criminal court entail?

References

Board of Child Care. (2017). Retrieved from https://www.boardofchildcare.org/.

Cammack Children's Center. (2018). Retrieved from http://cammack.org/.

Chapman, C., Blevins, T., Jones, A., & Walsh, L. (2016). *The annual statistical report on circuit, family and magistrate courts: The West Virginia court system 2016 data.* Charleston, WV: Administrative Office of the Supreme Court of Appeals of West Virginia. Retrieved from http://www.courtswv.gov/public-resources/press/Publications/2016AnnualReportData.pdf.

Cox, S. M., Allen, J. M., Hanser, R. D., & Conrad, J. J. (2014). *Juvenile justice: A guide to theory, policy, and practice.* Thousand Oaks, CA: Sage.

Gately, G. (2015, April). *West Virginia eases strict truancy law.* Retrieved from http://jjie.org/2015/04/08/west-virginia-eases-strict-truancy-law/.

Hess, K. M., Orthmann, C. H., & Wright, J. P. (2013). *Juvenile justice* (6th ed.). Belmont, CA: Cengage Learning.

Hockenberry, S., & Puzzanchera, C. (2017, April). *Juvenile court statistics 2014.* Pittsburgh, PA: National Center for Juvenile Justice. Retrieved from https://www.ojjdp.gov/ojstatbb/njcda/pdf/jcs2014.pdf.

National Institute of Justice (NIJ). (2017). *Drug courts* (NCJ 238527). Washington, DC: U.S. Department of Justice, Office of Justice Programs. Retrieved from https://www.ncjrs.gov/pdffiles1/nij/238527.pdf.

Stein, D. M., Deberard, S., & Homan, K. (2013). Predicting success and failure in juvenile drug treatment court: A meta-analytic review. *Journal of Substance Abuse Treatment, 44*(2), 159–168. doi: 10.1016./j.jsat.2012.07.002 2013.

Supreme Court of Appeals of West Virginia. (2009). *Juvenile probation in West Virginia 2008–2009.* Retrieved from http://www.courtswv.gov/court-administration/probation/Juvenile-probation-report.pdf.

West Virginia Division of Juvenile Services (WVDJS). (2018). *Community based programs.* (2018). Retrieved from https://djs.wv.gov/departments/Pages/Community-Based-Programs.aspx.

West Virginia Division of Juvenile Services (WVDJS). (2017, January). *West Virginia Division of Juvenile Services annual report for fiscal year 2016.* Retrieved from http://djs.wv.gov/annualreport/Documents/Annual%20Report%202016.pdf.

West Virginia Judiciary. (2016, February). *West Virginia juvenile law and procedure.* Retrieved from http://www.courtswv.gov/public-resources/CAN/juvenile-law-procedure/juvenile-law-procedure.html.

West Virginia Judiciary. (2017). *Drug courts.* Retrieved from http://www.courtswv.gov/lower-courts/juvenile-drug/juvenile-drug-court.html.

West Virginia Supreme Court of Appeals. (2013). *Adjudicated juvenile rehabilitation review Commission: 2013 Annual Report.* Retrieved from http://www.courtswv.gov/court-administration/juvenlie-justice-commission/2013%20Juvenile%20Justice%20report.pdf.

West Virginia Teen Court Association. (n.d.). Retrieved from http://www.wvteencourtassociation.org/.

Whitehead, J. T., & Lab, S. T. (2013). *Juvenile justice: An introduction.* Waltham, MA: Anderson Publishing.

Youth Academy. (2018). *Youth academy program description.* Retrieved from http://academyprograms.org/youthAcademyProgramDescription.cfm.

Legal References

Schall v. Martin, 467 U.S. 253 (1984).

W. Va. Code §28-3-1 (2017).

W. Va. Code §45-5-16(a) (2017).

W. Va. Code §49-1-1 (2017).

W. Va. Code §49-1-2 (2017).

W. Va. Code §49-1-4 (2017).

W. Va. Code §49-1-4(13) (2017).

W. Va. Code §49-1-4(15)(A) (2017).

W. Va. Code §49-1-4(15)(B) (2017).

W. Va. Code §49-1-4(15)(C) (2017).

W. Va. Code §49-2-907(a) (2017).

W. Va. Code §49-4-702 (2017).

W. Va. Code §49-4-702(d)(1) (2017).

W. Va. Code §49-4-702(d)(4) (2017).

W. Va. Code §49-4-704(a)(1) (2017).

W. Va. Code §49-4-706(a)(3) (2017).

W. Va. Code §49-4-709(b) (2017).

W. Va. Code §49-4-710 (2017).

W. Va. Code §49-4-710(d)(1) (2017).

W. Va. Code §49-4-710(d)(2) (2017).

W. Va. Code §49-4-710(d)(3) (2017).

W. Va. Code §49-4-710(e) (2017).

W. Va. Code §49-4-710(f) (2017).

W. Va. Code §49-4-724 (2017).

W. Va. Code §49-5-2 (2017).

W. Va. Code §49-5-8 (2017).

W. Va. Code §49-5-8(a) (2017).
W. Va. Code §49-5-8(b)(6) (2017).
W. Va. Code §49-5-9 (2017).
W. Va. Code §49-5-11 (2017).
W. Va. Code §49-5-13 (2017).
W. Va. Code §49-5-13(d) (2017).
W. Va. Code §49-5-13(d)(b) (2017).
W. Va. Code §49-5-15 (2017).
W. Va. Code §45-5-16(a) (2017).
W. Va. Code §49-5-18 (2017).
W. Va. Code §49-5-101 (2017).
W. Va. Code §49-7-301 (2017).

Chapter 8

Victim Advocacy and Services

Jackson County courtroom. Courtesy of Silling Associates, Inc.

The study of the criminal justice system typically involves a widespread examination of law enforcement, courts, and corrections. Following this type of systems approach, it is not uncommon that discussions are often centered on the offender. Yet, for every crime committed, there is a victim. Crime victimization does not discriminate; victims can be male or female, young or old, fully abled or impaired. Many of them suffer in silence, not seeking help from the police or other social services, and many are plagued by years of grief, depression, and possibly serious financial losses.

West Virginia has many "pockets" of victims' services and programs and has many sections of the legal code devoted to expressing the rights of crime victims. For instance, victims are provided with the right to notice, the right to be present at criminal justice proceedings, hearings, or trials, the right to be heard, the right to protection, and the right to restitution, among others. However, while the state admirably speaks to the rights of victims, the problem is that these services are not centralized or unified. Another limitation is that a number of victim services and programs are not state funded, but instead operate as nonprofit agencies that depend on the support of grant funding and in some cases volunteers. Moreover, West Virginia is 1 of 14 states that does not include a set of victim's rights in the constitution (National Victims' Constitutional Amendment Passage, 2012). With that said, West Virginia is on track with the rest of the nation in that it has taken an integrative approach when combating domestic violence, intimate partner violence, and child abuse. While all types of victimization are acknowledged here, parts of this chapter will focus more exclusively on personal violence, domestic violence, sexual assault, and special populations of victims such as children and the elderly.

Victims' Rights

What is extraordinary is that more than 30 years ago, our federal and state systems had little in place to assist victims, and had made no national declarations of victims' rights. Even today, the U.S. Constitution does not contain an amendment outwardly addressing the rights of crime victims. Nationally, several important pieces of legislation fully establish and recognize the rights of victims. Also, since many victims of violent crimes are women, there are federal acts and programs that address violent crimes involving women more explicitly, as well as other special populations (i.e., mentally ill, immigrants, etc.).

One of the first significant pieces of crime victim legislation was the Victims of Crime Act (VOCA) of 1984 (42 U.S.C. § 10601) that was approved during the Reagan Administration. The act created federal- and state-assisted compensation funds for victims. Today, the federal program is housed in the Department of Justice. The national act outlined the mechanisms to establish resources where a portion of criminal fines would go into the fund (i.e., restitution to the victim) and a portion would go to the state's victims' assistance programs per the governor's discretion. Also included in this act were grant monies for providing states with funding to develop crime victim notification systems.

Ten years after VOCA, the second landmark piece of legislation in our country's history was the Violence Against Women Act (VAWA), which was part of the Violent Crime Control and Law Enforcement Act of 1994 (42 U.S.C. § 13701-14040). The act was sponsored by Senator Joe Biden and signed into law by President Bill Clinton (Seghetti & Bjelopera, 2012). This was unprecedented in that it was the first piece of legislation to recognize how women are disproportionately victims of violent crimes and to call openly for criminalizing violent acts against women. Jurisdictions across the country were encouraged to establish community-based and coordinated approaches to respond to domestic violence, sexual assault, and stalking. In addition, VAWA increased the penalties for chronic or repeat sex offenders and included a federal "rape shield law." The enforcement of protection orders, legal assistance for battered immigrants, and police training for cases involving elder abuse or abuse of the disabled were additional components of the statute. Like other federal legislation, grant funding was provided such as the STOP (Services, Training, Officers, Prosecutors) Program, among others. Last, a national domestic violence hotline was created.

Today, the impact of VAWA has been substantial and applauded. VAWA has strengthened efforts to prosecute crimes of rape, domestic assault, and stalking more effectively and to increase the penalties for these crimes. Since its initial enactment, VAWA has been reauthorized several times. More recently in 2013, albeit controversial among Republicans, the act extended protection to gays, lesbians, transgendered individuals, Native Americans, and immigrants. Another significant part of the reauthorization addressed combating human trafficking and protecting victims of trafficking. VAWA is scheduled to be reviewed for reauthorization by Congress in 2018.

Twenty years later, President George W. Bush signed the Crime Victims' Rights Act (CVRA) (18 U.S.C. §3771), which is part of the Justice for All Act that was passed by Congress in 2004. The main provisions of this legislation ensured that victims' rights are fully recognized and enforced in all federal criminal justice proceedings. While many of these same rights are explicitly stated in the VOCA, the CVRA paved the way for how victims are afforded the right to have a greater role in the justice process. In addition, the definition of "crime victim" further ensured that the rights of victims of financial crime were covered as well as victims of violent crime (Deem, Nerenberg, & Titus, 2013). Moreover, funding mechanisms were established to encourage states to comply with these provisions and actively promote victims' rights. As shown below, victims are guaranteed the right of protection, the right to be informed and heard, the right to restitution, and the right to be treated with respect and dignity. The rights of crime victims according to the CVRA include the following:

(1) The right to be reasonably protected from the accused.
(2) The right to reasonable, accurate, and timely notice of any public court proceeding, or any parole proceeding, involving the crime or of any release or escape of the accused.
(3) The right not to be excluded from any such public court proceeding, unless the court, after receiving clear and convincing evidence, determines that testimony by the victim would be materially altered if the victim heard other testimony at that proceeding.
(4) The right to be reasonably heard at any public proceeding in the district court involving release, plea, sentencing, or any parole proceeding.

(5) The reasonable right to confer with the attorney for the Government in the case.
(6) The right to full and timely restitution as provided in law.
(7) The right to proceedings free from unreasonable delay.
(8) The right to be treated with fairness and with respect for the victim's dignity and privacy.
(9) The right to be informed in a timely manner of any plea bargain or deferred prosecution agreement.
(10) The right to be informed of the rights under this section and the services described in section 503(c) of the Victims' Rights and Restitution Act of 1990 (42 U.S.C. 10607(c)) and provided contact information for the Office of the Victims' Rights Ombudsman of the Department of Justice (CVRA, 18 U.S.C. §3771(a)).

Victims' Rights Legislation

West Virginia brought victims' rights to the forefront with the Victim Protection Act of 1984 (W. Va. Code §61-11A-1). Parts of the state legislation echo similar sentiments to the federal acts previously reviewed. Before outlining victims' rights, the act begins by acknowledging how the experience for victims can be degrading and traumatizing. In ways, they are "used" for the purposes of prosecuting a crime or identifying an offender, yet crime victims may experience physical, psychological or financial damages and have needs that are left unmet. This part of the legislation signals that victims of serious crimes must not be neglected and must be provided with ample services. It is here that the term ***victim*** is defined as "a person who is a victim of a felony, or, where a death occurs during the commission of a felony or a misdemeanor" (W. Va. Code §61-11A-2). The code also stipulates the process for crime victims to provide testimony, the ordering of restitution, and the crime victims' compensation fund notification process. In addition, the legislation describes the victim impact statement and the fair treatment of crime victims and witnesses. Another important aspect included in the code is a section about notifying the victim about the offender's release, institutional commitment, or escape from state custody. All of these parts of the code are explained in more detail in this chapter.

Domestic Violence Legislation

Traditionally, domestic violence has been considered a personal and private matter and that the legal system should not interfere (Muraskin, 2012a). These days, domestic violence is seen as a public health concern and more of a priority for law enforcement than in previous years. Unlike other offenses, there is a complexity to this crime that cannot be overlooked, that is, the offender and abuser are often in a personal or close relationship with one another. With this said, Section 48-27-101 of the West Virginia code states that residents have the right to safety and security in their own home, to be "free from domestic violence" (W. Va. Code §48-27-101). In addition, the code asserts that domestic violence impacts everyone, regardless of race, ethnicity, or social class. Likewise, the effects of violence in the home are extremely detrimental to children who may not only witness violence but who may be victims of abuse as well. Last, the code claims that domestic violence is a crime that can be prevented, reduced, and even deterred, especially when treated seriously.

In the state of West Virginia, ***domestic violence*** or abuse means the occurrence of one or more of the following acts between family or household members,

> (1) Attempting to cause or intentionally, knowingly or recklessly causing physical harm to another with or without dangerous or deadly weapons;
> (2) Placing another in reasonable apprehension of physical harm;
> (3) Creating fear of physical harm by harassment, stalking, psychological abuse or threatening acts;
> (4) Committing either sexual assault or sexual abuse ...
> (5) Holding, confining, detaining or abducting another person against that person's will (W. Va. Code §48-27-202).

Domestic violence consists of two types. The first is ***domestic battery***, which the state code defines as "any person who unlawfully and intentionally makes physical contact of an insulting or provoking nature with his or her family or household member or unlawfully and intentionally causes physical harm to his or her family or household member" (W. Va. Code §61-2-28). The second type is ***domestic assault***, that is "any person who unlawfully attempts to commit a violent injury against his or her family or household member or unlawfully commits an act which places his or her family or household member in reasonable apprehension of immediately receiving a violent injury" (W. Va. Code §61-2-28). Domestic battery and domestic assault are misdemeanor crimes. The former could result in confinement in a county or regional jail for up to 12 months and/or a fine not to exceed $500. The penalty for the latter is confinement for up to six months and/or a fine not to exceed $100.

Sexual Assault Legislation

Throughout our history, sexual assault and rape were viewed only as "real" if perpetrated by a stranger (Muraskin, 2012b). Culturally, we have evolved to adopt the standard that "a rape is a rape regardless of whether it is done by someone you know (acquaintance), by someone you do not know (a stranger), or by your spouse (marital)" (Muraskin, 2012b, p. 244). It is important to understand the dynamics of this crime—sexual assault and rape are crimes of power and control. Another important aspect of sexual assault that is relevant in today's courtroom is the issue of consent. According to the West Virginia Code, a lack of consent is present when the victim is coerced, when the victim is unable to consent, or when the victim clearly does not agree to the conduct. Also, a person who is under 16 years of age, "who is mentally defective, mentally incapacitated, or physically helpless" cannot consent (W. Va. Code §61-8B-2).

West Virginia law contains three degree categories for sexual assault. Sexual assault in the first degree is a felony crime and if a person is convicted the penalty is a period of incarceration for 15 to 35 years, or a fine of $1,000 to $10,000 and imprisonment of 15 to 35 years (W. Va. Code §61-8B-3). The crime of sexual assault in the first degree in West Virginia is defined as a person a who:

> (1) engages in sexual intercourse or sexual intrusion with another person and, in so doing:
>
> (i) Inflicts serious bodily injury upon anyone; or
>
> (ii) Employs a deadly weapon in the commission of the act; or
>
> (2) The person, being fourteen years old or more, engages in sexual intercourse or sexual intrusion with another person who is younger than twelve years old and is not married to that person (W. Va. Code §61-8B-3).

Sexual assault in the second degree involves forced sexual intrusion without the person's consent or who does so with an individual who is "physically helpless" (W. Va. Code §61-8B-4). The penalty is prison for 10 to 25 years or a fine of $1,000 to $10,000, plus prison for 10 to 25 years. Last, sexual assault in the third degree involves sexual intrusion with a person who is "mentally defective or mentally incapacitated" or sexual intrusion or intercourse with a person under the age of 16 by a person who is 16 years of age or older (W. Va. Code §61-8B-5). In cases such as these, this is a felony offense punishable by one to five years in prison or a fine of no more than $10,000 and imprisonment of one to five years.

Crime Victimization

In the United States, there were approximately 5.7 million violent crime victimizations among individuals over the age of 12 in 2016, and among households there were 15.9 million reported property crimes (Morgan & Kena, 2017). This figure was obtained from the ***National Crime Victimization Survey (NCVS)*** that is compiled by the U.S. Census Bureau for the Bureau of Justice Statistics (BJS). Unlike the UCR mentioned in Chapter 2, the NCVS measures the nature of crime, the personal characteristics of victims (i.e., age, sex, race, ethnicity, education level, etc.), and the characteristics of the offender in an annual survey of about 130,000 households and 200,000 people over age 12 (Morgan & Kena, 2017). With this information, the NCVS provides yearly estimates of the total number of personal contact crimes such as assault, rape, robbery, aggravated assault, and household victimizations such as burglary, larceny, and vehicle theft. In this self-report survey, victims may disclose information about crimes that were and were not reported to the police. In a way, some of this data may lend itself to a better understanding of the "dark figure of crime" that was mentioned in Chapter 2, which is not captured by the UCR.

In 2014, there were close to 78,500 victims of crime in West Virginia (WVSP, 2014). Approximately half of these victims were individual citizens, and the remaining victims were businesses, the government, and society at large. As expected, and in accordance with UCR arrest trends, state police data showed that property crimes were the most prevalent (63%), followed by crimes against persons (23.0%). There were fewer victimizations that occurred in the category "crimes against society" (15.3%). The largest number of property crimes was larceny-theft (26%), followed by destruction of property/vandalism (17.2%). Assaults (93%) were the most common type of personal offense, and of the remaining personal offenses, 5% were forcible sex offenses. As stated in Chapter 2, crimes against society include offenses such as drug violations, gambling, and prostitution. Drug/narcotic offenses (89%) were the highest in this category.

Aside from the categories of crime victimization data that are presented above, violent crime victimization can be examined in more detail. For example, 12.6% of violent crime victims in West Virginia were age 18 and under; while 72% of violent crime victims were between the ages of 19 and 64 (WVSP, 2014). Nearly half of violent crime victims were between the ages of 26 and 54. In 2014, the majority of violent crime victims were female (56%) between the ages of 21 and 54 (70%). Approximately 20% of female crime victims were age 18 and younger, including infants. Elderly female victims of crime accounted for 2% of the total female victim population. The majority of male victims of violent crime were also between the ages of 21 and 54 (61%). Juvenile males accounted for 18% of the total male crime victims, while males age 65 and over accounted for 2% of male crime victims.

Domestic and Intimate Partner Violence

According to the West Virginia State Police (2014), there were 10,038 reported incidents of domestic violence. Of these, 19% involved an intimate partner, 17.4% involved a spouse, and 12.5% involved a boyfriend or girlfriend. The most common type of violence that occurred was simple assault (65%), followed by aggravated assault (20%), and intimidation (9%). About 62% of domestic violence incidents involved the use of a personal weapon such as hands, feet, fists, etc. A smaller portion of incidents did not involve any type of weapon (17%). Even fewer incidents (2%) involved the use of a firearm, handgun, rifle, or shotgun, similar to the use of knives or cutting devices (2.7%). Among these weapons alone, handguns were used most often.

As stated earlier, a disproportionate number of females are victims of domestic violence. In 2014, West Virginia females were more likely to be victims of domestic violence (71%) than males (29%) (WVSP, 2014). Generally, most victims of domestic homicide are female. However, in 2014 approximately 50% of West Virginia domestic homicide victims were male and six of these victims were age 10 and under. There were no domestic homicide victims between the ages of 11 and 24. Females were the majority (67%) of domestic homicide victims age 25 and over.

Those in law enforcement know that it is common for crime to occur at certain times of the day and during certain months. In the 2014 crime report, the West Virginia State Police showed that most domestic violence incidents occurred between 4:00 p.m. and midnight. Domestic violence was least likely to occur between the hours of 4:00 a.m. and 7:00 a.m. The number of reported domestic violence offenses remained steady between the months of March and August. The month in 2014 with the fewest reported incidents of domestic violence was February (WVSP, 2014).

Sexual Assault

National statistics show that one in six females will be a victim of attempted or completed forcible rape at some point during her lifetime (FRIS, 1998–2017a). This data coincides with state-level crime statistics. The majority of sexual assaults were perpetrated against those who were female (82.1%) (WVSP, 2014). The crimes included in this category were: forcible fondling, forcible rape, sexual assault with an object, statutory rape, forcible sodomy, and incest. Sexual assault victims were an average of 16 years of age, but the most common age of victimization (i.e., mode) was 14 years of age. Altogether, about 67.2% of sexual assault victims were juveniles. Nearly all adult victims (90%) were sexually assaulted by someone who was not a relative. In comparison, approximately 33% of juveniles were sexually assaulted by an offender who was a relative. Juveniles were more likely to be victims of forcible fondling (45%) while adult victims were more likely to be victims of forcible rape (40%).

While females are often the victims of sexual assault, it is important not to diminish the number of male victims who suffer from this crime. Estimates show that 1 in 21 West Virginia males will be a victim of either attempted or completed rape at some point in his lifetime (FRIS, 1998–2017a). A significant portion of male victims experienced their first rape at a very young age. In fact, 27.8% of males have been victims of a completed rape before age 10 (Black et al., 2011). Also, one in six boys will be a victim of sexual abuse. Similar results were shown by the NCVS, where it was reported that 9% of rapes and sexual assaults were perpetrated against males from 1995 to 2010 (Planty, Langton, Krebs, Berzofsky, & Smiley-McDonald, 2013). Boys and men are unlikely to report sexual abuse, and may experience a number of psychological, emotional, and relational problems. Feelings of inadequacy, fear, isolation, anger, or depression are not uncommon. In brief, for both male and female victims it is important to encourage them to report the crime and to reiterate that sexual assault or abuse is not their fault.

Victims' Services

Many programs and offices throughout West Virginia provide services to crime victims. State-driven services are offered through several avenues. First, services are found within the West Virginia Division of Corrections' (WVDOC) Victim Services Program. Second, additional services are provided by the West Virginia Parole Board, and third, with the Crime Victims' Compensation Fund. For children who may be abused, neglected, or witness violence in the home, assistance comes from Child Protective Services (CPS), which is housed in the Department of Health and Human Resources (DHHR). Similarly, elderly or disabled individuals are protected by Adult Protective Services (APS). Last, and throughout many counties, the prosecuting attorney's office has a victim assistance program.

For victims of domestic violence and sexual assault, a number of support services are carried out by several nonprofit agencies that have served West Virginians for decades. For example, victims of domestic violence and sexual assault have sought refuge through a number of shelters established by victims' advocacy groups, and "help" hotlines. Organizations such as the West Virginia Foundation for Rape Information and Services (FRIS) and the West Virginia Coalition Against Domestic Violence (WVCADV) have been instrumental in assisting victims with the immediate help and resources they need, and in bringing awareness to the state about domestic abuse, sexual assault, and stalking. With the dedication of these agencies, coordinated efforts exist to provide first responders with the most effective and humanizing ways to treat and assist victims of sexual assault and domestic violence.

State- and County-Supported Victims' Services

West Virginia Division of Corrections, Victim Services

The WVDOC's Victim Services is predicated on ensuring that offenders take ownership for their behavior (i.e., accountability) and that victims are given high-quality direct services, often by the way of a victim advocate. The victims' services provided by the WVDOC are twofold. The first is the Victim Information and Notification Everyday (VINE) system. VINE or Vinelink, as it is sometimes called, is a telephone system where upon request, a victim is notified about custody status and WVDOC location of an offender (WVDOC, 2007–2017b). This can happen in three ways. Registered crime victims can call a toll free number to receive information about the offender any time of the day. Or, instead of dialing into VINE to obtain information, the victim can register for automated calls. For instance, the victim will receive a phone call or email (the third option), should they choose this option, about when the offender is in custody, including the type of custody (i.e., work release, parole, etc.). Also, the victim can be notified if the offender has escaped, has died, or when a parole hearing is scheduled, as well as when the offender is released.

Second, in West Virginia, like other states, crime victims have the right to be informed of and to attend parole board hearings. Even though the victim may be informed of the parole hearing through VINE, a victim services representative can provide extended support and coordination of additional services. For instance, the representative will assist the victim by developing a safety plan and coordinate efforts with any local, state or national entity, plus the prosecutor's office, as needed (WVDOC, 2007–2017a). At a parole hearing, they may administer a written statement to the board or speak directly to the offender at the hearing. Victims are permitted to have a support person with them at the hearing or a victim advocate. To ensure the victim's safety and to provide support, they are escorted by security staff. In order to go through the process, the victim must be comfortable with the fact that they may be in the presence of the offender, but they do not have to be in direct physical contact with the offender.

West Virginia Victim Compensation Fund

In 1981, the West Virginia Legislature created a crime victim compensation program (W. Va. Code §14-2A) that is housed in the court of claims. This program provides restitution to crime victims as a result of any personal injury and economic loss (up to $35,000) that they may have suffered or to the victim's family if the crime resulted in the death of a loved one (up to $50,000) (West Virginia Legislature, 2018). In order to receive compensation, the crime must be reported to the police within 72 hours. The claim for compensation itself must be filed within two years. Personal injury crimes covered in the act include those such as malicious assault, assault and battery, child abuse/molestation, domestic violence, driving under the influence, reckless driving, vehicle homicide (negligent homicide), murder, or other part one index crime, as well as kidnapping and hunting accidents.

Victim Assistance Programs: Prosecuting Attorney's Offices

Across the state, most counties contain a victim assistance program; some of these programs are commonly housed within the prosecuting attorney's office and include a victim advocate. A ***victim advocate*** is a trained professional who assists victims and survivors of crime in securing their rights, providing direct support services, or making referrals. More specifically, advocacy involves but is not limited to informing the victim of their legal rights, explaining criminal justice proceedings, and referring the victim to additional programs and resources (W. Va. Code §48-26-202). During the process, the advocate will also help the victim develop a victim impact statement to be sent to the probation office, and prepare the paperwork for the crime victim's compensation fund, if desired. More specifically, the ***victim impact statement (VIS)*** is a document completed by the victim or victim's family and incorporated into the presentence report by a probation officer. The VIS typically contains the following information:

> … the identity of the victim, an itemization of any economic loss suffered by the victim as a result of the offense, a description of the nature and extent of any physical or psychological injury suffered by the victim as a result of the offense, the details of any change in the victim's personal welfare, lifestyle or family relationships as a result of the offense, whether there has been any request for psychological or medical services initiated by the victim or the victim's family as a result of the offense and such other information related to the impact of the offense upon the victim as may be required by the court (W. Va. Code §61-11A-3).

Non-Profit Victim Services

The West Virginia Coalition Against Domestic Violence

The West Virginia Coalition Against Domestic Violence (WVCADV) is a nonprofit agency that provides protection to men, women, and children who are victims of domestic violence. The other part of the WVCADV mission is to provide collaborative networks to reduce domestic violence in West Virginia. There are seven main areas of services and initiatives that the coalition office provides, such as public awareness, public policy development, community organizing, training and education, technical assistance, statewide partnerships, and prevention programs (WVCADV, 2015).

Today, West Virginia has 14 domestic violence programs/shelters in the state. The Census of Domestic Violence Services provides a 24-hour snapshot of the services provided by these programs. During one 24-hour period in 2016, domestic violence service providers answered 115 hotline calls and served 352 victims in-person (NNEDV, 2017). One hundred sixty-one of these victims, including children, were in need of shelter. And 191 children and adults on that day received counseling and legal advocacy services, which did not include housing. On September 14, 2016, all of the agencies provided support and advocacy for individual victims, and the majority provided advocacy and support for children. Nearly all (71%) of the programs provided emergency shelter. Less than half provided support/advocacy to young adults and teens who were victims of dating violence (43%) and less than half provided transportation services (43%) for victims. On that day, well over half of the programs (86%) engaged in rural outreach services.

The West Virginia Foundation for Rape Information and Services

West Virginia Foundation for Rape Information and Services (FRIS) is a statewide coalition dedicated to providing intervention and prevention services to combat dating violence, stalking, and sexual assault, as well as crimes that are sexually violent in nature. The professional network was established in 1982, and today there are nine rape crisis centers that comprise the coalition. They are: CONTACT (Huntington), Family Refuge Center (Lewisburg, WV), HOPE Inc. (Fairmont, WV), Rape and Domestic Violence Information Center (Morgantown, WV), REACH The Counseling Connection (Charleston, WV), Sexual Assault Help Center (Wheeling, WV), Shenandoah Women's Center (Martinsburg, WV), Women's Aid in Crisis (Elkins, WV), and the Women's Center (Beckley, WV). Despite the center's location, each one serves multiple or surrounding counties, and provides crisis intervention, advocacy, support, and counseling services free of charge to victims. Moreover, each center is dedicated to community education and awareness.

According to the 2015–2016 annual report, FRIS was devoted to an array of projects and services, which included sexual violence prevention and awareness, intercollegiate partnerships, stalking awareness, SANE and SART trainings, as well as legislative initiatives. When it comes to prevention and awareness efforts, for example, many are carried out in tandem with the DHHR. FRIS (2016) has also developed a number of partnerships with many colleges and universities and provided resource toolkits for the purposes of campus training. Awareness and prevention efforts such as these are important and necessary given the fact that one in five college females are sexually assaulted (Krebs, Lindquist, Warner, Fisher, & Martin, 2007). Beyond the university and college level, FRIS also collaborates with the Rural Advocacy Network. As mentioned earlier, partnerships with the SANE advisory board and the West Virginia SART make up two other important initiatives and are described next.

In the 1970s, some of the first ***Sexual Assault Nurse Examiner (SANE)*** programs were established in the country by professional nursing organizations in conjunction with victim advocate and rape crisis centers (Campbell, Patterson, & Bybee, 2012). Ultimately, the mission of these programs was "to meet the needs of the sexual assault victim by providing immediate, compassionate, culturally sensitive, and comprehensive forensic evaluation and treatment by trained, professional nurse experts" (Ledray, 2008, p. 7). Registered nurses undergo 40 hours of training in the classroom and 40 to 96 hours of training in a clinical setting (Campbell et al., 2012) to learn how to identify physical trauma, document injuries, and collect evidence (FRIS, 1998–2017b). In order to reduce or avoid additional physical or psychological trauma, SANE uses noninvasive techniques to obtain medical forensic evidence that may be used in future court proceedings.

Most, but not all, SANE programs include a ***Sexual Assault Response Team (SART)***. SARTs are "comprised of professionals who work to coordinate an immediate, quality, multidisciplinary, victim-centered response to sexual assaults in a community" (FRIS, 1998–2017a, para. 1). Response team members are comprised of representatives from law enforcement, hospitals (i.e., SANE), rape crisis centers, as well as the prosecuting attorney's office (Greeson & Campbell, 2013). As each plays a role in this process, it is imperative to coordinate the emergency response, to complete a full medical investigation, to provide emotional support and referrals, and to review the evidence in order to decide if it is best to prosecute the offender.

Child Victims' Services and Advocacy

One of the most troubling aspects of working in the criminal justice system is seeing children who suffer from maltreatment oftentimes by their own parents or caregivers. Child maltreatment may be in the form of physical abuse, emotional abuse, sexual abuse, or neglect. Child abuse and neglect are inexcusable, but as stated earlier in Chapter 2, what compounds this problem are the financial difficulties that plague many West Virginians, coupled with residents who struggle with drug addiction. To serve children, a very vulnerable population, state and nonprofit agencies coordinate efforts to ensure the protection of youth and the prosecution of offenders.

According to the West Virginia code, ***child abuse*** refers to the physical, mental, or emotional harming or threatening of a child. Specifically, it states "a parent, guardian or custodian who knowingly or intentionally inflicts, attempts to inflict or knowingly allows another person to inflict, physical injury or mental or emotional injury, upon the child or another child in the home" (W. Va. Code §49-1-3(A)). This definition includes physical injury that is caused by excessive corporal punishment. Physical injury can be detected by bruises, bites, cuts, abrasions, or burns on the child's body (Barnes, Harper, Prillman, & Davis, 2016). Mental or emotional injury can be more difficult to discern. For children whose parents have a history of degrading, rejecting, or berating them, it is not uncommon for the child to exhibit physical characteristics such as a speech disorder, a failure to thrive, or behavioral indicators such as sucking, rocking back and forth, or conduct disorders, to name a few (Hess, Orthmann, & Wright, 2013).

In this same section of the code, ***child sexual abuse*** refers to the attempted or completed act of sexual intercourse, sexual intrusion, or sexual contact with a child by a relative or guardian (W. Va. Code §49-1-3(15)(A)). The law explicitly states that this includes acts that are conducted with children under the age of 16 or with a child over 16 even if the youth consented and did not suffer any physical or mental harm. Also, it includes acts where sex organs are shown to a child for the parent, guardian, or custodian's sexual gratification. Another important part of the code defines ***sexual exploitation,*** which is an act where a parent or guardian "persuades, induces, entices or coerces a child to engage in sexually explicit conduct" (W. Va. Code §49-1-3(17)(A)). Sexual abuse can also be difficult to identify without a medical examination unless signs of pregnancy or a venereal disease are present (Hess et al., 2013). However, children may exhibit behaviors such as not wanting to change clothes for gym class, bizarre sexual behavior or sophistication, or runaway behaviors.

Last, the most common type of child maltreatment is neglect (Hess et al., 2013). In essence, ***child neglect*** is the inattention to a child's needs, resulting in physical or mental harm or threatened harm by a parent or caregiver. The West Virginia Code defines child neglect in two parts:

> (i) ... a present refusal, failure or inability of the child's parent, guardian or custodian to supply the child with necessary food, clothing, shelter, supervision, medical care or education, when such refusal, failure or inability is not due primarily to a lack of financial means on the part of the parent, guardian or custodian; or (ii) Who is presently without necessary food, clothing, shelter, medical care, education or supervision because of the disappearance or absence of the child's parent or custodian (W. Va. Code §49-1-3(11)(A)).

Children who show signs of neglect will often be hungry, dressed inappropriately given the season, have poor hygiene, or be unsupervised (Hess et al., 2013). Behaviorally, the child may steal food, arrive for school early, and leave late. Also, they may be fatigued, participate in drug and alcohol use, delinquency, and other illegal behaviors.

National research showed that 74.8% of children were neglected and 18.2% were physically abused (Children's Bureau, 2018). Approximately 8.5% were sexually abused and 5.6% of children were psychologically maltreated. Recent statistics showed that "1,750 children died of abuse and neglect at a rate of 2.36 children per 100,000 children in the population" (Children's Bureau, 2018, p. 53). Among violent crimes in our state, 12.6% of crime victims were under the age of 18 (WVSP, 2014). Fifty-four percent were female and 45% were male youth. The state police also reported that there were 1,203 incidents of domestic violence that involved child victims. This included victims who were identified as a grandchild, stepchild, or child of an intimate partner. Of these youth, four children were murdered (WVSP, 2014).

Child Protective Services

The most extensive mechanism by which child victims are served is through Child Protective Services (CPS). CPS is housed within the Bureau of Families and Children, which is part of the Department of Health and Human Resources (DHHR). CPS workers undergo hours of training and field supervision in order to identify problems in the home, manage cases, and improve family conditions, and facilitate healthy lifestyles. Their role involves gathering detailed information about each child and the child's family, assessing the need for intervention, especially if the child's safety is jeopardized or if the child is in imminent danger (Barnes et al., 2016). As described in the CPS policy, the process involves "intake assessment, family functioning assessment, safety planning (if necessary), family assessment, service provision, case evaluation, and case closure" (Barnes et al., 2016, p. 16). It is understood that CPS workers are inextricably linked to the family court and work collaboratively with law enforcement, among other criminal justice professionals.

Court-Appointed Special Advocates

Court Appointed Special Advocates (CASA) are trained volunteers who handle cases involving child abuse and neglect in all civil cases. They serve as a "voice" for the child and make recommendations on what is in the best interests of the child. The program was created in Seattle, Washington, in 1977 (CASA, 2017). Currently there are more than 1,000 community-based programs throughout the country; of those, about 12 programs are housed in West Virginia, serving close to 30 counties. The role of the CASA is recognized in Chapter 49 of the state code. Upon the completion of 30 hours of training, CASAs are sworn in and take an oath of confidentiality. They are appointed by circuit court judges, and brought into the process after a case of abuse or neglect has been reported and a petition has been filed. The CASA prepares a report based on the child's background including his/her financial situation, substance abuse, mental status, and education status, etc. A lot of information is secured by conducting interviews with the child, and the child's parents or guardians. While the CASA will be present in court and provide testimony, they cannot be cross-examined. Depending on the case, the CASA will continue to monitor the case until it is closed.

TEAM for West Virginia Children

One of the first comprehensive efforts to prevent child abuse and to advocate for children is the TEAM for West Virginia Children, founded in 1986 (TEAM, 2018). TEAM stands for "To Eliminate Abuse and Maltreatment." Today, the organization is supported by private, state, and national grant funding in order to provide programming, training, and advocacy on behalf of West Virginia's children. Some of the initiatives led by TEAM for West Virginia Children are the Circle of Parents Program, the Western Regional Court Appointed Special Advocate Program (CASA), and the Mountain State Healthy Families Program, just to name a few.

West Virginia Child Advocacy Network

The West Virginia Child Advocacy Network (WVCAN) is a non-profit organization that was established in 2006. The home office is located in Charleston and there are 20 child advocacy centers throughout the state (WVCAN, 2018b), which served 3,900 children during the fiscal year of 2016–2017. The child advocacy centers provide a neutral space where members of the Multidisciplinary Team (MDT) can meet. The MDTs are typically comprised of victim advocates, law enforcement, prosecutors, child protective service workers, and mental health and medical professionals. Overall, the goal of the team is to do what is in the best interest of the child. In addition, the team works to investigate crimes perpetrated against children, to provide child-friendly approaches that diminish the number of times the child is interviewed, and to coordinate medical and mental health services. Another component of WVCAN is to raise awareness about child abuse and to educate the public about how to report it. In 2017 alone, WVCAN was successful in providing 3,550 forensic interviews and 687 medical exams to children in West Virginia (WVCAN, 2018a). They also provided therapeutic services to approximately 937 children.

Spotlight: Elder Abuse

Recent predictions show that by 2050, 83 million elderly Americans will make up 21% of the total population (Ortman, Velkoff, & Hogan, 2014). Presently, elderly individuals comprise 15.2% of our population nationwide. The projected increase in the number of individuals 65 and older is largely influenced by factors such as an increased life expectancy, which can be attributed to medical advances and health campaigns. Per the last U.S. Census Bureau estimates in 2017, there were 341,381 West Virginians ages 65 and older (18.8% of the state population), which is recognizably higher than the national percentage. Given these numbers, West Virginia's population of elderly individuals will most likely exceed 21% by 2050. Currently, Kanawha, Cabell, and Wood counties have the largest populations of individuals who are 65 and older. Aside from age alone, and equally important, in 2016 West Virginia had higher percentages of individuals who were visually impaired (8.5% West Virginia; 4.7% United States), hearing impaired (13.3% West Virginia 5.8% United States), cognitively impaired (16.4% West Virginia; 10.8% United States), and who have difficulty walking (22.3% West Virginia; 10.8% United States) (Shanholtzer, 2018). Results show that the majority of those with some type of impairment are often 65 and older.

As stated earlier, victims can be of any age. The West Virginia Department of Health and Human Resource's Bureau of Children and Families extends protections to those who are 18 years of age or older. Also known as Adult Protective Services (APS), this agency was designed to protect aged, impaired, or disabled adults from abuse, neglect, or financial exploitation. Like CPS,

APS intervention is guided by a process through which an assigned case manager will investigate, assess, and assist victims with the necessary tools and resources. This includes individuals who are in nursing homes, senior residential facilities, or at home.

Research shows that anywhere from 7% to 10% of elderly individuals have been abused each year, and like other crimes, much of the abuse goes unreported (NCEA, n.d.). Elder mistreatment, which includes abuse and neglect, refers to:

> (a) intentional actions that cause harm or create a serious risk of harm (whether or not harm is intended) to a vulnerable elder by a caregiver or other person who stands in a trust relationship to the elder or (b) failure by a caregiver to satisfy the elder's basic needs or to protect the elder from harm (Bonnie & Wallace, 2003, p. 1).

In one study, Acierno et al. (2010) found that the types of elder maltreatment that were most prevalent included, financial abuse by a family member (5.2%), potential neglect (5.1%), followed by emotional abuse (4.6%). Fewer had reported physical abuse (1.6%) and sexual abuse (.06%). Although these crimes were not as prevalent, they still signify the need for more social support and resources for the elderly. In comparison, Hughes, Lund, Gabrielli, Powers, and Curry (2011) found that disabled individuals were are at an increased risk for abuse. Results such as these at the national level suggest that APS in West Virginia will need continued resources and support in order to protect these vulnerable individuals.

Key Terms and Definitions

Child abuse: Knowingly or intentionally inflicting or attempting to inflict or knowingly allowing another person to inflict, physical injury or mental or emotional injury, upon a child or another child by a parent, guardian, or custodian in the home.

Child neglect: The inattention to a child's needs, resulting in physical or mental harm or threatened harm by a parent or caregiver.

Child sexual abuse: The attempted or completed act of sexual intercourse, sexual intrusion, or sexual contact with a child.

Court-Appointed Special Advocates (CASA): Trained volunteers who handle cases involving child abuse and neglect in all civil cases.

Domestic assault: Unlawfully attempting to commit a violent injury against a family or household member or unlawfully committing an act that places a family or household member in reasonable apprehension of immediately receiving a violent injury.

Domestic battery: Unlawfully and intentionally making physical contact of an insulting or provoking nature with a family or household member or unlawfully and intentionally causing physical harm to a family or household member.

Domestic violence: Attempting or intentionally causing physical harm, sexual assault, or sexual abuse to another with or without dangerous or deadly weapons and creating fear of physical harm by harassment, stalking, psychological abuse, or threatening acts.

National Crime Victimization Survey (NCVS): An annual household survey about crime victims that is compiled by U.S. Census Bureau for the Bureau of Justice Statistics (BJS).

Sexual Assault Nurse Examiner (SANE): A trained nurse expert who assists victims of sexual assault by providing immediate, compassionate, culturally sensitive, and comprehensive forensic evaluation and treatment.

Sexual Assault Response Team (SART): A group of community professionals who work to coordinate an immediate, high-quality, multidisciplinary, victim-centered response to sexual violence.

Sexual exploitation: An act where a parent or guardian persuades, induces, entices, or coerces a child to engage in sexually explicit conduct.

Victim: A person who is a victim of a felony, or where a death occurs during the commission of a felony or a misdemeanor.

Victim advocate: A trained professional who assists victims and survivors of crime in securing their rights, providing direct support services, or making referrals.

Victim Impact Statement: A document prepared by the victim or victim's family and used in court that includes a description of financial losses, a description of the nature and extent of any physical or psychological injury suffered by the victim, details of any change in the victim's personal welfare, lifestyle, or family relationships, and/or details of the need for psychological or medical services as a result of the offense.

Select Internet Sources

Team for West Virginia Children: https://teamwv.org/.

Victim Information and Notification Everyday (VINE): http://www.wvdoc.com/wvdoc/victimservices/vine/tabid/58/default.aspx.

West Virginia Foundation for Rape and Information Services (FRIS): http://www.fris.org/.

West Virginia Coalition Against Domestic Violence (WVCADV): http://www.wvcadv.org/.

West Virginia Crime Victims Compensation Fund: http://www.legis.state.wv.us/joint/victims/eligibility.cfm.

Review and Critical Thinking Questions

1. What are the rights of crime victims? How are federal and state rights similar? How do they differ?
2. Who is most likely to be a victim in the state of West Virginia? Who is the most likely to be impacted by violent crimes? Why?
3. Why is domestic violence such a complex crime? What are ways in which police officers can be trained to deal with these complexities when responding to a domestic violence call?
4. What types of assistance and programs are available to victims of domestic violence and sexual assault in the state?
5. What services are provided to child victims?

References

Acierno, R., Hernandez, M., A., Amstadter, A. B., Resnick, H. S., Steve, K., Muzzy, W., & Kilpatrick, D. G. (2010). Prevalence and correlates of emotional, physical, sexual, and financial abuse and potential neglect in the United States: The national elder mistreatment study. *American Journal of Public Health, 100*(2), 292–297.

Barnes, L., Harper, C., Prillman, M., & Davis, K. (2016, March). *Child protective services policy*. Charleston, WV: West Virginia Department of Health and Human Resources, Bureau for Children and Families, Office of Children and Adult Services. Retrieved from http://dhhr.wv.gov/bcf/policy/Documents/Child%20Protective%20Services%20Policy.pdf.

Black, M. C., Basile, K. C., Breiding, M. J., Smith, S. G., Walters, M. L., Merrick, M. T., Chen, J., & Stevens, M. R. (2011). *National intimate partner and sexual violence survey: 2010 summary report*. Atlanta, GA: National Center for Injury Prevention and Control, Centers for Disease Control and Prevention.

Bonnie, R., & Wallace, R. (2003). *Elder mistreatment: Abuse, neglect and exploitation in an aging America*. Washington, DC: National Academies Press.

Campbell, R., Patterson, D., & Bybee, D. (2012). Prosecution of adult sexual assault cases: A longitudinal analysis of the impact of a sexual assault nurse examiner program. *Violence Against Women, 18,* 223–244. doi: 10.177/1077801212440158.

Children's Bureau. (2018). *Child maltreatment 2016.* Washington, DC: U.S. Department of Health & Human Services, Administration for Children and Families, Administration on Children, Youth and Families, Children's Bureau. Retrieved from https://www.acf.hhs.gov/sites/default/files/cb/cm2016.pdf.

Court Appointed Special Advocates (CASA). (2017). *About us.* Retrieved from http://www.casaforchildren.org/site/c.mtJSJ7MPIsE/b.5301303/k.6FB1/About_Us__CASA_for_Children.htm.

Deem, D., Nerenberg, L., & Titus, R. (2013). *Victims of financial crime.* In R. C. Davis, A. J. Lurigio, & S. Herman (Eds.), *Victims of crime* (4th ed.) (pp. 185–210). Thousand Oaks, CA: Sage.

Foundation for Rape Information and Services (FRIS). (2016). *Annual report 2015–16.* Retrieved from http://www.fris.org/Resources/PDFs/Reports/15-16-AnnualReport.pdf.

Foundation for Rape Information and Services (FRIS). (1998–2017a). *Sexual assault response teams (SARTS).* Retrieved from http://www.fris.org/SARTs/SARTs.html.

Foundation for Rape Information and Services (FRIS). (1998–2017b). *What is a forensic medical exam?* Retrieved from http://www.fris.org/SANEs/WhatisExam.html.

Greeson, M. R., & Campbell, R. (2013). Sexual assault response teams (SARTs): An empirical review of their effectiveness and challenges to successful implementation. *Trauma, Violence, & Abuse, 14*(2), 83–95. doi: 10.1177/1524838012470035.

Hess, K. M., Orthmann, C. H., & Wright, J. P. (2013). *Juvenile justice* (6th ed.). Belmont, CA: Cengage Learning.

Hughes, R. B., Lund, E. M., Gabrielli, J., Powers, L. E., & Curry, M. A. (2011). Prevalence of interpersonal violence against community-living adults with disabilities: A literature review. *Rehabilitation Psychology, 56*(4), 302–319. doi:10.1037/a0025620.

Krebs, C. P., Lindquist, C. H., Warner, T. D., Fisher, B. S., & Martin, S. L. (2007). *The campus sexual assault (CSA) study* (221153). Washington, DC: National Institute of Justice.

Ledray, L. (2008). *Sexual assault nurse examiner development and operation guide.* Minneapolis: Sexual Assault Resource Service (NCJ 170609). Washington, DC: U.S. Department of Justice, Office of Justice Programs, Office for Victims of Crime. Retrieved from https://www.ncjrs.gov/ovc_archives/reports/saneguide.pdf.

Morgan, R. E., & Kena, G. (2017, December). *Criminal victimizations, 2016* (NCJ 251150). Washington, DC: U.S. Department of Justice, Office of Justice Programs, Bureau of Justice Statistics. Retrieved from https://www.bjs.gov/content/pub/pdf/cv16.pdf.

Muraskin, R. (2012a). Domestic violence or intimate partner violence. In R. Muraskin (Ed.), *Women and justice: It's a crime* (5th ed.) (pp. 282–287). Upper Saddle River, NJ: Prentice Hall.

Muraskin, R. (2012b). It's not sex, it is rape! In R. Muraskin (Ed.), *Women and justice: It's a crime* (5th ed.) (pp. 238–245). Upper Saddle River, NJ: Prentice Hall.

National Center on Elder Abuse (NCEA). (n.d.). *Statistics/data.* Retrieved from https://ncea.acl.gov/whatwedo/research/statistics.html#23.

National Network to End Domestic Violence (NNEDV). (2017). *Domestic violence counts: West Virginia summary (2016).* Washington, DC: author. Retrieved from https://nnedv.org/mdocs-posts/census_2016_handout_state-summary_west-virginia/.

National Victims' Constitutional Amendments Passage. (2012). *Victim's rights amendments adopted in more than three states.* Retrieved from http://www.nvcap.org/.

Ortman, J. M., Velkoff, V. A., & Hogan, H. (2014, May). *An aging nation: The older population in the United States.* Washington, DC: U.S. Census Bureau.

Planty, M., Langton, L., Krebs, C., Berzofsky, M., & Smiley-McDonald, H. (2013, March). *Female victims of sexual violence, 1994–2010* (NCJ 240655). Washington, DC: U.S. Department of Justice, Bureau of Justice Statistics. Retrieved from https://www.bjs.gov/content/pub/pdf/fvsv9410.pdf.

Seghetti, L. M., & Bjelopera, J.P. (2012, May). *The violence against women act: Overview, legislation, and federal funding.* CRS Report for Congress. Washington, DC: Congressional Research Services.

Shanholtzer, B. (2018). *West Virginia behavioral risk factor surveillance system report, 2016.* Charleston, WV: West Virginia Department of Health and Human Resources, Health Statistics Center. Retrieved from http://www.wvdhhr.org/bph/hsc/pubs/brfss/2016/BRFSS2016.pdf.

Team for West Virginia Children (TEAM). (2018). Retrieved from https://teamwv.org/.

United States Census Bureau. (2017). *State and county quickfacts.* Retrieved from https://www.census.gov/quickfacts/fact/table/WV,US/PST045217.

West Virginia Child Advocacy Network (WVCAN). (2018a). *About, Results.* Retrieved from https://wvcan.org/about/results/.

West Virginia Child Advocacy Network (WVCAN). (2018b). *About, Why the CAC model works.* Retrieved from https://wvcan.org/about/.

West Virginia Coalition Against Domestic Violence (WVCADV). (2015). Retrieved from http://www.wvcadv.org/.

West Virginia Division of Corrections (WVDOC). (2007–2017a). *Services provided.* Retrieved from http://www.wvdoc.com/wvdoc/VictimServices/ServicesProvided/tabid/61/Default.aspx.

West Virginia Division of Corrections (WVDOC). (2007–2017b). *VINE: Victim Information & Notification Everyday.* Retrieved from http://www.wvdoc.com/wvdoc/VictimServices/VINE/tabid/58/Default.aspx.

West Virginia Legislature. (2018). *West Virginia legislature's crime victims compensation fund.* Retrieved from http://www.wvlegislature.gov/Joint/victims.cfm.

West Virginia State Police (WVSP). (2014). *Crime in West Virginia 2014.* Charleston, WV: author. Retrieved from https://www.wvsp.gov/about/Documents/CrimeStatistics/2014wvcrimes.pdf.

Legal References

Crime Victims' Rights Act, 18 U.S.C. §3771 (2004).

Victims' Rights and Restitution Act, 34 U.S.C. §20141 (1990).

Victims of Crime Act, 42 U.S.C. §10601 (1984).

Violence Against Women Act, 42 U.S.C. §13701-14040 (1994).

Violent Crime Control and Law Enforcement Act, 42 U.S.C. §13701-14040 (1994).

W. Va. Code §14-2A (2017).

W. Va. Code §48-26-202 (2017).

W. Va. Code §48-27-101 (2017).

W. Va. Code §48-27-202 (2017).

W. Va. Code §49-1-3 (2017).

W. Va. Code §49-1-3(11)(A) (2017).

W. Va. Code §49-1-3(15)(A) (2017).

W. Va. Code §49-1-3(17)(A) (2017).

W. Va. Code §61-2-28 (2017).

W. Va. Code §61-8B-2 (2017).

W. Va. Code §61-8B-3 (2017).

W. Va. Code §61-8B-4 (2017).

W. Va. Code §61-8B-5 (2017).

W. Va. Code §61-11A-1 (2017).

W. Va. Code §61-11A-2(2017).
W. Va. Code §61-11A-3 (2017).

Chapter 9

The Drug Problem

Moonshine stills confiscated by State Police, Greenbrier County, ca. 1926–1928. Courtesy of the West Virginia State Archives, West Virginia State Police Collection.

Our nation's war on drugs has a long and complex history. It is no different for the state of West Virginia, where the cost of drug and alcohol abuse is rather alarming. In a report from the West Virginia Partnership to Promote Community Well-being and the West Virginia Prevention Resource Center (WVPRC) drug and alcohol abuse costs the state more than $1.6 billion dollars annually ("West Virginia cost," 2011). Other estimates indicate that the opioid crisis alone costs the state $8.8 billion dollars per year (Eyre, 2018b). While alcohol and marijuana seem to be the most prevalent and widely consumed drugs, many jurisdictions struggle with areas permeated by heroin, crack cocaine, and prescription drug abuse. National news accounts have drawn attention to the state's opioid crisis and the number of drug overdose deaths that has reached epidemic proportions. Data from the West Virginia Health Statistics Center revealed that in 2015 the:

> West Virginia resident drug overdose mortality rate of 35.5 is more than twice as high as the United States mortality rate of 14.7 per

> 100,000. West Virginia has the highest age-adjusted mortality rate in the nation and over a third higher than the next highest state, Kentucky (Haddy, 2017, p. 4).

Given these figures, it is important to place the drug problem in context with certain socio-demographic variables. West Virginia, for example, is one of the most rural states in the nation. The unemployment rate was 5.4% in January of 2018, which was slightly higher than the national rate of 4.1% (Bureau of Labor Statistics, 2018), and 17.9% of West Virginians lived below the poverty level in 2016, according to United States Census Bureau (2017) estimates. Conditions such as these, along with a struggling state economy that was dependent on the coal industry, certainly exacerbate the drug abuse problem in our state.

Drug abuse and addiction is a major concern for many behavioral, health, and criminal justice agencies. To begin, substance abuse research is regularly compiled by the West Virginia Department of Health and Human Resources' (DHHR) Bureau for Behavioral Health and Health Facilities, in order to inform policy and programmatic responses. One mechanism that has assisted residents is the Help4WV hotline, which was launched in 2015 (Loftin, 2016). Despite emergency hotlines, which aim to help those who have fallen victim to drug abuse problems, the illegal possession, manufacturing, and distribution of illegal drugs is still a criminal act and of utmost importance to law enforcement, prosecutors, and judges. In turn, it is also a concern for probation and parole officers who supervise offenders in the community. It is equally important for those who treat addicts in our state's prisons and jails, as well as in our state's mental health and nonprofit addiction recovery facilities. Last, with drug abuse and addiction prevalent in many West Virginia homes, children may be in harm's way, requiring Child Protective Services (CPS) to intervene.

In this chapter, some of the statutory approaches to regulate drugs, as well as various types of drugs, are described, but a deeper discussion goes beyond the scope of this text. Thus, this chapter explores some of the main drugs that plague our state, including alcohol, marijuana, cocaine/crack cocaine, heroin, fentanyl, oxycodone, methamphetamine, and designer drugs.

The Drug-Crime Connection

Most of the research to date has examined how drugs are related to crime. The causal direction often studied is one where drug use leads directly to crime. Conversely, research studies have explored other angles where crime leads to potential drug use (Gaines, 2014). Regardless, the research overwhelmingly demonstrates that there is a drug-crime connection, particularly for violent crimes such as murder, rape, and robbery. Aside from street drugs, it cannot be ignored that alcohol is also a drug commonly involved in the commission of a crime, and it is often associated with domestic violence offenses. It is important to note that not all drug users commit all crimes. Even more so, there are certain types of drugs that are linked to certain types of crimes more than others. In the end, law enforcement has to be involved despite the debate that drug use is a "victimless" crime.

Before proceeding, it is essential to define a couple of key terms. Among those in the health professions, the term ***drug addiction*** is defined as "a chronic, relapsing brain disease that is characterized by compulsive drug seeking and use, despite harmful consequences" (NIDA, 2014, p. 5). Among law enforcement and in a legal context, ***drug abuse*** is considered "the non-sanctioned use of substances controlled in Schedules I through V of the CSA" (DEA, 2017a, p. 36). In other words, "when controlled substances are used in a manner or amount inconsistent with the legitimate medical use, it is called drug abuse" (DEA, 2017a, p. 36).

National and State Drug Laws

The first and most aggressive federal drug statute indicating the government's need to address drug addiction, treatment, and the regulation and manufacturing of drugs was Title II of the Comprehensive Drug Abuse Prevention and Control Act of 1970 (Abadinsky, 2014), which was later amended to the Controlled Substances Act of 1990, or CSA. The act placed illicit substances into five classes or schedules based on the potential for abuse (i.e., dependency), accepted or accredited medical use, and a process for categorizing narcotics, stimulants, depressants, hallucinogens, and other hazardous chemicals or substances. The classification of drugs are shown in Table 9.1, but a more extensive review of each drug and the federal penalty it carries can be found in the Drug Enforcement Administration's (DEA) resource guide titled, *Drugs of Abuse* (2017a).

Similar to other states, West Virginia followed suit with adopting a Uniform Controlled Substances Act (W. Va. Code §60A). Section §60A-2-201 of the code describes how the state board of pharmacy can make recommendations to the legislature about which "substances should be added to or deleted from the schedules of controlled substances." These recommendations are based on seven criteria and mirror what is listed in Section 201(c), [21 U.S.C. §811(c)] of the Controlled Substances Act, including:

Table 9.1. National Classification of Controlled Substances

Category	Potential for Abuse	Medical Use & Properties	Types
Schedule I	High potential for abuse; the most dangerous drugs of all the drug schedules with potentially severe psychological or physical dependence.	The drug has no currently accepted medical use in treatment in the United States.	Heroin, lysergic acid diethylamide (LSD), marijuana (cannabis), methaqualone (quaalude), and peyote
Schedule II	Less abuse potential than Schedule I drugs; but still potentially leading to severe psychological or physical dependence. These drugs are also considered dangerous.	The drug or other substance has a currently accepted medical use in treatment in the United States or a currently accepted medical use with severe restrictions.	Cocaine, hydrocodone, methamphetamine, methadone, morphine, oxycodone (OxyContin), fentanyl, and opium
Schedule III	Moderate to low potential for physical and psychological dependence. Schedule III drugs abuse potential is less than Schedule I and Schedule II drugs but more than Schedule IV.	The drug or other substance has a currently accepted medical use in treatment in the United States.	Combination products with less than 15 milligrams of hydrocodone per dosage unit (Vicodin), products containing less than 90 milligrams of codeine per dosage unit (Tylenol with codeine), ketamine, and anabolic steroids
Schedule IV	Low potential for abuse and low risk of dependence; limited physical dependence or psychological dependence relative to the drugs or other substances in Schedule III.	The drug or other substance has a currently accepted medical use in treatment in the United States.	Alprazolam (Xanax), clonazepam (Clonopin), diazepam (Valium), and Zolpidem (Ambien)
Schedule V	Lower potential for abuse than Schedule IV and consist of preparations containing limited quantities of certain narcotics. Schedule V drugs are generally used for antidiarrheal, antitussive, and analgesic purposes; Abuse of the drug or other substance may lead to limited physical dependence or psychological dependence relative to the drugs or other substances in Schedule IV.	The drug or other substance has a currently accepted medical use in treatment in the United States; most are available as over-the-counter preparations.	Cough preparations with less than 200 milligrams of codeine or per 100 milliliters (Robitussin AC), Lomotil, Motofen, Lyrica, Parepectolin

Source: Drug Enforcement Administration (DEA). (2017a). *Drugs of abuse: A DEA resource guide*. Washington, DC: Drug Enforcement Administration, U.S. Department of Justice. Retrieved from https://www.dea.gov/pr/multimedia-library/publications/drug_of_abuse.pdf (table modified).

> (1) The actual or relative potential for abuse; (2) The scientific evidence of its pharmacological effect, if known; (3) The state of current scientific knowledge regarding the substance; (4) The history and current pattern of abuse; (5) The scope, duration and significance of abuse; (6) The potential of the substance to produce psychic or physiological dependence liability; and (7) Whether the substance is an immediate precursor of a substance already controlled ... (W. Va. Code §60A-2-201).

The state pharmacy board also has the power to add or delete any substances to the schedule in emergency situations. However, the power of the board does not include authority over nonnarcotic substances that are federally approved and sold over the counter without a doctor's prescription, or to any products such as distilled spirits, wine, malt beverages, or tobacco (W. Va. Code §60A-2-201).

Other than defining how substances are to be classified, the law in West Virginia explicitly states that it is illegal to "manufacture, deliver, or possess with intent to manufacture or deliver, a controlled substance" (W. Va. Code §60A-4-401). The penalties are based on the schedule of the drug where Schedule I and II drugs, for example, may have a higher penalty, especially if they are narcotics. The code states that manufacturing, possessing, or intending to manufacture or sell all Schedule I, II, III, and IV drugs is a felony offense. The penalties are as follows:

> (i) A controlled substance classified in Schedule I or II, which is a narcotic drug, is guilty of a felony and, upon conviction, may be imprisoned in the state correctional facility for not less than one year nor more than fifteen years, or fined not more than twenty-five thousand dollars, or both;
> (ii) Any other controlled substance classified in Schedule I, II or III is guilty of a felony and, upon conviction, may be imprisoned in the state correctional facility for not less than one year nor more than five years, or fined not more than fifteen thousand dollars, or both;
> (iii) A substance classified in Schedule IV is guilty of a felony and, upon conviction, may be imprisoned in the state correctional facility for not less than one year nor more than three years, or fined not more than ten thousand dollars, or both;
> (iv) A substance classified in Schedule V is guilty of a misdemeanor and, upon conviction, may be confined in jail for not less than six months nor more than one year, or fined not more than five thousand dollars, or both: *Provided,* That for offenses relating to any substance

classified as Schedule V in article ten of this chapter, the penalties established in said article apply (W. Va. Code §60A-4-401).

The simple use of alcohol is not prohibited if the person is over the age of 21. However, alcohol-related offenses mainly come into play when a person is operating a motor vehicle. The code stipulates that not only is it illegal to operate a vehicle while under the influence of alcohol, but also any controlled substance or other type of drug (W. Va. Code §17C-5-2). The law also states that being under the influence of a combination of alcohol, any controlled substance, inhalant substance, or any type of other drug is prohibited. Moreover, drivers ages 21 or older are considered driving under the influence of alcohol when they have a blood-alcohol concentration (BAC) of .08. For those under 21, the BAC is .02. The amount of jail time and fines varies depending on whether it is the driver's first, second, or third offense. The statutory code also outlines additional penalties when drunk driving causes the death of another individual or when it causes bodily injury.

Arrests, Sentence Data, and Traffic Offense Data Related to Alcohol

Upon examining West Virginia NIBRS data, there were 10,484 arrests for drug violations and 361 arrests for drug equipment violations in 2016 (NIBRS, 2016). Moreover, the state police reported 10,123 drug/narcotic offenses, which included attempts (attempts typically involve offenses where the alleged individual had intent, but was unsuccessful in committing the crime). The West Virginia State Police also make concerted efforts to disrupt the flow of drugs being trafficked into the state by way of Washington, DC, and Baltimore. For example, as part of the Washington-Baltimore, High Intensity Drug Trafficking Areas (HIDTA) initiative, field troops in Berkeley and Jefferson counties made 202 traffic stops and 45 felony drug arrests in one month alone (WVSP, 2016). The illegal narcotics seized during the month of June totaled $238,038. Moreover, among the state troopers involved in drug diversion efforts, 188,535 marijuana plants were eradicated and 171 clandestine laboratories were dismantled.

As mentioned in Chapter 6, 11.4% of offenders in state prison were serving time for a drug offense in 2017 (WVDOC, 2017). Of this figure, the majority (81.4%) were serving time for the primary offense of manufacturing and/or delivering a Schedule I, II, III, or IV controlled substance or controlled narcotic substance. A smaller percentage of offenders, 13.4%, were incarcerated in a state facility for operating a clandestine laboratory. It is also noteworthy that while manufacturing and selling drugs is a problem, it is also a contributing factor in domestic offenses. For example, substance abuse was linked to 45.7% of domestic violence cases in 2012, according to the West Virginia Coalition Against Domestic Violence (Gwilliam, 2013).

Data based on the National Highway Safety Traffic Administration and the Uniform Crime Report revealed that in 2015, 9,086 DUI arrests were made for drivers who were impaired (Justice, Reed, & Tipton, 2017). Kanawha County had the largest number of DUI arrests with 911, followed by Cabell County with 724, and Monongalia County with 621. Another way to examine the problem is by examining the number of fatalities that occur as a result of drinking and driving using the Fatality Analysis Reporting Systems (FARS), which contains state-level information. According to FARS, in 2015, 268 West Virginians lost their lives as a result of a driver who was impaired (NHSTA, 2015). Also in 2015, 22% of West Virginians killed in car crashes involved a driver with a blood-alcohol level of 0.01 or higher. Among West Virginia youth, fewer (16.7%) reported riding in a car with a driver who had consumed alcohol than the national percentage (20%) in 2015 (CDC, 2015b). Also, fewer West Virginia high school students (6.3%) reported driving drunk compared to youth across the nation (7.8%). Eleventh graders reported the most incidents of drunk driving or riding in the car with a person who had consumed alcohol.

Drug Abuse among West Virginia Youth

Since drug use is common among youth, it is important to examine these trends in comparison to youth nationwide. Data presented in Table 9.2 was largely obtained from the Youth Risk Behavioral Surveillance System (YRBS), a biannual survey that is sponsored by the Centers for Disease Control and the West Virginia Department of Education. It can be seen that most high school students in the state largely use or have tried marijuana as opposed to other forms of illegal substances (CDC, 2015a). The second most common drug reported in 2015 was synthetic marijuana, and results showed that more West Virginia youth reported that they had tried it in comparison to high school students in the country. Specifically, 14.6% of West Virginia high school youth reported using synthetic marijuana compared to 9.2% of all high school students in the United States. West Virginia youth also reported slightly more use of illicit drugs such as ecstasy (6.7%), heroin (3.5%), methamphetamine (4.7%), and steroid pills without a doctor's prescription (4.6%). High school youth in the state reported a greater use of injecting drugs as well. In addition, among all of the drugs listed, twelfth graders in comparison to ninth, tenth, and

Table 9.2. Comparison of Reported Substance Abuse among High School Students in West Virginia and the United States, 2015

	% of High School Students in West Virginia	% of High School Students in the United States
Students Reporting First Using Marijuana before Age 13	8.4%	7.5%
Students Reporting Any Use of Marijuana in the Past 30 Days	16.5%	21.7%
Students Reporting Any Use of Marijuana in Their Lifetime	34.7%	38.6%
Students Reporting Any Use of Synthetic Marijuana in Their Lifetime	14.6%	9.2%
Students Reporting Any Use of Cocaine (or form of) in Their Lifetime	4.6%	5.2%
Students Reporting Any Use of Ecstasy (MDMA) in Their Lifetime	6.7%	5.0%
Students Reporting Any Use of Steroid Pills or Shots in Their Lifetime	4.6%	3.5%
Students Reporting Any Use of Methamphetamines in Their Lifetime	4.7%	3.0%
Students Reporting Any Use of Heroin in Their Lifetime	3.5%	2.1%
Students Reporting Use of Any Drugs via Injection in Their Lifetime	3.5%	1.8%

Source: Centers for Disease Control and Prevention (CDC). (2015b). *Youth Risk Behavioral Surveillance System (YRBSS). West Virginia 2015 and United States 2015 results*. Retrieved from https://nccd.cdc.gov/youthonline/app/Results.aspx?LID=WV.

eleventh graders were more likely to report using synthetic marijuana, ecstasy, methamphetamines, and steroids without a doctor's prescription one or more times in their lifetime. Approximately 4.1% of freshmen and seniors reported using heroin at least once in their lifetime. More sophomores reported currently using marijuana (18.9%) and using marijuana before age 13 (10.3%) than any other grade level.

With all the drugs listed in Table 9.2, high school males were more likely to report using an illegal substance in their lifetime more so than females with the exception of females, who were more likely to report using marijuana one or more times in their lifetime. Gender differences, albeit small differences, were found among males who reported using steroids without a doctor's prescription (7.2% males vs. 1.9% females), methamphetamine (6.8% males vs. 2.6% females), cocaine (6.3% males vs. 2.8% females), and ecstasy (8.4% males vs. 4.9% females) (CDC, 2015a). West Virginia high school males had a higher percentage of reported use of synthetic marijuana, ecstasy, methamphetamine, and heroin compared to all male high school students in the United States. Among these illicit substances, West Virginia high school males reported the highest rates of using synthetic marijuana (14.8%) at least once in their lifetime in comparison to high school males in the United States (10.3%).

Commonly Abused Drugs in West Virginia

Alcohol

Normally, a discussion about alcohol would not be included alongside illicit drugs. However, alcohol use cannot be ignored as it is often abused and connected to most criminal activity. Throughout our country's history, it has been consumed for ritual, recreational, and therapeutic purposes (Siegel & Inciardi, 2004). Yet overconsumption and public intoxication heightened the questionable nature of alcohol, labeling it a social ill as our country transformed during the 1800s–1900s. Even before most street drugs became a concern, the use of alcohol was largely attacked, and a temperance movement began, ultimately leading to the Eighteenth Amendment, where the manufacture, sale, and transportation of intoxicating liquors was prohibited in 1920. Later, it was repealed with the Twenty-First Amendment in 1933; the only case where an amendment to the constitution was rescinded.

Alcohol is not listed as a controlled substance; instead, it is regulated (Abadinsky, 2014). It is an organic compound otherwise known as ethanol that is created in a process of fermentation, commonly found in beer, wine, and liquor. As a depressant, it is known to impact the central nervous system, producing a calming or sedative effect. However, for some, it stimulates the central nervous system, where the user may experience a sense of excitement and become more uninhibited or talkative. The absorption of alcohol into the bloodstream is known to be faster for women than men, and a genetic influence of alcohol has been well documented in the research. Persistent abuse of alcohol is known to have many severe effects on a person's heart, liver, intestinal system, nervous system, and endocrine system. Numerous research studies also document the damaging effects of alcohol to a fetus (i.e., fetal alcohol syndrome).

Data from the National Survey on Drug Use and Health (NSDUH), which is sponsored by the Substance Abuse and Mental Health Services Administration (SAMHSA) showed that from 2015–2016, 40.71% of West Virginians 12 and older were currently using alcohol in comparison to 51.21% of those in the country (SAMSHA, 2017). When asked about using alcohol in the past 30 days, fewer West Virginians (22.59%) ages 12 and older reporting using alcohol versus 24.58% of those in the United States. While the rate of current alcohol use was slightly higher for the United States as a whole, results were similar to West Virginians when it came to binge drinking and using alcohol in the past year. For instance, from 2015–2016, 15.33% of West Virginians reported binge drinking and close to 12.71% of Americans reported binge drinking in the rest of the nation. In another data set, known as the Treatment Episode Data Set (TEDS), sponsored by SAMHSA, alcohol was found to be the primary drug for 26.1% of treatment admissions among West Virginia male and female adults compared to 18.7% of adults in the country in 2015 (SAMSHA, 2018). Alcohol abuse was notably higher among West Virginia males (73.2%) than females (26.8%). Also, those found to be treated for alcohol were mostly 46 to 50 years of age.

Marijuana

Marijuana (or marihuana) is a derivative of the hemp plant recognized scientifically as *Cannabis sativa* (Inciardi, 2002). The plant is known for its long, narrow, fan-shaped leaves. The only part of the plant that has pharmaceutical properties is THC or delta-9-tetrahydrocannabinol. Although it can be consumed in food or drink, it is most commonly smoked, which contributes to the main physical consequences, such as an irritation of the lungs, much like tobacco products. The effects for some marijuana users vary, but most experience a state of euphoria and then a period of sedation (Mechoulam, 2000). The sedative effects of the drug often results in sensory impairment, that is, delays in motor skills where perceptions of time and distance are altered. Many users experience hallucinations as well. For occasional users and regular users, anxiety and panic are common adverse effects as well as an increased risk of motor vehicle accidents (Hall, 2009). Over the long term, regular users are more likely to suffer from chronic bronchitis. Last, in a longitudinal study of users and non-users, cannabis use from ages 14 to 21 was associated with psychosocial consequences later in life (ages 21 to 25), including decreased degree attainment, reduced income, and decreased life satisfaction, just to name a few (Fergusson & Boden, 2008).

Drug paraphernalia confiscated by Cabell County probation officers. Courtesy of Chris May and Matt Meadows.

Once legal, marijuana became the spotlight drug in the 1930s with the scare tactics and rhetoric of Harry Anslinger, who was the newly appointed Commissioner of the Treasury Department's Bureau of Narcotics. To support his anti-marijuana campaign, he wrote, *Marijuana: Assassin of Youth* (Anslinger & Cooper, 1937), spinning tales of the "devil drug," the insidious reefer man, and crimes of violence, murder, and suicide that he attributed to the consumption of the marijuana. Given Anslinger's position with the bureau, he was able to persuade Congress to classify the drug as a narcotic, thereby criminalizing the drug under the 1937 Marihuana Tax Act, despite disagreements from the American Medical Association. In the 1970s, the act was repealed after the case *Leary v. United States* (1969). Shortly thereafter, marijuana was placed under the Controlled Substances Act, and it is classified as a Schedule I narcotic even though it is not an actual narcotic. Today, the drug is trafficked mostly by way of Mexico, although a large number of growers exist in the United States. In 2017, DEA intelligence reported that from Mexico, marijuana enters primarily along the southwest border. Mexican drug cartels and transnational criminal organizations continue to traffic drugs using very sophisticated methods. Not only are drugs smuggled in traditional ways at points of entry into the United States via passenger vehicles, there also are tunnels leading into the United States from Mexico that are used for transport, unmanned aerial systems, and drones. From these points of entry, drugs are then divided and distributed through networked channels across the country to cities such as Phoenix, Los Angeles, Chicago, and Atlanta.

Marijuana is one of the leading drugs that plagues not only West Virginians but the entire country (DEA, 2017b). In the United States, reports show that marijuana remains the most commonly abused drug, and its use has increased since 2007 (NIDA, 2015). Most who turn to illicit substance abuse begin with marijuana and usually when they are in their late teens and early 20s. This is also reflected in state-wide data gathered from the National Survey on Drug Use and Health (NSDUH) as 16.56% of 18- to 25-year-olds reported the most use of marijuana in the past year followed by 5.94% of 12- to 17-year-olds. Reports showed that marijuana also was the most common drug used in the past year compared to cocaine and heroin (SAMSHA, 2017). Also, using state data and information from NSDUH, 6.76% of West Virginians ages 12 and older reported using marijuana in the past month over the 2015–2016 time period compared to 8.60% in the United States as a whole. Among Poison Center admissions in West Virginia, there were 41 reported exposures to marijuana in 2016 (WV Poison Center, 2016). Among treatment admissions in 2015, 14.1% of West Virginians were treated for marijuana, which was nearly identical to the 14.2% of adults treated for marijuana nationally (SAMSHA, 2018). There were far more admissions for males who used marijuana (63%) in comparison to females (37%). Those seeking treatment for marijuana use were mostly 21 to 25 years old (19.1%).

Medical Marijuana

As mentioned, marijuana is a Schedule I narcotic, and carries penalties for abuse, illegal possession, and distribution, but that has not prevented a conversation to expand its availability to those with a terminal illness. Following suit with other states, in April 2017, Governor Jim Justice signed the West Virginia Medical Cannabis Act (§16A-1-1) into law. This act allows licensed and trained physicians to prescribe marijuana in various forms such as pills, oils, topical ointments, gels, and tinctures to certified patients (W. Va. Code §16A-3-2).

Those who are eligible to be prescribed medical marijuana often suffer from conditions such as cancer, HIV/AIDS, Parkinson's disease, and multiple sclerosis, just to name a few. The process for issuing medical marijuana, and the criteria for diagnosing a patient is outlined in the state code (§16A-4-3) as follows:

> *Issuance of certification.*
> (a) *Conditions for issuance.*—A certification to use medical cannabis may be issued by a practitioner to a patient if all of the following requirements are met:
> (1) The practitioner has been approved by the bureau for inclusion in the registry and has a valid, unexpired, unrevoked, unsuspended license to practice medicine in this state at the time of the issuance of the certification.

(2) The practitioner has determined that the patient has a serious medical condition and has included the condition in the patient's health care record.
(3) The patient is under the practitioner's continuing care for the serious medical condition.
(4) In the practitioner's professional opinion and review of past treatments, the practitioner determines the patient is likely to receive therapeutic or palliative benefit from the use of medical cannabis, and other treatments, including treatments involving opioids, have proven ineffective or otherwise are contraindicated.

Restrictions and penalties for improper use of medical marijuana still apply. For one, medical marijuana cannot be smoked or grown by the patient (W. Va. Code § 16A-3-3). Also, physicians who falsely prescribe medical cannabis may be found guilty of a felony crime, which carries a penalty of one to five years' imprisonment. Those who manufacture medical marijuana are prohibited from dispensing it to those who are not legally and medically certified. Additional prohibitions exist for those who misuse an identification card and for family members who sell the drug to others.

Narcotics

The term *narcotic* is often misused and misunderstood. In a true pharmacological sense, ***narcotic*** refers to any natural derivative of the opium poppy, known scientifically as *Papaver somniferum* (Inciardi, 2002). This includes "opiates (drugs derived from the opium poppy) or ... opioids (synthetically produced opiates)" (Gaines, 2014, p. 118). For centuries, opiates have been used as analgesics or painkillers in Ancient Egypt, Southeast Asia, and the Middle East. Narcotics such as morphine and codeine are derived naturally from opium, while semisynthetic narcotics like heroin and oxycodone are derived from morphine (Inciardi, 2002). Other commonly known opioids include Oxymorphone (Opana®) and hydrocodone (Vicodin®), which are prescribed legally by a physician.

Heroin

Heroin is a Schedule I narcotic and as mentioned, a derivative of morphine that is refined from the opium poppy. Other names for the drug are "smack," "horse," "harry," "jones," "black tar," or "junk," just to name a few (Inciardi, 2002). First synthesized in 1874 by a German pharmacist, the drug can be consumed in multiple ways, including snorting, inhaling, smoking, or intravenous injection (Gaines, 2014). Some addicts prefer to inject the drug under the surface of the skin called "skin popping." Along with the "high," the user will experience a dry mouth, a warmth or flushing of the skin, and a state of drifting from drowsiness to wakefulness. Because heroin is so addictive, a physical dependency will occur where chronic users may experience negative health effects such as collapsed veins, liver and kidney disease, an infected heart lining, and constipation (NIDA, 2018). Also, for those who inject the drug intravenously and share needles, there is an increased risk of contracting HIV and hepatitis C.

In the 1960s and 1970s, much of the illicit opium was manufactured and transported from Southeast Asia (Inciardi, 2002). Most of the activity came from the countries of Myanmar (once Burma), Thailand, and Laos, also known as the Golden Triangle. Increased competition and trafficking came in the 1970s and 1980s from the Golden Crescent, which is made up of the countries of Pakistan, Iran, and Afghanistan. Today, large quantities of heroin are still seized in these regions. For the United States, organized drug cartels traffic heroin from where it is produced in Columbia and Mexico (DEA, 2017b).

Using data obtained from the West Virginia Health Statistics Center, there was a fivefold increase in heroin overdose deaths from 2010 to 2015 (Haddy, 2017). Statewide there were 201 deaths as a result of heroin overdoses in 2015. Cabell County had the highest death rate of 54.7 deaths per 100,000 people in the population. The two other leading counties in heroin overdose deaths were Kanawha County and Berkeley County. Most deaths as a result of a heroin overdose occurred among those ages 26–34 from 2012 to 2015 and among males. In terms of reported heroin treatment admissions from West Virginia Poison Centers, there were 327 reports of heroin use in 2016, which was substantially higher from the previous years (WV Poison Center, 2016). Substance abuse treatment data (TEDS) showed that in 2015, a slightly higher percentage of female (53.8%) treatment admissions were reported for heroin use than males (46.2%) (SAMSHA, 2018).

Fentanyl

Yet another synthetic opioid, fentanyl, has become increasingly popular and abused. ***Fentanyl*** was introduced to the market as an anesthetic in the 1960s (DEA, 2017a). The Schedule II narcotic is far more potent than heroin and is 100 times more potent than morphine. It is produced in clandestine labs in either a powder or tablet form. It may also be produced as patches or lozenges known as lollipops. Illegal manufacturers are known to produce it in combination with cocaine or heroin. If combined with heroin, the drug is most likely injected. The other forms are either snorted or smoked.

With the discussion of heroin taking center stage, it is important to recognize that a large number of overdose deaths occur as a result of fentanyl. Data from the West Virginia Health Statistics Center showed that fentanyl overdoses tripled from 2010 to 2015 (Haddy, 2017). In 2015 alone there were 180 overdose deaths in comparison to 201 deaths as a result of heroin and 182 deaths as a result of oxycodone. In 2015, most of the fentanyl-related overdoses occurred in Cabell County at a rate of 41.3 deaths per 100,000 people in the population, followed by Webster County (22.8 deaths per 100,000 people in the population), and Kanawha County (20.2 deaths per 100,000 people in the population).

Prescription Drug Abuse

It has become widely known that prescription drugs can be used to achieve a certain "high" or to enhance the effects of alcohol and other drugs. Two of the drugs that are regularly abused are oxycodone and hydrocodone. Most prescription drugs are purchased on the street, abused from a legitimate prescription, or purchased from a family member or friend. Others obtain prescription drugs for illegal purposes by ***doctor shopping***, which is "when patients intend to deceive physicians to obtain controlled substances from multiple physicians in a short time frame" (Shaffer & Moss, 2009, p. 10). Others have defined doctor shopping as visiting numerous doctors to obtain prescriptions, or by simply stealing prescription tablets or stealing samples from doctor's offices or pharmacies (Griffin & Spillane, 2012). Often the standard is that the person tries to obtain drugs from five or more physicians. Withholding information from a physician about obtaining previous prescriptions of a controlled substance concurrently is illegal in the State of West Virginia (W. Va. Code §60A-4-410) and carries a possible sentence of nine months and/or a fine of no more than $2,500.

Oxycodone

Oxycodone is a Schedule II narcotic and prescription painkiller (branded as OxyContin® or as Percocet®) (Inciardi & Goode, 2004). Among users, it is also called "hillbilly heroin," "kicker," "ox," or "roxy" (DEA, 2017a). The drug's "true" intention and medical purpose is to treat chronic pain. And, for many who suffer from prolonged pain, it is one of the most effective analgesics on the market. For these legitimate purposes, it is prescribed and taken orally. However, others abuse the drug by crushing or snorting the pills or dissolving the pills and injecting the drug intravenously. Some may heat the tablet on a piece of foil in order to inhale the vapors (DEA, 2017a). Those who use OxyContin, like other drugs, will have a euphoric sensation, coupled with relaxation and drowsiness. The addictive properties of oxycodone are tremendous, and when used in combination with other drugs and/or alcohol, the effects can be fatal. Some of the side effects include a decreased heart rate and decreased respiration, which may lead to a coma or death.

OxyContin has been used since the Second World War. In 1995, Purdue Pharma was granted approval from the Food and Drug Administration to manufacture the drug (Griffin & Spillane, 2012). By 1999, reports of the drug's misuse given its addictive properties started to circulate. Certain parts of the country, including Appalachia, seem to be impacted the most. Mainly, some have claimed this is due to "***prescription drug diversion***, which involves the unlawful movement of regulated pharmaceuticals from legal sources to the illegal marketplace" (Inciardi & Goode, 2004, p. 165) or "doctor shopping" as mentioned earlier (Griffin & Spillane, 2012; Shaffer & Moss, 2009). Given the exponential increase in use of OxyContin, and the many West Virginians who became addicted, West Virginia sued Pharma Purdue. The lawsuit reached a settlement in 2004 and the state was granted $44.1 million (Thomas, 2004), even though the company claimed that it did not aggressively market the drug to state residents. Lawsuits against other drug companies by the state have followed. Despite such legal action, OxyContin has not been banned or reclassified from a Schedule II to a Schedule I drug, and it continues to beg the question of how medical treatment needs to be balanced with the potential for abuse.

In 2015, 182 deaths occurred as a result of the drug, falling second to heroin (Haddy, 2017). But unlike those who have succumbed to heroin, oxycodone was abused by those ages 55–64 (Sanders & Mullins, 2017). Table 9.3 displays the number of the most common opioids that were detected after a postmortem toxicology screening in West Virginia. Since many who abuse drugs use multiple drugs at a time (known as ***polypharmacy***), it is possible for the deceased to have had traces of multiple illicit substances found in their system. For example, in 2017, out of the 830 West Virginians who died as a result of a drug overdose, 86% had traces of several illicit drugs in their system (Sanders & Mullins, 2017). Research based on 2016 drug overdose data also shows that 90% of deceased females had more than one illegal substance in their system compared to 84% of males.

Aside from the illicit substances such as heroin and fentanyl, many of the drugs listed in Table 9.3 are by prescription only. Among decedents from 2010 to 2015, prescription drugs such as oxycodone were found most commonly in the system, followed by hydrocodone and oxymorphone (Haddy, 2017). Prior research from the WV Quitline in 2012 showed that 86.9% of callers claimed they purchased the prescription drug on the street whereas 40.2% acquired the drug from a legitimate doctor's order (Gwilliam, 2013). A little over 30% of callers reported they obtained the drug from a family member or friend.

Table 9.3. Top Ten Primary Opioids Recorded on Death Certificates in West Virginia, 2010–2015

Drug Type	2010	2011	2012	2013	2014	2015	Total
Oxycodone	223	224	182	200	200	182	1211
Hydrocodone	138	171	142	138	133	113	835
Heroin	34	41	67	157	165	201	665
Oxymorphone	77	182	72	32	48	54	465
Fentanyl	44	51	32	40	55	180	402
Methadone	83	61	65	55	39	32	335
Morphine	39	45	54	48	68	76	261
Tramadol	25	35	32	34	42	22	190
Buprenorphine	12	15	32	30	34	31	154
Codeine	11	11	10	50	16	17	115

Source: Haddy, L. (2017, August). *West Virginia drug overdose deaths: Historical overview 2001–2015.* Bureau for Public Health, West Virginia Department of Health and Human Resources. Retrieved from http://dhhr.wv.gov/oeps/disease/ob/documents/opioid/wv-drug-overdoses-2001_2015.pdf (Table 1, modified).

Stimulants

Stimulants are among the most widely used drugs in our country, namely caffeine and nicotine. However, there are other synthetic drugs and stimulants like amphetamine, methamphetamine, cocaine, and ecstasy that are more troublesome for those in the health and criminal justice professions (Gaines, 2014). ***Stimulants*** are chemical substances that impact the central nervous system by producing an increased state of alertness or awareness. It is not uncommon for stimulants to increase a person's blood pressure, heart rate, and disrupt their sleep.

Cocaine and Crack Cocaine

Cocaine is a Schedule II narcotic[1] that is derived from the coca plant (*Erythroxylon coca*) through a chemical process that involves refining the leaves

1. Technically, narcotics are drugs from the opiate family or derived from the poppy seed. Although confusing, drugs like cocaine, crack cocaine, and even marijuana are classified as narcotic drugs under the Controlled Substances Act of 1990.

into a powder form, otherwise known as cocaine hydrochloride or powder cocaine (Abadinsky, 2014). In its white, crystalline powder form, it is either snorted or injected (DEA, 2017a). Whether injecting or snorting cocaine, users will experience a "rush" or euphoria that is often paired with feelings of omnipotence. For instance, the user may become insensitive to pain or have illusions of great physical strength and intense alertness (Abadinsky, 2014). Tolerance of the drug develops quickly, so users will resort to injecting the drug intravenously or using higher doses of the drug in order to achieve the desired effects. Adverse effects of cocaine are numerous. It is not uncommon for users to suffer from delirium, hallucinations, and paranoia. Moreover, when coming down from the drug, users may experience depression, irritability, and insomnia. Others report a condition known as "cocaine bugs" or Magnon's syndrome, where users have the perception that bugs are crawling under the skin. Research has shown that with chronic abuse, the prefrontal and temporal cortex of the brain is damaged, resulting in intensified and irrational behaviors, plus the inability to make rational decisions, poor memory recall, and disinhibition. In addition, heavy use leads to an increased heart rate and blood pressure. With damage to the heart, cocaine can lead to vascular disease and aneurysms in heart arteries. Ultimately, this may lead to a heart attack, stroke, or death.

The earliest accounts of cocaine stem from the sixteenth century and the Andes region of South America. In Austria, cocaine was first isolated from the plant by chemist Albert Niemann in the 1880s (Musto, 2004). With this discovery, the drug gained popularity throughout Europe and the United States and was even advocated by renowned psychiatrist, Sigmund Freud.

> By 1885, the major U.S. manufacturer, Parke, Davis, & Co., of Detroit and New York, was selling cocaine and coca in 15 forms, including coca-leaf cigarettes or cheroots, cocaine inhalant, a Coca Cordial, cocaine crystals, and cocaine in solution for hypodermic injection (Musto, 2004, p. 226).

With small traces of cocaine, the elixir, Coca Cola, was marketed in 1886. Today, cocaine continues to be trafficked into the United States from Bolivia, Colombia, and Peru (Inciardi, 2002).

Freebase cocaine, or ***crack cocaine***, gained popularity in the 1980s, and is also a Schedule II narcotic and stimulant that is processed from cocaine hydrochloride in a heating process that involves a mixture of water and sodium bicarbonate (baking soda) (Abadinsky, 2014). Once heated, the drug takes the form of bars or chips that are then cut into "rocks." Crack cocaine is known as a cheaper alternative to powder cocaine and is usually smoked through a glass pipe or other handcrafted device made from jars, bottles, or cans (Inciardi, 2002). Some users will smoke crushed pieces of crack with tobacco or marijuana.

Compared to the entire country (3.2% of admissions in the U.S.), the percentage of individuals treated for smoked cocaine in 2015 was much lower in West Virginia (0.9% of admissions) (SAMSHA, 2018). Note that for the data that are reported here, "smoked cocaine mainly represents crack or rock cocaine, but can include cocaine hydrochloride (powder cocaine) when it is free-based" (Gwilliam, 2013, p. 113). There were more males (51.6%) in West Virginia who had treatment admissions for smoked cocaine compared to females (48.4%), and nationwide higher percentages of crack cocaine treatment admissions were documented for males than for females. In 2015, the majority of those seeking substance abuse treatment for crack cocaine were individuals ages 26 to 30 (16.1%). For cocaine that was consumed using methods other than smoking, estimates are more conservative as the exact method is not often reported. Treatment admissions for non-smoked cocaine in West Virginia was minimal (1%), compared to treatment admissions nationally of 1.8%. More than half of the treatment admissions for non-smoked cocaine were for males (55.9%), and there were substantially more treatment admissions for males nationally (68.6%).

Methamphetamine

Methamphetamine is a highly addictive derivative of amphetamine and is classified as a Schedule II stimulant. The origin of the drug can be traced back to 1887 when it was synthesized in Germany and later in Japan in 1893 (Anglin, Burke, Perrochet, Stamper, & Dawud-Noursi, 2000). Also known as "speed," "crystal," "chalk," or "ice," the drug can be taken orally, snorted, or smoked (NIDA, 2017a). For the user, methamphetamine produces a "rush" or a "high" as a result of an increased amount of dopamine that is released into the brain (Kremling, 2014). That is, users experience a sense of euphoria, prolonged energy, and invincibility, yet the drug also has been known to produce hallucinogenic effects as well as panic attacks. When used over a longer period, users may experience behavioral consequences such as increased anxiety, paranoia, insomnia, and violent tendencies (NIDA, 2017a). With long-term use, there are numerous physical consequences including extreme weight loss, tooth decay and loss (meth mouth), skin sores, and an increased likelihood of contracting an infectious disease (i.e., HIV and hepatitis B and C). Last, prolonged use will result in chemical and structural changes in the brain (Kremling, 2014) that may diminish the user's working memory and lead to other cognitive deficits.

The drug was used legally in the late 1960s to medically treat depression and obesity, but it also became widely popular with counterculture groups like the Hells Angels in California, where it was widely manufactured in underground drug labs. Today, Mexican Transnational Criminal Organizations (TCOs) are known to transport the drug by way of California and Arizona (DEA, 2017b). Production of methamphetamine peaked in the United States in 2004 (when nearly 25,000 labs were seized), however, the number of clandestine labs today are not only fewer in number, but smaller operations (roughly 3,000 labs were seized in the U.S. in 2016) in comparison to those in Mexico (see DEA, 2017b). For example, as of April 2017, Indiana had the highest number of methamphetamine lab incidents[2] in the country (945), followed by Michigan (655), and Ohio (474). In comparison, West Virginia had one of the lowest number of methamphetamine lab incidents (8) compared to other southern states and has seen a remarkable decrease since 2004 when 326 methamphetamine lab incidents were reported. However, even with a decreased number of labs, 127 methamphetamine overdose deaths occurred in 2017 (which is an increase by 500% in the past four years) and at least half of these cases involved fentanyl (Eyre, 2018a).

An additional and troubling aspect of methamphetamine is the fact that it is extremely dangerous to manufacture (Kremling, 2014). This poses added risks to those who are exposed to the chemicals during the production stages, such as neighbors or children. Furthermore, law enforcement must take extra precautions when called to the scene given that the labs are highly explosive. Information about the country's clandestine labs are collected by the National Clandestine Registry (NCLR), which is maintained by the Drug Enforcement Administration. This national registry includes detailed information about the lab or dump site location (i.e., state, county, address, and date the lab was found) (Wells & Weisheit, 2012). The database has existed since 2004, and contains useful information from state and local law enforcement that is reported to the DEA, but herein also lies the limitation as it is not a comprehensive list.

As part of the state's Uniform Controlled Substances Act, Article 10 includes the Clandestine Drug Laboratory Eradication Act (W. Va. Code §60A-10-1).

> A *clandestine drug laboratory* means the area or areas where controlled substances, or their immediate precursors, have been, or were attempted to be, manufactured, processed, cooked, disposed of or stored and all proximate areas that are likely to be contaminated as a result of

2. The DEA states that a methamphetamine lab incident includes reported meth-related incidents, involving labs, dumpsites, or any chemical and equipment seizures.

such manufacturing, processing, cooking, disposing or storing (W. Va. Code §60A-11-2).

Using the state clandestine drug lab property report, which is used more commonly among law enforcement agencies instead of the national database maintained by the DEA, there have been a total of 1,190 reported clandestine labs in the state from 2013–2017. It is evident by the number of reported clandestine drug labs in West Virginia that it was once a popular enterprise, but it has dwindled since 2014 (WV Clandestine Drug Lab Remediation Program, 2018). For instance, there were 423 reported labs in 2013 yet only 82 labs were reported in 2017. It is important to note that some of the data is limited in that the exact year is unreported. There are at least 22 labs for which the year was not reported. Also, Kanawha County had the largest number of reported clandestine labs from 2013 to 2017 (191 labs), followed by Wood County (106 labs) and Cabell County (58 labs). Both Mason and Upshur counties had 55 and 57 reported labs during the same time period, respectively.

Operating a clandestine lab is a felony offense and carries with it a penalty of 2 to 10 years in state prison or a fine of $15,000 to $25,000 or both (W. Va. Code §60A-4-411). Because these labs endanger public health and the environment, hazardous chemicals must be disposed of properly by certified professionals (see DEA's *Guidelines for law enforcement for the cleanup of clandestine drug laboratories*, 2005). This means that those convicted of operating a clandestine lab also are responsible for the cost of remediating the site.

Synthetic and Designer Drugs

Another growing concern is the number of synthetic drugs that are illegally produced for human consumption (Abadinsky, 2014). In the 1970s, some of the first ***designer drugs*** were produced in home-based labs, mostly synthetic opioids (German, Fleckenstien, & Hanson, 2014). Today, designer drugs have become increasingly popular. More precisely, designer drugs are defined as "synthetic compounds developed to provide rewarding effects similar to illicit drugs of abuse (e.g., opioids, amphetamines, and marijuana), while circumventing existing legislative classification and penalty" (German et al., 2014, p. 2).

Bath Salts

Bath salts are Schedule I stimulants that are derived from one of any three cathinones, known also as a "monoamine alkaloid found in khat (*Catha edulis*), a shrub whose leaves are chewed or dried as tea" (Miotto, Streibel, Cho, &

Wang, 2013, p. 2). Bath salts can be snorted, smoked, injected intravenously, or consumed orally when in pill form (German et al., 2014). Those who manufacture the drug sell it in small attractive packaging with names like "Cloud Nine," "Ivory Wave," "White Lightening," or "Vanilla Sky" (DEA, 2017a). In addition, packaging will include the phrase "not for human consumption" in order to avoid being charged with violating the Analogue Enforcement Act (German et al., 2014).

Today, illicit bath salts can be obtained from gas stations, convenience stores, as well as the Internet (Miotto et al., 2013). For some users, bath salts produce desirable effects such as an increased sense of alertness, increased energy, and numbness (Miotto et al., 2013). However, severe adverse effects are known to occur. For example, among emergency room reports, tachycardia, hypertension, nausea, vomiting, and chest pain have been documented (German et al., 2014; Miotto et al., 2013).

K2/Spice

The drug ***K2/Spice*** is also chemically manufactured and produced and has been classified as a Schedule I drug. More precisely, it is a brand of "synthetic designer drugs that are intended to mimic THC, the main active ingredient of marijuana" that is sold as a type of herbal incense or potpourri (DEA, 2017a, p. 88). Most individuals obtain the drug from tobacco or head shops in which they may be sold "as packets of incense, potpourri, or room deodorant" (Abadinsky, 2014, p. 114). Like marijuana, it can be smoked. Some may refer to it as "Black Magic," "Smoke," "Genie," "Crazy Clown," or "Sence" (DEA, 2017a). Given the THC compounds that make up this drug, the effects are similar to that of marijuana. Users also may experience paranoia, delusions, and may become agitated (DEA, 2017a). The possible additional adverse side effects are increased heart rate, blood pressure, and vomiting.

In West Virginia, Poison Centers reported the highest number of bath salt exposures in 2011 (259), perhaps when the drug had gained the most popularity among the public (Gwilliam, 2013). However, in 2012, there was a marked decrease in bath salt exposures (45) and only 10 exposures were reported in 2016 (WV Poison Center, 2016). Synthetic THC exposures were not nearly as high. Eighty-eight synthetic THC exposures were reported by West Virginia Poison Centers in 2011, 60 in 2012, and 41 in 2016 (Gwilliam, 2013; WV Poison Center, 2016). However, caution must be used when interpreting the data on calls made in reference to synthetic marijuana. That is, data for both marijuana and synthetic marijuana were combined. In addition, treatment for bath salts was not reported or may have been combined with other drug categories.

Spotlight: Substance Abuse and Pregnancy

Illicit drug use during pregnancy is a major public health concern. The deleterious effects of cigarette smoking and drinking alcohol while pregnant are well documented. Across the nation, most reports indicate that pregnant women have the highest rates of alcohol use, illicit drug use, and smoke cigarettes during the first trimester (SAMHSA, 2013). Even though the use of illicit drugs and alcohol may decrease during the mother's pregnancy during the second and third trimesters, the neonatal effects are still extraordinary. The umbrella term that is often used in these cases is ***neonatal abstinence syndrome (NAS).*** NAS is a set of withdrawal conditions that a newborn exhibits as a result of the mother's drug dependency during pregnancy. In the past, the term was more exclusively used for cases where infants were addicted to narcotics, but now, it is used to explain the withdrawal conditions from any type of drug. Current research shows that in the state of West Virginia, 14 out of every 100 infants born have at least one substance in their system (Holdren, 2017) and require detoxification procedures.

Nationally, treatment admissions data (TEDS) revealed that in 2012, 63.8% of pregnant women ages 15 to 44 were being treated for drugs alone, whereas 7% were being treated for alcohol abuse alone (SAMSHA, 2013). Nearly 28% of pregnant women were seeking treatment for a combination of alcohol and drug abuse. With greater attention on opioids, research has also shown that from 2007 to 2012, 2.8% of pregnant women ages 15 to 44 reported misusing an opioid (such as heroin or a prescribed opioid-based pain reliever) in comparison to 3.6% of non-pregnant women in the same age group (Smith & Lipari, 2017). The misuse is more common during the first trimester and dwindles substantially during the second and third trimesters.

Compared to national rates in 2013 where 8% of women reported drinking alcohol during the last three months of their pregnancy, only 2.4% of pregnant women in West Virginia reported doing so (WV DHHR, 2016a). Even though tobacco is not an illicit drug per se, smoking during the last three months of pregnancy often leads to an increased likelihood of low birth weight. According to Pregnancy Risk Assessment Monitoring System (PRAMS) report, in 2013, 41.4% of pregnant women in West Virginia smoked three months before pregnancy, and about 25% smoked during the last three months of pregnancy (WV DHHR, 2016b). Overall, these percentages are twice as high as those found among pregnant women in the United States.

Numerous research studies have been conducted to further understand the impact of illicit drugs and the adverse effects on newborns. For example, a meta-analysis of 31 studies on prenatal cocaine exposure was associated with pre-term birth, low birth weight, small gestational age, and reduced birth weight, among others (Gouin, Murphy, & Prakesh, 2011). Lindsay and Burnett (2013) explained that there are similar consequences for heroin abuse such as poor fetal growth, preterm birth, and low birth weight. The harmful effects of prescription opioid abuse is less understood, but still leads to NAS. On the other hand, the use of ecstasy is linked to an increased risk of congenital abnormalities, namely cardiovascular and musculoskeletal abnormalities. Above all, more research is needed and even here, the research is limited as some of the effects of a single illicit drug alone are difficult to determine as some mothers may also smoke cigarettes regularly, abuse alcohol, or abuse a combination of other illicit drugs.

Given the fact that the effects of illicit drugs, alcohol, and tobacco are predominantly linked to low birth weight or preterm birth, it is important to remember that the developmental deficits affecting behavior and cognition later in life can be just as devastating. Children may experience difficulty paying attention, and/or have impaired language and learning skills, sometimes coupled with behavioral problems (NIDA, 2017b). Some youth may even have a higher rate of drug addiction during adolescence. For example, Minnes et al. (2014) found that youth who were exposed to cocaine prenatally had higher rates of using marijuana, alcohol, and tobacco at age 15, but they did not have higher rates of using cocaine compared to a group of youth who were not exposed to cocaine in the womb.

In a study of newborns in West Virginia, Stitely, Calhoun, Maxwell, and Nerhood (2009) found that of the 759 umbilical cord samples tested, 142 were positive for drugs and/or alcohol. More specifically, 46% tested positive for cannabinoids, 28% for opiates, 27% for alcohol, 12% of benzodiazepines, 10% for methadone, and smaller percentages of amphetamines. Hospitals in the state that had the highest percentages of women who tested positive for drug abuse were Raleigh General Hospital, Cabell Huntington Hospital, and Charleston Area Medical Center. On the other hand, Wheeling Hospital, Thomas Memorial Hospital, and Charleston Area Medical Center had the highest percentages of pregnant women who tested positive for alcohol. In brief, they concluded, "one in five infants born in West Virginia has a significant drug exposure" (Stitely et al., 2009, p. 48).

The alarming number of infants born with a drug addiction has led many area hospitals to create neonatal therapeutic units; however, at times, some of these units are full and there is no space for infants who are going through drug withdrawal. Hospitals are unable to place these infants in the NICU as these spaces are reserved for those infants with other life-threatening conditions (Nelson, 2013a). This does not mean that NAS infants do not require serious attention or critical care. Many hospitals like Charleston Area Medical Center and Cabell Huntington Hospital have partnered with nonprofit agencies, like Lily's Place, a pediatric addiction recovery center (Nelson, 2013b). Depending on the severity of NAS, infants may experience long periods of wakefulness, irritability, difficulty self-soothing, tremors, regurgitation, a poor sucking reflex, frequent diarrhea, and weight loss, just to name a few. Infants going through withdrawal require low levels of stimulation, and a warm and quiet room, with more frequent but smaller feedings. In the end, these step-down facilities serve a much needed purpose, but hopefully with increased education and prenatal care, they will not become the norm around the state.

Key Terms and Definitions

Alcohol: A regulated organic compound otherwise known as ethanol that is created in a process of fermentation, commonly found in beer, wine, and liquor.

Bath salts: Schedule I stimulants that are derived from one of any three cathinones, known also as a monoamine alkaloid found in Khat, a shrub whose leaves are chewed or dried as tea.

Clandestine drug laboratory: The area or areas where controlled substances, or their immediate precursors, have been, or were attempted to be, manufactured, processed, cooked, disposed of, or stored, and all proximate areas that are likely to be contaminated as a result of such manufacturing, processing, cooking, disposing, or storing.

Cocaine: A Schedule II narcotic that is derived from the coca plant (*Erythroxylon coca*) through a chemical process that involves cultivating the leaves into a powder form, otherwise known as cocaine hydrochloride or powder cocaine.

Crack cocaine: A Schedule II narcotic and stimulant that is processed from cocaine hydrochloride in a heating process that involves a mixture of water and sodium bicarbonate (baking soda).

Designer drugs: Synthetic compounds developed to provide rewarding effects similar to illicit drugs of abuse (e.g., opioids, amphetamines, and marijuana), while circumventing existing legislative classification and penalty.

Doctor shopping: Deceptive methods to obtain controlled substances from physicians or pharmacies.

Drug abuse: The nonsanctioned use of substances controlled in Schedules I through V of the CSA; when drugs are used in a manner or amount inconsistent with the medical or social patterns of a culture.

Drug addiction: A chronic, relapsing brain disease that is characterized by compulsive drug seeking and use, despite harmful consequences.

Fentanyl: A Schedule II narcotic and very potent synthetic opioid that is often combined with other illegal substances such as heroin and methamphetamine.

Heroin: A Schedule I narcotic and derivative of morphine that is refined from the opium poppy.

K2/Spice: A Schedule I synthetic drug that is intended to mimic THC, the main active ingredient of marijuana; it is often sold as a type of herbal incense or potpourri.

Marijuana (or marihuana): A derivative of the hemp plant recognized scientifically as *Cannabis sativa.*

Methamphetamine: A highly addictive derivative of amphetamine and is classified as a Schedule II stimulant.

Narcotic: Any natural derivative of the opium poppy, known scientifically as *Papaver somniferum.*

Neonatal Abstinence Syndrome (NAS): A set of withdrawal conditions that a newborn exhibits as a result of the mother's drug dependency during pregnancy.

Oxycodone: A Schedule II narcotic and prescription painkiller that is branded as OxyContin® or as Percocet®.

Polypharmacy: Simultaneously using multiple drugs.

Prescription drug diversion: The unlawful movement of regulated pharmaceuticals from legal sources to the illegal marketplace.

Stimulants: Chemical substances that impact the central nervous system by producing an increased state of alertness or awareness.

Select Internet Sources

Drug Enforcement Administration (DEA): https://www.dea.gov/index.shtml.

Help4WV: https://www.help4wv.com/

Lily's Place: https://www.lilysplace.org/.

West Virginia DHHR, Bureau for Behavioral Health and Health Facilities: http://dhhr.wv.gov/bhhf/Pages/default.aspx.

Critical Thinking and Review Questions

1. What is the Controlled Substances Act? How are chemical substances classified?
2. What type of drug abuse is most prevalent among West Virginians? Are certain types of drugs used more commonly among high school students than adults? Which ones?
3. Which type of drug is associated with the largest number of overdose deaths in West Virginia? Why is this type of drug so commonly abused?
4. What types of programs or policy initiatives have been created by the state to combat drug abuse and drug overdoses? What else can be done?
5. How are newborns affected by drugs and alcohol that were consumed during their mother's pregnancy?

References

Abadinsky, H. (2014). *Drug use and abuse: A comprehensive introduction* (8th ed.) Belmont, CA: Wadsworth/Cengage Learning.

Anglin, M. D., Burke, C., Perrochet, B., Stamper, R., & Dawud-Noursi, S. (2000, June). History of the methamphetamine problem. *Journal of Psychoactive Drugs, 32*(2), 137–141.

Anslinger, H. J., & Cooper, C. R. (1937, July). Marijuana: Assassin of youth. *American Magazine,* 18–19, 151–153.

Bureau of Labor Statistics. (2018). *Local area unemployment statistics.* Retrieved from https://www.bls.gov/lau/.

Centers for Disease Control and Prevention (CDC). (2015a). *Youth Risk Behavioral Surveillance System (YRBSS). West Virginia 2015 results.* Retrieved from https://nccd.cdc.gov/youthonline/app/Results.aspx?LID=WV.

Centers for Disease Control and Prevention (CDC). (2015b). *Youth Risk Behavioral Surveillance System (YRBSS). West Virginia 2015 and United States 2015 results.* Retrieved from https://nccd.cdc.gov/youthonline/app/Results.aspx?LID=WV.

Drug Enforcement Administration (DEA). (2005). *DEA's Guidelines for law enforcement for the cleanup of clandestine drug laboratories.* Retrieved from http://www.justice.gov/dea/resources/img/redbook.pdf.

Drug Enforcement Administration (DEA). (2017a). *Drugs of abuse: A DEA resource guide.* Washington, DC: Drug Enforcement Administration, U.S.

Department of Justice. Retrieved from https://www.dea.gov/pr/multimedia-library/publications/drug_of_abuse.pdf.

Drug Enforcement Administration (DEA). (2017b). *2017 National drug threat assessment, October 2017*. Retrieved from https://www.dea.gov/docs/DIR-040-17_2017-NDTA.pdf.

Eyre, E. (2018a, December 2). Meth-related overdose deaths hit record number in WV. *Charleston Gazette Mail*. Retrieved from https://www.wvgazettemail.com/news/health/meth-related-overdose-deaths-hit-record-number-in-wv/article_67cb7c01-fba3-5dbc-80c8-f9913e07dfde.html.

Eyre, E. (2018b, February 6). Opioid epidemic costs WV $8.8 billion annually study says. *The Charleston Gazette-Mail*. Retrieved from https://www.wvgazettemail.com/news/health/opioid-epidemic-costs-wv-billion-annually-study-says/article_1cd8aaa5-78eb-5fd5-8619-3a0a1c086e66.html.

Fergusson, D. M., & Boden, J. M. (2008). Cannabis use and later life outcomes. *Addiction, 103*, 969–976. doi:10.1111/j.1360-0443.2008.02221.x.

Gaines, L. K. (2014). The psychopharmacology and prevalence of drugs In L. K. Gaines & J. Kremling (Eds.), *Drugs, crime, and justice* (3rd ed) (pp. 105–138). Long Grove, IL: Waveland Press.

German, C., Fleckenstein, A. E., & Hanson, G. R. (2014). Bath salts and synthetic cathinones: An emerging designer drug phenomenon. *Life Sciences, 97*, 2–8.

Gouin, K., Murphy, K., & Prakesh, S. S. (2011). Effects of cocaine use during pregnancy on low birthweight and preterm birth: Systematic review and metanalyses. *American Journal of Obstetrics & Gynecology, 204*(4), 1.e1-1.e12. doi: 10.1016/j.ajog.2010.11.013.

Griffin, O. H., & Spillane, J. F. (2012). Pharmaceutical regulation failures and changes: Lessons learned from OxyContin abuse and diversion. *Journal of Drug Issues, 43*(2), 164–175. doi: 10.1177/0022042612467990.

Gwilliam, M. (2013). *West Virginia behavioral health epidemiological profile*. Charleston, WV: West Virginia Department of Health and Human Resources, Bureau for Behavioral Health and Health Facilities, Division on Alcoholism and Drug Abuse. Retrieved from http://www.dhhr.wv.gov/bhhf/resources/Documents/2013_State_Profile.pdf.

Haddy, L. (2017, August). *West Virginia drug overdose deaths: Historical overview 2001–2015*. Bureau for Public Health, West Virginia Department of Health and Human Resources. Retrieved from http://dhhr.wv.gov/oeps/disease/ob/documents/opioid/wv-drug-overdoses-2001_2015.pdf.

Hall, W. (2009). The adverse health effects of cannabis use: What are they, and what are their implications for policy? *International Journal of Drug Policy, 20*, 458–466.

Holdren, W. (2017, December 13). 14% of babies exposed to drugs. *The Register-Herald*. Retrieved from http://www.register-herald.com/news/of-babies-exposed-to-drugs/article_eb3cb535-17f0-5d07-945d-8f12a747f09e.html.

Inciardi, J. A. (2002). *The war on drugs III: The continuing saga of the mysteries and miseries of intoxication, addiction, crime, and public policy*. Boston, MA: Allyn and Bacon.

Inciardi, J. A., & Goode, J. L. (2004). OxyContin: Miracle medicine or problem drug? In J. A. Inciardi & K. McElrath (Eds.), *The American drug scene: An anthology* (pp. 163–173). Los Angeles, CA: Roxbury Publishing.

Justice, J., Reed, P., & Tipton, B. (2017, July). *West Virginia highway safety plan: Federal fiscal year 2018*. Charleston, WV: West Virginia Governor's Highway Safety Program. Retrieved from https://www.nhtsa.gov/sites/nhtsa.dot.gov/files/documents/west_virginia_fy2018_hsp.pdf.

Kremling, J. (2014). The scourge of methamphetamine. In. L. K. Gaines, & J. Kremling (Eds.), *Drugs, crime, and justice* (3rd ed.) (pp. 150–177). Long Grove, IL: Waveland Press.

Lindsay, M. K., & Burnett, E. (2013, March). The use of narcotics and street drugs during pregnancy. *Clinical Obstetrics and Gynecology, 56*(1), 133–141.

Loftin, K. L. (2016, February 26). Help 4 WV connects West Virginians with substance abuse and behavioral health services. *Appalachian Health News*. Charleston, WV: WV Public Broadcasting. Retrieved from http://wvpublic.org/post/help-4-wv-connects-west-virginians-substance-abuse-and-behavioral-health-services#stream/0.

Mechoulam, R. (2000). A Cannabis tale. *Science Spectra, 21*, 44–50.

Minnes, S., Singer, L., Min, M. O., Wu, M., Lang, A., & Yoon, S. (2014). Effects of prenatal cocaine/polydrug exposure on substance abuse by age 15. *Drug and alcohol dependence, 134*, 201–210.

Miotto, K., Striebel, J., Cho, A. K., & Wang, C. (2013). Clinical and pharmacological aspects of bath salt use: A review of the literature and case reports. *Drug and alcohol dependence, 132*, 1–12. doi: 1111/j.1521-0391.2012.00240.x.

Musto, D. F. (2004). America's first cocaine epidemic. In J. A. Inciardi & K. McElrath (Eds.), *The American drug scene: An anthology* (pp. 225–229). Los Angeles, CA: Roxbury Publishing.

National Highway Safety Traffic Administration (NHTSA). (2015). *Fatality analysis reporting system (FARS) encyclopedia, Persons killed by state and highest driver blood alcohol concentration (BAC) in crash—State: West Virginia, year: 2015*. Retrieved from https://www-fars.nhtsa.dot.gov/States/StatesAlcohol.aspx.

National Incident Based Reporting System (NIBRS). (2016). *Agency tables by state: West Virginia.* Federal Bureau of Investigation, Uniform Crime Report. Retrieved from https://ucr.fbi.gov/nibrs/2016/tables/data-tables.

National Institute on Drug Abuse (NIDA). (2014). *Drugs, brains, and behavior: The science of addiction.* National Institutes of Health U.S. Department of Health and Human Services. Retrieved https://d14rmgtrwzf5a.cloudfront.net/sites/default/files/soa_2014.pdf.

National Institute on Drug Abuse (NIDA). (2015, June). *DrugFacts: Nationwide trends.* Retrieved from https://www.drugabuse.gov/publications/drugfacts/nationwide-trends.

National Institute on Drug Abuse (NIDA). (2017a, February). *Methamphetamine.* Retrieved from https://www.drugabuse.gov/publications/drugfacts/methamphetamine.

National Institute on Drug Abuse (NIDA). (2017b, April). *Sex and gender differences in substance use.* Retrieved from https://www.drugabuse.gov/publications/drugfacts/substance-use-in-women.

National Institute on Drug Abuse (NIDA). (2018, January). *Heroin.* Retrieved from https://www.drugabuse.gov/publications/drugfacts/heroin.

Nelson, C. (2013a, June 5). Drug-addicted infant rates worry doctors. *Charleston Daily Mail.* Retrieved from http://www.charlestondailymail.com/News/201306040191.

Nelson, C. (2013b, May 29). Lily's Place to soothe infants born addicted to drugs. *Charleston Daily Mail.* Retrieved from http://www.charlestondailymail.com/News/201305280119.

Sanders, S., & Mullins, C. (2017, December 20). *2016 West Virginia overdose fatality analysis: Healthcare systems utilization, risk factors, and opportunities for intervention.* Charleston, WV: West Virginia Department of Health and Human Resources. Retrieved from https://dhhr.wv.gov/bph/Documents/ODCP%20Reports%202017/2016%20Overdose%20Fatality%20Analysis%20final%20rv.pdf.

Shaffer, E. G., & Moss, A. H. (2009). Physicians' perceptions of doctor shopping in West Virginia. *West Virginia Medical Journal, 106*(4), 10–14. Retrieved from www.wvsma.com/Journal.aspx.

Siegal, H. A., & Inciardi, J. A. (2004). A brief history of alcohol. In J. A. Inciardi and K. McElrath (Eds.), *The American drug scene: An anthology.* Los Angeles, CA: Roxbury Publishing.

Smith, K., & Lipari, R. (2017, January 17). Women of childbearing age and opioids. *The CBHSQ Report: January 17, 2017.* Rockville, MD: Center for Behavioral Health Statistics and Quality, Substance Abuse and Mental

Health Services Administration. Retrieved from https://www.samhsa.gov/data/sites/default/files/report_2724/ShortReport-2724.html.

Stitely, M. L., Calhoun, B., Maxwell, S., Nerhood, R., & Chaffin, D. (2009). Prevalence of drug use in pregnant West Virginia patients. *West Virginia Medical Journal, 106*(4), 48–52.

Substance Abuse and Mental Health Services Administration (SAMHSA). (2013, July). Trends in substances of abuse among pregnant women and women of childbearing age in treatment. *The TEDS Report.* Rockville, MD: Author. Retrieved from http://www.samhsa.gov/data/spotlight/spot110-trends-pregnant-women-2013.pdf.

Substance Abuse and Mental Health Services Administration (SAMSHA). (2017). *2015–2016 National Survey on Drug Use and Health: Model-Based Prevalence Estimates (50 States and the District of Columbia).* Rockville, MD: Center for Behavioral Health Statistics and Quality, Substance Abuse and Mental Health Services Administration. Retrieved from https://www.samhsa.gov/data/sites/default/files/NSDUHsaePercents2016/NSDUHsaePercents2016.pdf.

Substance Abuse and Mental Health Services Administration (SAMSHA). (2018, January). *Substance abuse treatment admissions by primary substance of abuse, according to sex, age group, race, and ethnicity among admissions aged 12 and older, 2015, West Virginia.* Rockville, MD: Center for Behavioral Health Statistics and Quality, Treatment Episode Data Set (TEDS). Retrieved from https://wwwdasis.samhsa.gov/webt/quicklink/WV15.htm.

Thomas, L., Jr. (2004, November 6). Maker of OxyContin reaches settlement with West Virginia. *New York Times.* Retrieved from http://www.nytimes.com/2004/11/06/business/06drug.html?_r=0.

United States Census Bureau. (2017). *State and county quickfacts.* Retrieved from https://www.census.gov/quickfacts/fact/table/WV,US/PST045217.

Wells, L. E., & Weisheit, R. A. (2012). Crime and place: Proximity and the location of methamphetamine laboratories. *Journal of Drug Issues, 42*(2), 178–196. doi:10.1177/0022042612446594.

West Virginia Clandestine Drug Lab Remediation Program. (2018). *Clandestine drug lab properties listings.* Retrieved from https://www.wvdhhr.org/rtia/Meth.asp.

West Virginia cost of drug and alcohol abuse: $1.6 billion a year. (2011, May 2). *Alcoholism & Drug Abuse Weekly, 23*(17), 4–5. doi: 10.1002/adaw.20279.

West Virginia Department of Health and Human Resources (WV DHHR). (2016a). *Prevalence of mothers who drank alcohol before and during pregnancy among women in West Virginia compared to women in the US.* Retrieved from http://www.wvdhhr.org/wvprams/pdf/Analytic_Reports/Analytic_Report_November_2016_Alcohol.pdf.

West Virginia Department of Health and Human Resources (WV DHHR). (2016b). *Prevalence of mothers who smoked before, during and after pregnancy among women in West Virginia compared to women in the US.* Retrieved from http://www.wvdhhr.org/wvprams/pdf/Analytic_Reports/Analytic_Report_October_2016_Smoking.pdf.

West Virginia Division of Corrections (WVDOC). (2017). *West Virginia Division of Corrections, Annual report: FY 2017.* Charleston, WV: Office of Research and Planning. Retrieved from http://www.wvdoc.com/wvdoc/Portals/0/documents/2017-Annual-Report.pdf.

West Virginia Poison Center (2016). *Annual report 2016.* Retrieved from http://wvpoisoncenter.org/media/6523/wv-poison-center-annual-report-2016.pdf.

West Virginia State Police (WVSP). (2016). *West Virginia State Police 2015–2016 annual report.* Charleston, WV: author. Retrieved from https://www.wvsp.gov/about/Documents/AnnualReports/2016annualReport.pdf.

Legal References

1970 Controlled Substances Act. 21 U.S.C. 812.

Leary v. United States, 395 U.S. 6 (1969).

W. Va. Code § 16A-1-1 (2017).

W. Va. Code § 16A-3-2 (2017).

W. Va. Code § 16A-3-3 (2017).

W. Va. Code § 16A-4-3 (2017).

W. Va. Code § 17C-5-2 (2017).

W. Va. Code § 60A-2-201 (2017).

W. Va. Code § 60A-4-401 (2017).

W. Va. Code § 60A-4-410 (2017).

W. Va. Code § 60A-4-411 (2017).

W. Va. Code § 60A-10-1 (2017).

W. Va. Code § 60A-11-2 (2017).

Chapter 10

Counterterrorism and Homeland Security

West Virginia Intelligence Fusion Center. Courtesy of the West Virginia Intelligence Fusion Center.

The attacks of September 11, 2001, are unequivocally the single biggest factor shaping the United States response to terrorism for the twenty-first century. *Terrorism*, as defined by the U.S. Code, "means premeditated, politically motivated violence perpetrated against non-combatant targets by subnational groups or clandestine agents" (United States Department of State, Bureau on Counterterrorism, 2017, p. 446). It can be further subdivided as ***international terrorism*** and ***domestic terrorism***, with international implying involvement of people or territory in more than one country, as opposed to domestic terrorism, which is limited to citizens of a country attacking within its own borders. In this context, the attacks of 2001 were classified as acts of international terrorism, which have been relatively uncommon in the United States. Conversely, numerous acts of domestic terrorism have occurred, with the bombings of the Alfred P. Murrah Building in Oklahoma City in 1995 and at the Boston Marathon in 2013 being the most widely publicized. While the focus of this text is more specific to West Virginia, unlike other topics in this book, the state-level approach to counterterrorism and homeland security is directly tied into the national strategy as envisioned at the federal level. Therefore, a fundamental understanding of what this entails is warranted.

As a result of more recent terrorist events, in particular 9/11, the concept of ***homeland security*** is relatively new to most Americans; yet ***counterterrorism*** is not so new. While there are numerous definitions of counterterrorism, it can be defined as the use of personnel and resources to preempt, disrupt, or destroy terrorists and their support networks (Kushner, 2003). The prefix, "counter," implies a proactive response, which can be in the form of aggressive or offensive strategies. These plans commonly include legislation, intelligence gathering, and diplomacy. However, counterterrorism is not always synonymous with homeland security, which involves more reactive or defensive strategies to keep the country safe from terrorism (Gaines & Kappeler, 2012). For example, target-hardening approaches or enhanced security measures that can serve as deterrents would be a part of homeland security approaches, although proactive methods can be implemented as well. Moreover, counterterrorism has a broader focus both internationally and domestically; whereas, homeland security focuses on securing the United States within its borders. A crucial point to make here is that there are various definitions of homeland security, as there are of terrorism and counterterrorism, which complicates the situation for the agencies involved, including law enforcement. For example, homeland security also includes emergency responses to natural disasters and catastrophes, which broadens the mission for these organizations (Oliver, Marion, & Hill, 2015). Regardless, one can quickly see that there is a definite overlap between counterterrorism and homeland security; thus, discussion of one automatically infers discussion of the other.

An in-depth analysis of counterterrorism and homeland security is beyond the scope of this chapter, but we will briefly look at the strategies employed in West Virginia to support the *War on Terror* in the context of the National Strategy for Homeland Security (NSHS). The primary mission of the NSHS is to keep the country safe from risks both international and domestic. This is achieved primarily by way of two state entities: 1) the West Virginia Division of Homeland Security and Emergency Management, and 2) the West Virginia Intelligence Fusion Center, both of which are discussed in this chapter. However, to get a better understanding of the current status of counterterrorism policy and legislation, it is important to begin with a brief, but broader perspective.

The Evolution of Counterterrorism in the United States

The United States has been involved in activities that can be characterized as counterterrorism dating back to shortly after its independence from England. In 1798, the country adopted the Alien and Sedition Acts. These laws sought to repress domestic protest in response to what was seen as a threat from the French at the time, although it could be argued that the acts were more a matter of national security then counterterrorism (Bora, 2012). The Force Act and the Ku Klux Act of 1871 were additional measures taken to fight domestic terrorism, primarily by "expanding the powers of the government" (Fagan, 2006, p. 51). After the turn of the century, the Espionage Act of 1917 and the Sedition Act of 1918 were added to target subversive activities against the government. However, the real impetus of U.S. counterterrorism policies did not develop until after the Second World War (Bora, 2012).

Post-World War II

After the conclusion of the war in 1945, a number of new strategies emerged, primarily aimed at limiting the influence of communism in the United States. It is here that terrorism was included as part of the political agenda. Any sort of political dissent was now labeled terroristic in nature. Senator Joseph McCarthy became the lead architect in this nationwide battle for combating the communist spread in the 1950s, which by default now included terrorism. This led to the passage of the Communist Control Act in 1954 (Fagan, 2006). In essence, this act deprived anyone labeled a communist of his or her legal and constitutional rights. Shortly thereafter, the Federal Bureau of Investigation (FBI) introduced COINTELPRO (Counterintelligence Program), in order to target political activity that was deemed to be radical in nature. This initiative lasted for nearly two decades, consuming thousands of Americans in its wake (Bora, 2012). By the 1970s, the United States was heavily entrenched in the Cold War against the Soviet Union; therefore, the policies developed during this period primarily addressed the government's authority in fighting the Cold War. Subsequently, the U.S. Department of Justice, through the Attorney General's office, issued the Levi Guidelines of 1976 and the Smith Guidelines of 1983, for the FBI. These policies dictated the Bureau's authority in conducting domestic intelligence as well as initiating investigations prior to the commission of criminal acts (EPIC, n.d.).

Counterterrorism in the Modern World

With the fall of the Berlin Wall came the end of the Cold War in the late 1980s. With it dawned the modern age of terrorism as we know it today.[1] Indeed, many of the policies of the previous two centuries mainly centered "on the prohibition of propaganda, deportation of enemies of the state, and the expansion of governmental powers," while "the new focus would include laws and directives defining the role of government agencies that would be responsible for responding to and preventing various types of terrorist activities" (Bora, 2012, p. 185–186). During the Reagan administration, five National Security Decision Directives were delivered in an attempt to streamline the U.S. government's response to terrorist activity. These directives (30, 179, 180, 205, and 207) would be further developed and refined for the current counterterrorism strategy that is now in place. According to Fagan (2006), listed below are each of these directives and its purpose:

- Directive 30 is aimed at prevention and response to the hijacking of commercial airlines;
- Directives 179 and 180 helped establish the Task Force on Combating Terrorism, which is responsible for holding government agencies accountable in the event of an attack;[2]
- Directives 205 and 207, subtitled State-Sponsored Terrorism and Non-Concessions Policy, is aimed at nations that pose a threat to U.S. national security through state sponsorship.[3]

During the Clinton era, much of the profile of the current stance on counterterrorism would be established, although initially, domestic terrorism was the primary focus. The Freedom of Access to Clinic Entrances Act (FACE) was passed in 1994. Under this law, individuals who obstructed and/or threatened others at entrances to clinics and other healthcare providers that offered abortion services would be criminalized. A year later, as a result of the Oklahoma City bombing, identifying U.S. target vulnerability both domestically and

1. Many of the former Cold War players turned to tactics of terrorism to achieve political or social change. For example, members of Afghanistan's Taliban government were former allies of the U.S., as mujahedeen freedom fighters, who were compelled to drive out the Soviets during their occupation of Afghanistan from 1979–1989.

2. These were partly responsible for expanding the Federal Air Marshal Program.

3. Libya was the primary concern when these directives were issued, but later Cuba, North Korea, Iran, Iraq, Sudan, and Syria would be added to the list of concerns (U.S. Department of State, 2004).

internationally became the primary concern. Similar to the Reagan administration, presidential directives and other critical legislation would be the primary tool to deal with terrorism (Fagan, 2006). The first of Clinton's directives, Presidential Decision Directive 39, was adopted in 1995. This order "revisited the role of the federal agencies involved in the event of a terrorist attack" as well as increased the agencies that would be responsible for the response[4] (Bora, 2012, p. 186). Directive 39 also addressed scenarios where weapons of mass destruction may be used, and how to plan against and respond to such an event.

Also in 1995, the United States Congress passed the Omnibus Counterterrorism Act for the stated purpose of strengthening our ability to deal with terrorism. However, due to lack of specificity, a year later the Anti-Terrorism and Effective Death Penalty Act of 1996 replaced it. This legislation was meant to be more comprehensive by including "justice for victims of terrorism and mandating capital punishment at the federal level for acts of terrorism" (Bora, 2012, p. 186). However, it was criticized for possible civil liberties violations (Nacos, 2006). In reality, the 1996 act was essentially several previous pieces of legislation that had stalled during the previous 10 years, but were combined and put forth again in response to the bombings that took place at the World Trade Center in 1993 and then the 1995 Oklahoma City attack. The main controversy, however, centered more on the aspects of law enforcement authority at the domestic level (Griset & Mahan, 2003). Nonetheless, the act would serve as the cornerstone for the soon-to-be-adopted Uniting and Strengthening America by Providing Appropriate Tools Required to Intercept and Obstruct Terrorism Act (USA Patriot Act), which would prove to be even more controversial.

Post-9/11

The pivotal moment in the evolution of U.S. counterterrorism efforts would be the attacks of September 11, 2001. President George W. Bush would issue Executive Order 13224 two weeks following the attacks. The most important aspect of this mandate was to give the government the authority to freeze and seize assets of anyone who provided material support to terrorist organizations or their activities. A few months later, two other controversial measures were passed. One was the ***Enemy Combatant Executive Order***, which was issued on

4. The Department of Defense (DOD) and the Central Intelligence Agency (CIA) now have a more direct role.

November 13 and culminated with roughly 700 detainees at Guantanamo Bay, Cuba. This order gave the President of the United States the authority to hold anyone indefinitely if he or she was deemed to be an enemy combatant against the United States, which in the context of the War on Terror were persons suspected of alliances with al Qaeda or the Taliban. As an enemy combatant, these individuals would not be entitled to their constitutional rights, including access to legal counsel or notification of charges (Nacos, 2006). This executive order was criticized for several reasons: 1) it would violate the Geneva Convention's stipulation regarding the capture and treatment of prisoners of war; 2) it would increase the power of the executive branch of government by giving the President the power to dictate who was an enemy combatant; and 3) as an enemy combatant, the prisoner would be subjected to military justice rather than civilian justice, which lies with the judicial branch (i.e., the courts). Again, this would diminish the power of another branch of government as well as our system of checks and balances (Fagan, 2006). This last issue is further compounded by the fact that persons tried in military tribunals do not have access to the civilian appellate process, especially the right to be heard by the U.S. Supreme Court. Many of the controversial aspects that existed with this directive were also found in the other policy, which actually predated the Enemy Combatant Executive Order by 17 days. On October 26, 2001, Congress passed the ***USA Patriot Act***, which was intended to deter, convict, and punish terrorist acts against the United States by breaking down legal obstacles and providing enhanced investigative tools for law enforcement.

Undeniably, the Patriot Act is one of the most hotly debated, yet most significant pieces of counterterrorism legislation to be adopted by the government in United States history. However, state and local governments had strong reservations about its passage. As a result, more than 150 state and local government entities passed countermeasures in objection to certain aspects of the law (Fagan, 2006). The Act (USA PATRIOT ACT, 2001) incorporates the following 10 Titles:

I. Enhancing Domestic Security Against Terrorism
II. Enhanced Surveillance Procedures
III. International Money Laundering Abatement and Anti-terrorist Financing Act of 2001
IV. Protecting the Border
V. Removing Obstacles to Investigating Terrorism
VI. Providing for Victims of Terrorism, Public Safety Officers and Their Families
VII. Increased Information Sharing for Critical Infrastructure Protection
VIII. Strengthening the Criminal Laws Against Terrorism

IX. Improved Intelligence
X. Miscellaneous

Title II regarding enhanced surveillance arguably contains the most controversial aspects. Many civil libertarians feared that, just like giving the President more authority under the Enemy Combatant Executive Order, the Patriot Act would expand the power of law enforcement by giving them more authority to collect information on private citizens and groups. Moreover, the police also are a part of the executive branch, and once again the system of checks and balances may be compromised (Martin, 2017). Also at the heart of the debate is the Fourth Amendment and the right against unwarranted searches and seizures, which may be jeopardized if police are not required to inform individuals of an imminent search. However, in spite of these arguments, the government continues to "maintain that the act is necessary, and the fact that another attack on the United States has been avoided justifies its existence" (Bora, 2012, p. 188).

The USA Patriot Act was only one step toward a comprehensive counterterrorism strategy post-9/11, so the efforts did not stop there. The Ashcroft Guidelines, named after the U.S. Attorney General at the time, also further defined standards for the FBI and other federal agencies concerning investigative practices and intelligence gathering. This allowed federal law enforcement to start using private databases to develop predictive models to thwart another attack on American soil. Finally, the culmination of all of these efforts eventually led to the signing of the Homeland Security Bill by President Bush in November 2002. This bill was the basis for the creation of the newest federal office, the Department of Homeland Security (DHS) in March 2003.

The development of DHS entailed the "largest reorganization of federal agencies in the nation's history. Twenty-two agencies were shifted to DHS from across the federal level, including the Secret Service, Immigration and Naturalization Service, and Customs Service" (Bora, 2012, p. 188). Initially, the plans also included relocating the FBI and CIA to this new department. Ultimately, they were left alone, but today they both work directly with DHS regarding counterterrorism (Nacos, 2006). In fact, the FBI is still considered the lead investigative agency in acts of domestic terrorism.[5]

Along with DHS and the FBI, another crucial piece of the counterterrorism picture is the ***National Counterterrorism Center (NCTC),*** which was founded in 2004 through the Intelligence Reform and Terrorism Prevention Act. This

---

5. In regard to international terrorism, the CIA and the DOD have the primary role of "taking the fight to the terrorists" before they can strike U.S. borders.

center is a joint operational planning intelligence organization. The staff of the NCTC is comprised of personnel from a number of different agencies with the primary goal of integrating and analyzing all intelligence related to terrorism and counterterrorism. It is headed by the Office of the Director of National Intelligence (DNI).

Homeland Security

The United States *National Strategy for Homeland Security (NSHS)*, as it was first defined in July 2002, and which formed the basis for passage of the Homeland Security Bill in November of that same year, was based on three key strategic objectives in order of priority: "1) prevent terrorist attacks within the United States; 2) reduce America's vulnerability to terrorism; and 3) minimize the damage and recover from attacks that do occur" (Homeland Security Council, 2002, p. vii). In support of this strategy, there were six key areas of focus.

1. Intelligence and warning: this would include the ability to detect and monitor potential threats before they can occur within our borders.
2. Border and transportation security: this incorporates airline security and inspection of cargo shipments at various entry points into the country to prevent illegal people or weapons from coming across our borders.
3. Domestic counterterrorism: this consists mostly of investigative activities by federal law enforcement agencies that focus on identification and apprehension of terrorists.
4. Protection of critical infrastructure and key assets: this includes ensuring the physical security of national parks, landmarks, federal buildings and installations, as well as critical infrastructure such as bridges, power plants, and waterways.
5. Defense against catastrophic threats: this incorporates preventing terrorists from obtaining weapons of mass destruction and introducing strategies to mitigate the effects of those weapons if used.
6. Emergency preparedness and response: this includes efforts to diminish the effects of future terrorist attacks and includes creation of federal response plans and the provision of equipment and training to first responders.

However, once the Department of Homeland Security was firmly in place in 2003, the mission areas of the NSHS have continued to be refined, but all six areas are still incorporated into the current strategy in some form or another (Homeland Security Council, 2007).

The Department of Homeland Security

The NSHS has had a significant impact on the newest organization within the federal government structure, the Department of Homeland Security. However, there is still a great deal of confusion regarding the role of DHS. This is partly a result of the newness of the concept. Furthermore, an additional layer of bureaucracy has now been created, adding to an already-existing plethora of red tape. The Department has a central vision, reinforced with five core mission statements in support of that vision. These all correspond to the national strategy defined previously. Thus, the vision of DHS is "to ensure a homeland that is safe, secure, and resilient against terrorism and other hazards" (DHS, 2012, p. 2). The core missions are: 1) preventing terrorism and enhancing security; 2) securing and managing our borders; 3) enforcing and administering our immigration laws; 4) safeguarding and securing cyberspace; and 5) ensuring resilience to disasters.

The common perception of most Americans in regard to DHS is based on firsthand experience. That is to say, the Transportation Security Administration (TSA), which is a critical agency within DHS, is tasked with the protection of civilian aircraft through target-hardening strategies. Through enhanced security measures and use of air marshals, the TSA is the frontline defense for securing air transportation from terrorism (Dempsey & Frost, 2013).

Other agencies within DHS that play a visible role in counterterrorism include U.S. Customs and Border Protection (CBP), U.S. Immigration and Customs Enforcement (ICE), and the U.S. Coast Guard (USCG), just to name a few. However, the Department of Homeland Security is quick to point out that the national strategy is heavily dependent on state and local authorities to be effective. Terrorism is a crime, after all; thus, it must first be addressed at the local level. In fact, the routine patrol officer on the streets is on the frontline of homeland security and counterterrorism. This means they have to be trained to spot warnings and collect intelligence from all sources available. This implies that each state must incorporate its own policies and guidelines in support of the overall mission of homeland security. In West Virginia, this is coordinated through the West Virginia Division of Homeland Security and Emergency Management (DHSEM), as well as the West Virginia Intelligence Fusion Center (WVIFC).

West Virginia's Homeland Security Strategy

While at first glance, West Virginia would seem an unlikely target for a terrorist event, it is indeed vulnerable to such a threat. According to former West Virginia Homeland Security Advisor, James Spears (2007):

> Our State is home to over one hundred chemical plants, multiple coal-fired power plants, hundreds of miles of natural gas transmission lines, a port that is the 6th busiest in America in terms of tonnage, miles of coal mines, and a burgeoning coal bed methane gas industry and robust locks and dams systems. West Virginia occupies a critical place in the nation's electrical grid. There is a multitude of public and private critical infrastructure in this state that interfaces with the economy, communications, energy and other integral resources that are critical to the continuity of life in the eastern portion of the United States (p. 4).

While these threats are of serious concern, they are secondary, as Spears goes on to state in his address at the U.S. Senate Select Committee on Intelligence Reform Hearing in 2007:

> It is no secret that Washington D.C. and New York City are at the top of the international terrorist hit list and that today's terrorists are looking at how to inflict the most catastrophic of blows on our nation. Therefore, it is not unreasonable, nor should we overlook the potential of a terrorist chemical, nuclear, biological or radiological attack on our nation's capital. Should this occur, it is of great concern to West Virginia, that vast numbers of Americans will evacuate the Baltimore-Washington area in a chaotic uncontrolled exodus (Spears, 2007, p. 5).

Given these vulnerabilities, much of the homeland security strategy developed at the state level reinforces the mission of the NSHS, as previously mentioned. Five strategic goals make up this state initiative.

1. Strengthen Policy and Unify Management
2. Enhance Preparedness for Preparedness for All-Hazard Incidents
3. Protect Critical Infrastructure and Key Resources
4. Facilitate Interoperability
5. Prepare West Virginia for a Mass Evacuation

These five goals require cooperation from agencies at all levels, including federal, state, and local organizations. These are not limited to law enforcement. In fact, all first responders, hospitals, schools, and public agencies have a role in the success of this strategy. However, the bulk of the workload of counterterrorism, intelligence, and emergency management is conducted by the state's Division of Homeland Security and Emergency Management.

Division of Homeland Security and Emergency Management

As with most states, West Virginia's mandate for protection against terrorism came by way of the birth of DHS. In support of DHS's mission, the West Virginia Division of Homeland Security and Emergency Management[6] (DHSEM) has the stated mission "to ensure the protection of life and property by providing coordination, guidance, support and assistance to local emergency managers and first responders" (WVDHSEM, 2018, para. 1). This organization is considered an all-hazards agency; thus, it is not a single-focus entity. Three divisions make up its purpose: 1) preparedness and response, 2) technological hazards, and 3) mitigation and recovery. The first component is "responsible for the coordination and operation of the State Emergency Operations Center," which also "includes the Homeland Security Area Liaisons, the Watch Center, Planning, Training, and Exercises" (WVDHSEM, 2018, para. 5). The second facet of technological hazards coordinates "activities related to radiological and hazardous materials planning and response," which includes, "the Radiological Emergency Preparedness (REP) program, Tier II reporting, the Toxic Report Inventory Program, and the administration of the State Emergency Response Commission (SERC)" (WVDHSEM, 2018, para. 6). The final branch of mitigation and recovery deals with floodplain management, as well as hazard mitigation as a result of natural and man-made disasters, and individual assistance after such events. In addition, preemptive programs to prevent such catastrophes are developed. Within all three of these divisions, homeland security is a key component. As such, this is accomplished partly in collaboration with the state's Intelligence Fusion Center.

For the purposes of homeland security organization, West Virginia is divided into six zones (see Figure 10.1). These zones also correspond to the zones used by the West Virginia State Police, which makes structural sense in that facilitation of state-wide information from a law enforcement body would naturally start with the state police.

---

6. This agency is part of the West Virginia Department of Military Affairs and Public Safety.

Figure 10.1. Regional Breakdown of West Virginia Homeland Security Zones

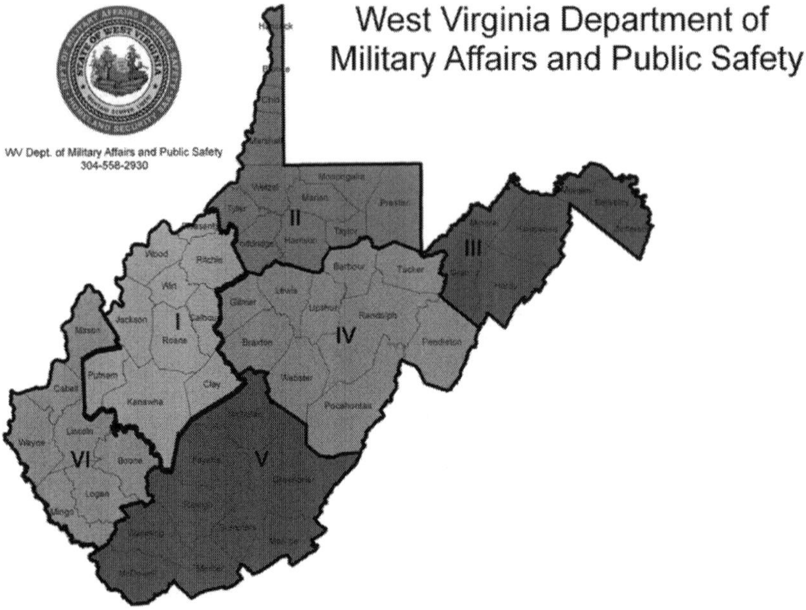

Source: *West Virginia homeland security strategy.* (2010). Retrieved from https://dhsem.wv.gov/Homeland%20Security/Documents/West%20Virginia%20Homeland%20Security%20Strategy.pdf.

West Virginia Intelligence Fusion Center

One integral component of homeland security is intelligence. The West Virginia Intelligence Fusion Center (WVIFC) was established in 2008, and falls under the West Virginia Department of Military Affairs and Public Safety (DMAPS). The Fusion Center works very closely with the DHSEM and the Homeland Security Advisor (who also serves as the director of DHSEM).

The fusion center concept was initiated by the weaknesses identified in the country's intelligence system, as well as the lack of cooperation between law enforcement agencies prior to 9/11. Today, all 50 states have fusion centers, with some states having more than one. There are total of 79 at this time. ***Fusion centers*** can be viewed as partnerships between public and private agencies. In fact, beyond intelligence analysts, other key personnel from various federal and state law enforcement agencies are involved in the process. According to the 'About' page from website for the West Virginia Intelligence Fusion Center (2018, para. 1):

> A fusion center is a collaborative effort of two or more agencies that provide resources, expertise, and information to the center with the goal of maximizing their ability to detect, prevent, investigate, and respond to criminal and terrorist activity. Intelligence processes through which information is collected, integrated, evaluated, analyzed, and disseminated are a primary focus.
>
> Data fusion involves the exchange of information from different sources including law enforcement, public safety, and the private sector. Relevant and actionable intelligence results from analysis and data fusion. The fusion process helps agencies be proactive and protect communities.

As such, the mission of the West Virginia Intelligence Fusion Center is "to anticipate, identify, prevent, and monitor criminal activity and all other hazards and to responsibly distribute that intelligence to its stakeholders while both protecting the rights of its citizens and guarding the rights and integrity of law enforcement and private industry" (WVIFC, 2018, para. 1).

It is important to note that fusion centers in general are not without controversy. Initially, the goal seemed clearly to be a tool to assist in counterterrorism; however, civil libertarians fear they have gone beyond their mandate and engage in other activities akin to spying (Monahan & Palmer, 2009). It is true that they have taken on the task of assisting local law enforcement agencies in basic policing, but again, it can be argued that counterterrorism first starts at the street level. Nonetheless, the three key areas of concern with these centers are: (1) level of effectiveness given the financial cost; (2) mission "creep" into areas beyond their mandate; and (3) violation of civil liberties, especially in the realm of the First Amendment (Monahan & Palmer, 2009).

Spotlight: OSIX-Open Source Intelligence Exchange

In collaboration with DHS and the state fusion center, a unique initiative is unfolding in West Virginia. The Open Source Intelligence Exchange (OSIX) is a partnership between these two agencies and universities to establish secure labs run by student analysts, who in turn provide intelligence reports to public and private agencies based on information that is publicly available on the Internet via websites, archival documents, blogs, and social networking sites such as Facebook and Twitter. OSIX programs use students from varied disciplines, such as digital forensics, history, political science, anthropology, psychology, and international affairs in addition to traditional students in homeland security and criminal justice and criminology. This allows a more holistic view of issues from various lenses. For example, anthropology students would be able to identify cultural aspects of communication, and political science students would be better able to assess political movements.

The OSIX initiative is set up to support security threats and opportunities presented by new and emerging information technologies (NET), and the labs serve four primary objectives (The Open Source Intelligence Exchange, n.d., para. 2):

1. Identify and assess NET that pose a national security or law enforcement threat. Analysts at OSIX continually monitor developments in information technology and related fields to spot NET that could be used by bad actors.
2. Exploit NET to identify and assess national security and law enforcement threats. Terrorists and criminals aren't the only ones who can use NET to their advantage. OSIX applies the latest NET tools and techniques to gain unique insight into "traditional" threats from terrorist groups, rogue states, arms dealers, drug traffickers, and organized crime.
3. Develop tools, techniques, and methodologies for exploiting NET for intelligence and law enforcement purposes. As OSIX studies NET, we constantly learn new and better ways to exploit them for intelligence purposes. OSIX is dedicated to capturing these "lessons learned" and passing them on to our colleagues in the US national security and law enforcement communities.
4. Leverage OSIX's expertise in NET to provide operational support to the US national security and law enforcement communities. Exploitation of NET for intelligence purposes is a new phenomenon. Most intelligence and law enforcement agencies are unfamiliar with the concept and lack the ability to put it into practice. OSIX will offer its services, consistent with applicable federal and state law, to US intelligence and law enforcement agencies seeking to use NET to advance their mission.

Considering these objectives, the use of students to carry them out is prudent, as the younger generation of adults is already technologically savvy having grown up with computers and the Internet from the time of their infancy. For many, envisioning a world without the easy access to information at their fingertips or social interaction through Facebook is unimaginable. Furthermore, students bring a valuable skill to the intelligence gathering mission in that they are not biased by preconceived notions that may otherwise affect professional analysts. Due to turnover of students at these labs, there is always a fresh perspective. Moreover, the experience greatly benefits students as well by providing practical experience, increasing their skill sets, developing solid critical thinking abilities, and learning to work as a team. In the end, the opportunity makes them more marketable when competing for high demand internships and employment opportunities.

Currently there are six labs in the country, three of which are in West Virginia alone: one at Fairmont State University, one at Glenville State College, and the most recent one established in 2013 at Marshall University. The OSIX lab at Fairmont was the first to be established in 2009 and is the "applied research component of the university's National Security and Intelligence (NSI) program" (Fairmont State University, n.d., para. 1). A few examples of the type of activities that the Fairmont students have been involved in are provided below by the current director of the program, David Abruzzino (Fairmont State University, 2011, para. 6, 7, 8).

> "A few months ago we picked up on discussion about huge pro-democracy protests in Iran. We set up a 24-7 operations center, monitored events in real time, and sent update reports to a number of government agencies. We provided them with information that they were not getting through other channels in terms of location of protests, size, what people were saying, and what was happening on the ground. This information wasn't available through other sources because there was a total media blackout, so traditional media was banned from the country. Our information was coming from local Iranians on site through Twitter and Facebook. When the Iranian government started cracking down, we were able to provide regular updates about tanks being spotted on a particular street, soldiers firing in a particular square, and those sorts of things. Based off of this event, our group began to look at the Middle East more broadly and decided to compile a weekly report which is now going to a variety of customers in the national security community. Right now, we are solely grant funded. Our ultimate goal is to contract our services out to the government and private sector so that we can not only fund ourselves, but be a source of revenue for the university."
>
> The students of OSIX also participated in U.S. President Barack Obama's visit to the memorial service in Beckley, West Virginia for those lost in the Upper Big Branch Mine Disaster in April 2010. The team of 11 students supported the West Virginia Intelligence Fusion Center during the visit. Through their monitoring of the web and social media, they were able to provide useful information to the Fusion Center that was passed on to the Secret Service.

> "I provided top level director support, but at the end of the day the students were responsible for getting the work done and for taking care of the management of tasks. The Fusion Center told us that at least one of the reports we provided caused the Secret Service to say, 'Wow, we didn't know that.' Working with students and the level of enthusiasm they bring is remarkable," Abruzzino said.

A more recent example involves the Marshall OSIX program and its collaboration with the non-profit group Operation Underground Railroad (O.U.R.) in the fall of 2017 to help arrest suspected child sex traffickers abroad. With the help of OSIX reports generated from intelligence gathered by students, the information was used "to support O.U.R. child rescue operations in Latin America, the Caribbean and Southeast Asia. To date, this intelligence has assisted in the liberation of almost forty child trafficking victims in Latin America, and in the arrest of some ten suspected traffickers" (Operation Underground Railroad, 2018, para. 10). While not homeland security focused, this example demonstrates the potential of these types of programs in open source intelligence collection tasks that can assist law enforcement.

As with fusion centers, the OSIX labs may garner some level of scrutiny as well. In fact, the actions that are assigned to each lab primarily come from the West Virginia Intelligence Fusion Center. Each student goes through a background check and receives extensive training on privacy issues before being allowed to participate. In fact, most of the trainings are provided by DHS. In the end, the OSIX labs in West Virginia are proving to be an important component of the state's homeland security mission, as well as an asset to state and local law enforcement.

Key Terms and Definitions

Counterterrorism: The use of personnel and resources to preempt, disrupt, or destroy terrorists and their support networks.

Domestic terrorism: Acts of terrorism limited to citizens of a country attacking within its own borders.

Enemy Combatant Executive Order: This order gave the President of the United States the authority to hold anyone indefinitely if he or she was deemed to be an enemy combatant against the United States, which in the context of the War on Terror were persons suspected of alliances with al Qaeda or the Taliban.

Fusion centers: Can be viewed as partnerships between public and private agencies. Beyond intelligence analysts, other key personnel from various federal and state law enforcement agencies are involved in the process.

Homeland security: Reactive or defensive strategies to keep the country safe.

International terrorism: Acts of terrorism that involve people or territory in more than one country.

National Counterterrorism Center (NCTC): Was founded in 2004 through the Intelligence Reform and Terrorism Prevention Act. This center is a joint operational planning intelligence organization.

National Strategy for Homeland Security (NSHS): (1) Prevent terrorist attacks within the United States; (2) reduce America's vulnerability to terrorism; and (3) minimize the damage and recover from attacks that do occur.

Terrorism: Premeditated, politically motivated violence perpetrated against non-combatant targets by subnational groups or clandestine agents.

USA Patriot Act: Intended to deter, convict, and punish terrorist acts against the United States by breaking down legal obstacles and providing enhanced investigative tools for law enforcement.

Select Internet Sources

National Counterterrorism Center (NCTC): **http://www.nctc.gov/index.html.**

OSIX-Fairmont: **http://www.fairmontstate.edu/collegeofliberalarts/academics/open-source-intelligence-exchange.**

Regional Information Sharing System: **https://www.riss.net/.**

U.S. Department of Homeland Security: **http://www.dhs.gov/.**

West Virginia Division of Homeland Security and Emergency Management: **http://www.dhsem.wv.gov/.**

Review and Critical Thinking Questions

1. How is counterterrorism theoretically distinguishable from homeland security?

2. Are there any similarities between the post-World War II hunt for communists and the post-9/11 hunt for enemy combatants?

3. What are some of the threats to civil liberties as a result of the increase in focus on protecting the nation from a terrorist attack?

4. Is the strong link between the state's homeland security strategy to the NSHS a threat to state autonomy? If so, how? If not, why?

5. Are fusion centers a threat to individual privacy rights? Explain why or why not.

References

Bora, D. J. (2012). Historical look at the evolution and effectiveness of state counterterrorism strategies: Laws, policies, and operational tactics post-1945. In F. G. Shanty (Ed.), *Counterterrorism: From the cold war to the war on terror, volume one—combating modern terrorism (1968–2011)* (pp. 185–188). Santa Barbara, CA: Praeger/ABC-CLIO.

Dempsey, J. S., & Frost, L. S. (2013). *Police* (2nd ed.). Belmont, CA: Cengage Learning.

Electronic Privacy Information Center (EPIC). (n.d.). *The Attorney General's guidelines*. Retrieved from http://epic.org/privacy/fbi/.

Fagan, J. (2006). *When terrorism strikes home: Defending the United States.* Boston: Pearson Publishing.

Fairmont State University. (n.d.). Open Source Intelligence Exchange. Retrieved from http://www.fairmontstate.edu/collegeofliberalarts/academics/open-source-intelligence-exchange.

Fairmont State University. (2011, September 1). Saving lives one mouse click at a time. *FSU Now.* Retrieved from http://www.fairmontstate.edu/fsunow/academics/saving-lives-one-mouse-click-time.

Gaines, L. K., & Kappeler, V. E. (2012). *Homeland security*. Boston, MA: Prentice Hall Publishing.

Griset, P. L., & Mahan, S. (2003). *Terrorism in perspective.* Los Angeles: Sage Publishing. Homeland Security Council. (2002, July). *National strategy for homeland security.* Retrieved from http://www.dhs.gov/publication/first-national-strategy-homeland-security.

Homeland Security Council. (2007, October). *National strategy for homeland security.* Retrieved from http://www.dhs.gov/national-strategy-homeland-security-october-2007.

Kushner, H. W. (2003). *Encyclopedia of terrorism.* Thousand Oaks, CA: Sage.

Martin, G. (2017). *Essentials of terrorism: Concepts and controversies* (4th ed.). Los Angeles: Sage.

Monahan, T., & Palmer, N. A. (2009). The emerging politics of DHS fusion centers. *Security Dialogue, 40*(6): 617–636. doi: 10.1177/0967010609350314.

Nacos, B. (2006). *Terrorism and counterterrorism: Understanding threats and responses in the post-9/11 world.* New York: Penguin Academics.

Oliver, W. M., Marion, N. E., & Hill, J. B. (2015). *Introduction to homeland security: Policy, organization, and administration.* Burlington, MA: Jones and Bartlett Publishing.

Operation Underground Railroad (O.U.R.). (2018, February 15). Marshall University students and staff assist in the liberation of almost forty child trafficking victims. Retrieved from http://ourrescue.org/blog/marshall-university-students-staff-assist-liberation-almost-forty-child-trafficking-victims/.

Spears, J. (2007, January). *U.S. Senate Select Committee on Intelligence: Intelligence reform* hearing. Retrieved from http://fas.org/irp/congress/2007_hr/012507spears.pdf.

The Open Source Intelligence Exchange. (n.d.). Retrieved from https://www.fairmontstate.edu/collegeofliberalarts/academics/open-source-intelligence-exchange.

United States Department of Homeland Security (DHS). (2012, February). *Department of Homeland Security strategic plan: Fiscal years 2012–2016.* Retrieved from http://www.dhs.gov/strategic-plan-fiscal-years-fy-2012-2016.

United States Department of State. (2004, April). *Patterns of global terrorism 2003.* Washington, DC: Author. Retrieved from http://www.state.gov/documents/organization/31912.pdf.

United States Department of State, Bureau on Counterterrorism. (2017, July). *Country reports on terrorism 2016.* Retrieved https://www.state.gov/documents/organization/272488.pdf.

West Virginia Division of Homeland Security and Emergency Management (WVDHSEM). (2018). *About DHSEM.* Retrieved from http://www.dhsem.wv.gov/about/Pages/default.aspx.

West Virginia homeland security strategy. (2010). Retrieved from https://dhsem.wv.gov/Homeland%20Security/Documents/West%20Virginia%20Homeland%20Security%20Strategy.pdf.

West Virginia Intelligence Fusion Center (WVIFC). (2018). Retrieved from https://fusioncenter.wv.gov/.

Legal References

Uniting and Strengthening America by Providing Appropriate Tools Required to Intercept and Obstruct Terrorism (USA PATRIOT Act) Act of 2001, Pub. L. No. 107-56. 115 Stat. 272 (2001).

About the Authors

Kimberly A. DeTardo-Bora is a Professor of Criminal Justice and Criminology at Marshall University, where she serves as graduate director. In 2003, she received her Ph.D. in Criminology from Indiana University of Pennsylvania. She has published in a variety of scholarly venues such as *Action Research*, *Corrections Compendium*, *Security Journal*, and *Women and Criminal Justice*. She has co-authored grant-funded research projects regarding the evaluation of the Court Appointed Special Advocate (CASA) Programs in West Virginia, the West Virginia STOP Violence Against Women Project, and the O.N.E. Wheeling Weed and Seed Program. Dr. DeTardo-Bora has more than 18 years of teaching experience in higher education in the state of West Virginia.

Dhruba J. Bora is a Professor of Criminal Justice and Criminology as well as Director of the School of Forensic and Criminal Justice Sciences at Marshall University. He received his Ph.D. in Criminology from Indiana University of Pennsylvania, and his dissertation was on *The Influence of Emotional Intelligence on Deviant Behavior*. He also has worked on several grants funded by the U.S. Department of Justice in the area of community policing and domestic violence and has published in the areas of campus safety and security, crime prevention, and counterterrorism. Dr. Bora has been teaching criminal justice in the state of West Virginia since 1997.

Wendy Perkins is an Assistant Professor of Criminal Justice and Criminology at Marshall University. In August 2014 she received her Ph.D. in Criminal Justice from the University of Cincinnati. She has published in the *Journal of School Violence* and is a reviewer for the *Journal of Interpersonal Violence*. Her research agenda focuses on (1) sexual victimization and (2) women in policing. She was the recipient of the 2017 Sarah Denman Fellowship. Her research for this fellowship focused on rape myth acceptance among college students from Appalachia. She is a former police officer and victim service provider, and has extensive experience training police officers and victim advocates about sex crimes and domestic violence investigations. She has been involved in the criminal justice field for 26 years, and has been in higher education for nine years.

Index